IN THE VATICAN

IN THE VATICAN

Peter Hebblethwaite

OXFORD UNIVERSITY PRESS
1987

Oxford University Press, Walton Street, Oxford OX2 6DP

Oxford New York Toronto
Delhi Bombay Calcutta Madras Karachi
Petaling Jaya Singapore Hong Kong Tokyo
Nairobi Dar es Salaam Cape Town
Melbourne Auckland

and associated companies in
Beirut Berlin Ibadan Nicosia

Oxford is a trade mark of Oxford University Press

First published 1986 by Sidgwick and Jackson
First issued, with a new preface, as an Oxford University Press
paperback 1987

British Library Cataloguing in Publication Data

Hebblethwaite, Peter
In the Vatican.
1. Vatican City
I. Title
945'.634   DG796

ISBN 0-19-283063-5

Printed in Great Britain by
Richard Clay Ltd.
Bungay, Suffolk

'He who travels in the barque of Peter had better not look too close into the engine-room.' (Mgr Ronnie Knox, quoted by Penelope Fitzgerald)

Contents

List of Plates

Preface to the Paperback Edition

Aggiornamento or 'A Glut of Occurrences'

'A week', Harold Wilson observed, 'is a long time in politics.' But for the Vatican which notoriously 'thinks in centuries', a week or a year is hardly more than a blink. Yet the last few months have been packed with incident. Marshall McLuhan talked of an eighteenth-century newspaper that announced it would appear twice a week, 'or more often if there were a glut of occurrencies'. There has undoubtedly been 'a glut of occurrencies' in the Vatican.

The purpose of this new preface is to bring the story up to date. The Vatican is a moving target. Though the general picture changes slowly, the detail alters in subtle ways so that knowledge not renewed quickly becomes ignorance. On the whole my analysis has been confirmed by subsequent events – sometimes depressingly so. Cardinal Ratzinger has moved on somewhat from 'liberation theology' and begun the onslaught on moral theologians with the suspension from teaching of Fr Charles Curran of the Catholic University of Washington. The U.S. Church feels even more the Vatican's favourite target after strange goings-on in Seattle. Archbishop Raymond Hunthausen, best known as a peace activist, remains Archbishop but has been flanked by an auxiliary (suffragan in Anglican terms) who is responsible for the marriage tribunal, priests leaving the ministry, clergy training, worship and all moral issues relating to health care and ministry to homosexuals. The auxiliary, Bishop Donal Wuerl, was well known in Rome because he used to work in the Congregation for the Clergy. He at first denied that he was being sent to Seattle as a Vatican watch-dog. But this fiction can no longer be sustained. Thus my remark on p. 129 that 'it would be virtually impossible to dismiss a European or American Archbishop' needs some modification. It is possible to hamstring an archbishop.

On other matters I have yielded to superior evidence and changed my mind. Cardinal John J. O'Connor, for example, needs a more nuanced portrait than the one I draw on pp. 101-3. Rather more importantly, it appears that Pope John Paul II has changed *his* mind on liberation theology. That suggestion needs examination. Then there have been moves on the 'reform' of the Roman Curia, while the Extraordinary Synod, at the end of 1985, recommitted the Church, a little warily, to the Second Vatican Council (1962-5).

The reform of the Roman Curia remains an enigma wrapped up in a mystery. Pope John Paul prefers to call it a 'revision' rather than a 'reform', perhaps because 'reform' would imply weaknesses and inadequacies in the present system. Anyway, there exists a plan for the revision of the Roman Curia. Officially, only about two hundred people have seen it. It was debated in a private meeting of Cardinals in the Vatican on 21-23 November 1985. Both plan and meeting were secret. However, it is known that the main proposals concern the Secretariat for Christian Unity (S.P.U.C. from its Italian initials), and the Council for the Public Affairs of the Church – the rough Vatican equivalent of a foreign ministry.

The conflict between Secretariat and Congregation for the Doctrine of Faith described in chapter 13 was to be resolved by the simple device of turning it into a 'council' wholly subordinate to the C.D.F. Bureaucratic minds pointed out that 'secretariat' was a term unknown to canon law. This was precisely the reason Pope John XXIII used it when he founded the Secretariat in 1960: it left space for unforeseen developments as ecumenism made unpredictable progress. The term 'council' is used for toothless bodies that are merely advisory. Thus a 'council for Christian Unity' would not be headed by a cardinal and would carry little weight on the status-conscious Roman scene. However, that was the proposal put forward in November 1985. The task of this new body would be (to quote the official explanation), 'that of study, promotion and pastoral animation without exercising any ordinary acts of government'. But S.P.U.C. had in the past clearly performed such acts by, for example, producing documents and guidelines of its own for the universal Church. The proposal before the Cardinals was therefore designed to cut the Secretariat down to size.

Three English-speaking cardinals took the lead in opposing this unfortunate proposal. Joseph Bernadin (Chicago), Basil Hume (Westminster), and Tomas O Fiach (Armagh), strongly urged that whatever its intentions, the proposal would be perceived by other Christians as gravely damaging to the ecumenical cause. They enlisted as their spokesman Cardinal Francis Arinze – as a black Nigerian he could not be accused of axe-grinding for the developed world, and he had not yet been so long in the Vatican (at the Secretariat for Non-Christian Religions) that he had forgotten what life was like in an ordinary diocese. No amount of verbal juggling, Arinze pointed out, could convince one's fellow-Christians that the subordination of the post-conciliar secretariats to Cardinal Ratzinger's C.D.F. represented a great ecumenical advance. It just could not be done. And it was not true.

The counter-suggestion was made that if the category of 'secretariat' had at all costs to be abolished in the name of 'rationalization', then it would be better to make S.P.U.C. a fully-fledged Roman Congregation headed by a cardinal. The bureaucratic question merges with the deeper one: how far is Pope John Paul personally committed to the ecumenical cause? One will get a hint of an answer when Cardinal Jan Willebrands finally retires as President of S.P.U.C. He passed the official retirement age of 75 on 4 September 1984. If someone inexperienced in dealing with fellow-Christians is named to the post, whatever his status, grave damage will be done. That such fears were not the product of an over-heated imagination was proved by a remark of Dr Howard Root, the full-time Anglican observer at the Vatican:

> Quite highly placed, very level-headed and widely experienced members of the Curia itself were showing signs of being more frightened than I have ever known them to be since the Council. No doubt there were many reasons for this. I suspect that a strong factor was the uncertainty felt by many about just what the present Pope feels about ecumenical and other matters (*Newsletter of the Friends of the Anglican Centre in Rome*, Spring 1986, p. 8).

The 'revisionist' plan also put a question-mark against the Council for the Public Affairs of the Church. Set up by Paul VI in 1967 it is responsible for running the Vatican diplomatic service, overseeing the Press Office, and handling all dealings with governments. The proposal was that this body should be hived off from the Secretariat of State proper (see chapter 6), and become the 'Congregation for Relations with Governments'. That looked like an enhancement of its status, but in fact, as Archbishop Achille Silvestrini, its present head, argued with some vigour, the Council can only function effectively if it is in day-to-day contact with the Holy Father. It needs to send a telegram of condolence *now* to the victims of outrage or catastrophe, and cannot work at the leisurely rhythm of other Roman departments, which can take up to two years to produce a document.

So, for a variety of reasons, the Cardinals were not at all happy about the proposals for the 'revision' of the Roman Curia. They sent them back for further study. They asked for a 'theological prelude', because one can only say how the Curia should be organized if one knows what it is for. This book unwittingly contributed to this preliminary theological work. Meanwhile, the highly secret commission working on the project was 'enlarged'. Their names leaked out by accident in March 1986. Retired Cardinal Sebastiano Baggio presides over a study commission that has five more Cardinals, Italian Opilio Rossi, Nigerian Francis Arinze, Venezuelan José Rosalio Castillo Lara, French-Canadian Edouard Gagnon and Austrian Salesian Alfons Steckler. Two Italian curial prelates, Giovanni Marra and Bruno Bertagna, complete the team. Apart from Arinze, these names do not inspire much confidence about the future of the Secretariat for Christian Unity. Gagnon, for example (see p. 179), believes that the American Church is 'in material schism' and would sack 90 per cent of its moral theology professors. Curran is only a sighting-shot. At the moment, the proposals for curial reform have disappeared into the black hole reserved for future plans: nothing is ever 'going to happen' in the Vatican, you have to wait until it is announced. What will be announced will be a *fait accompli*, probably in August when the press can't find anyone to comment intelligently about it.

If reforming the Curia was an obscure question, accessible only to a small group of initiates or Vatican-watchers (*Vaticanisti* is the Italian term), the Extraordinary Synod brought reporters flocking to Rome on a scale not seen since the days of the Vatican Council it was designed to commemorate. For many the celebration of twenty years after Vatican II was a nostalgic trip down memory lane. Misty-eyed veterans of the Council reminisced about famous victories long ago, when the Good and the Bad Guys seemed a lot easier to identify. Washington Redemptorist Fr Francis X. Murphy re-incarnated 'Xavier Rynne', his *alter ego*, and produced a book on the Synod under this *nom de guerre*. I too wrote a book on the Synod (*Synod Extraordinary*, Darton, Longman and Todd), so I needn't devote too much space to it here.

The participants in the Synod all declared that it was 'a great success'. But when questioned about the precise nature of its achievement they became rather coy and tongue-tied. The reason was, quite simply, that the main achievement of the Synod was negative. It had *not* followed the programme of 'restoration' set out by Cardinal Joseph Ratzinger in a series of interviews published as *The Ratzinger Report*. To do him justice, Ratzinger never espoused the line of dissident traditionalist Archbishop Marcel Lefebvre, who said that Vatican II was in error because it had meekly succumbed to secularism, Protestantism, Freemasonry, Zionism and international Communism. Ratzinger on the contrary held that Vatican II was a Good Thing. His quarrel – so he said – was not with Vatican II itself, but with the faulty interpretations of it that had become fashionable. He was especially worried by those who did whatever they liked in the name of 'the spirit of Vatican II'.

Believing that the Church was 'manifestly falling apart in more than one or two places', Ratzinger laid the blame for this state of affairs squarely on the shoulders of theologians who, with the pernicious doctrine of 'anonymous Christianity' (Karl Rahner), had undermined evangelism and 'opened the Church indiscriminately to an agnostic and hostile world'. Moral theologians, especially in the United States, had compromised with a secular ethic, imagining that 'they have to choose between clashing with their society and clashing with their bishops'. Ratzinger claimed they had opted to clash with their bishops. This judgement had some harsh consequences in the real world. It was revealed only in March 1986 that Ratzinger had written to Charles Curran with some critical 'observations' as long ago as 10 May 1983. There were further exchanges in autumn 1985 with Curran stoutly defending his right to explore non-infallible teachings. What had begun as a 'dialogue' on the principles of moral theology from which the whole Church might benefit, soon became a 'confrontation' that led nowhere. Curran wanted to know who his accusers were. Ratzinger replied with the inquisitor's remark: 'Your own writings condemn you'. Curran's compromise of not teaching sexual ethics was rejected. The fall-out reached our shores when Kevin Kelly, appointed moral theology professor at Heythrop College, University of London, defended Curran in *The Times* (30 August 1986). The Catholic Theological Association of Great Britain – or strictly speaking those of its members who had not left their annual conference in Leeds – expressed their 'urgent concern at an apparent tendency in some recent actions of ecclesiastical authorities to compromise the legitimate exercise of responsible freedom in theological discussion and debate within the Church'. That was on 8 September 1986.

But all this was in the lap of the future in autumn 1985 when it seemed as though Ratzinger had set the agenda for the Synod and that his pessimism about Vatican II would prevail. Both assumptions proved false. On the way back from Africa in August 1985 Pope John Paul conceded that Cardinal Ratzinger had been expressing his own 'personal opinions' and not those of his office. However far-fetched, this remark licensed theological critics to set about Ratzinger with considerable zest. Again, as reports came in from the 104 episcopal conferences (benches of bishops) all over the world, it became abundantly clear that most bishops held that Vatican II was the work of the Holy Spirit, and that it had brought greater vitality to the Church which, despite growing secularization, now had a more adapted liturgy and an increasingly active laity. Ratzinger's systematic pessimism was rejected. When the Synod began, its *rapporteur*, Cardinal Godfried Danneels of Malines-Brussels, sharply put the boot in. Asked whether Ratzinger's book had any bearing on the work of the Synod, he replied, 'This Synod is not about anyone's book'.

There was some slight evidence that Ratzinger himself became aware that his office as Prefect of the Congregation for the Doctrine of Faith (see chapter 7) did not automatically equip him to pronounce on any theological topic anywhere in the world. He complained of being overworked and misunderstood. He did a thorough semantic job on the concept of 'restoration' in order to get off the hook on which he had impaled himself. 'Restoration', he now explained, did not have the natural sense of 'bringing it back the way it was', but meant rather 'the quest for a new balance after all the exaggerations of an indiscriminate opening to the world' (*The Ratzinger Report*, p. 37). This was a novel definition of 'restoration'.

Thus, by any ordinary definition, the Extraordinary Synod of 1985 was not a work of 'restoration'. Its final report – the first one ever to be published immediately after a Synod – stated with the utmost clarity:

> The end for which this Synod was convoked was the celebration, verification and promotion of Vatican II. With grateful hearts we feel that we have truly obtained this fruit, with God's assistance. Unanimously we have CELEBRATED the Second Vatican Council, from which have come forth many spiritual fruits for the universal Church and the particular Churches, as well as for the men of our time. Unanimously and joyfully we also VERIFY that the Council is a legitimate and valid expression and interpretation of the deposit of faith as it is found in sacred scripture and in the living tradition

of the Church. Therefore we are determined to PROGRESS further along the path indicated to us by the Council.

I have left this text in the translation provided by the Vatican Press Office at the end of the Synod. Rough-hewn, sexist ('the men of our time') and bizarre (in what sense can a Synod 'verify' a Council?) though it is, it gives one a sense of immediacy and explains why they all felt so pleased with themselves. Against all the prophets of woe, they endorsed Vatican II. That looks like a great achievement only if one had feared something else.

Yet if one looked at the fine print of the Final Report there were two features that gave grounds for disquiet, and suggested that Ratzinger, having made an initial concession, had clawed back some lost ground. First, the idea of the Church as the 'new people of God on the march' scarcely appears in the Final Report. Yet the Council placed the People of God at the centre of its understanding of the Church. Chapter 2 of *Lumen Gentium* is entirely devoted to it. There are many possible images of the Church in the New Testament: ark, sheep-fold, vineyard, bride of Christ, body of Christ and so on. But the most synthetic shorthand summing up of what the Church really is – according to *Lumen Gentium* – is the People of God. But in the Extraordinary Synod's treatment, the People of God is, as it were, squeezed between the emphasis on the Church as 'mystery' found in chapter 1 of *Lumen Gentium* and the Church as hierarchical institution found in chapter 3 of the conciliar constitution.

What is at stake here? The fact that Vatican II placed the People of God before the hierarchical constitution of the Church had great practical importance. It was more faithful to the New Testament and the patristic tradition. It asserted that the Church was essentially the new Messianic people on which the gifts of the Holy Spirit were showered.

The Greek expression for People of God, *laos tou theou*, was at the origin of our term laity and layperson. It stressed the equality in grace of all the baptized. Distinctions of office in the Church are, therefore, functional and, in some sense, secondary. So People of God would be the pivot for the Synod of 1987 on 'the role and vocation of the laity in the Church and in the world'. Since this was also an approach to the Church in which all Christians could find themselves, it had great ecumenical importance.

But conversely, the abandonment of the People of God as the starting-point for thinking about the Church would signify that all these insights would be thrown away on the dubious pretext that they were tainted with a dangerous dose of 'democratic' thinking. But the Church is not a democracy. *Q.E.D.*

Father Kenneth Baker, an American Jesuit whom no-one would accuse of being a liberal theologian, let the cat out of the bag by quoting an Italian newspaper, *La Repubblica*, which said that 'the expression "People of God" has been entombed by the Synod'. Baker thought this was a happy result. He explained: 'That may be a bit strong but it does reflect the almost total disappearance of the image from the speeches and documents of the Synod.' He also pointed out the similarities between this Final Report and the Ratzinger interview, 'especially in the concept of the Church as mystery of Christ and communion, rather than the People of God'. Baker also claimed that this Final Report 'must now be used when it comes to the authentic interpretation of Vatican II'. But this, says Professor Joseph A. Komonchak of the Catholic University of America, 'is a view which on substantive and formal grounds must be resisted' (*The Tablet*, 8 March 1986, p. 255). For it would mean that Vatican II had been repudiated on a crucial point.

Theological arguments, it should be clear, are not always as straightforward as they may appear. A hidden agenda is invariably at work. What is intended is not always what is stated. This could be seen in the way the Synod Final Report transformed the meaning of 'the signs of the times'. As used by Pope John XXIII and the Council, 'discerning the signs of the times' meant detecting the presence of the Holy Spirit in the positive trends of our age. John's encyclical *Pacem in Terris* hailed the end of colonialism, the emancipation of women and the advancement of the working-class as welcome 'signs of the times'.

But the Synod Final Report subverts this position. It says:

The Church as communion is the sacrament of the world's salvation. . . . In this context we affirm the importance and the great relevance of the pastoral constitution *Gaudium et Spes*. At the same time we observe that the signs of our times differ to some extent from those which the Council discerned, for today anguish and suffering have increased. All over the world today there is hunger, oppression, injustice, war, torture, terrorism and other kinds of violence of every kind. This obliges us to a new and more profound theological reflection, which interprets such signs in the light of the Gospel.

This suggests – perhaps is meant to suggest – that the reading offered of the signs of the times in 1964-5 was superficial and belonged to the overly-optimistic and self-deceiving 1960s. No doubt there is something in this. No doubt a 'theology of the cross' is always needed by believers to help them cope with disaster and failure. Yes, Christ suffers in Auschwitz and the Lebanon and South Africa and the Gulag Archipelago. The case of Irina Ratushinskaya, a Soviet Catholic sentenced to seven years hard labour for writing poems proves that. But that is not what the Council had in mind when it spoke of 'signs of the times'.

After this theological hard grind – it is sometimes necessary to split hairs in order to avoid starting them – it is a relief to return to the more humdrum world of personalities. Mgr George Higgins of the Catholic University of Washington tells me that I was unjust to Cardinal John J. O'Connor. I confess to excessive reliance on a secondary source and freely admit that O'Connor as a 'team-player' differs notably from O'Connor the loner. My Editor, Tom Fox, conceded that O'Connor's statements at the 1986 Catholic Press Association in Columbus, Ohio, were 'more subtle and reflective than what he said during the 1984 presidential election' (*National Catholic Reporter*, 20 June 1986). O'Connor has evidently progressed.

Moreover, that he is no longer an unconditional supporter of the Republican administration is proved by the following facts. He has spoken before a Congressional Committee against aid to the Contras in their war against Nicaragua. This infuriated the administration. *Item*, testifying before the Congressional Committee on Housing, O'Connor recommended directing funds from the MX missile project towards housing the poor. *Item*, his widely published telegram to President Reagan urging a change in his 'Biltberg itinerary' greatly upset the administration. In short, O'Connor is far from being the presidential poodle I depicted, and has supported the 'consistent ethic' stance of Bernadin from the outset. The remark quoted from *Corriere del la Sera* on p. 105 is now explained away as a 'joke'. Reporters asked him if he was close to Pope and President. According to my latest source, O'Connor replied, 'Some reporters seem to think that I am so close that each one calls me several times a week, and sometimes one has to wait because I am talking to the other.' Laughter greeted this sally.

So there was laughter in Rimini in August 1985, but in Brazil, on 12 April 1986, there were tears from the 320 bishops as a letter from Pope John Paul was read out to them. These were tears of joy, for the Pope now praised liberation theology and said it was 'not only opportune, but useful and necessary'. The Brazilian bishops hugged each other with delight and sang *Alleluias*. The day before Easter Sunday there had been a hint of what was to come. Franciscan Father Leonardo Boff, their chief theological adviser, was told that the ban imposing silence on him was lifted. There was, naturally, neither explanation nor apology. But it was one of the swiftest rehabilitations in Church history. They usually happen when the subject is well and truly dead. Thus there was talk among Dominicans in 1986 of rehabilitating Meister Eckhart, condemned in 1329. Boff was more fortunate. He was not asked to recant in centuries.

These various moves led commentators to speculate on this 'unique example of a change of mind by the Pope on a leading issue. He is usually credited with remarkable powers for listening, but then continuing as if he had heard nothing' (Peter Nichols, *The Times*, 18 June 1986). So had John Paul really changed his mind? Had he become a 'liberal'?

The best way to answer this question is to compare what John Paul said to the Brazilian bishops in this Easter letter of 1986 with his speech to them in Fortaleza, Brazil on July 10 1980. The address to the episcopal conference is always the most important part of any papal visit: away from TV cameras, the Pope speaks his mind uninhibitedly and gives the bishops his verdict on their pastoral policies. In Fortaleza in 1980 he was very critical of the Brazilian bishops. He treated 'base communities', on which they pinned their hopes, with suspicion. They must not be allowed to drift toward political goals. Then came the warning: 'We would all be happy if errors and deviations in the areas of Christ, the Church and Man were remote possibilities rather than an actual threat. But you know this is not so.' It was at Puebla in January 1979 that John Paul had first denounced this triad of errors concerning Christ (reducing him to a political liberator), the Church (inventing a popular Church that wells up from below), and Man (espousing false ideologies, *i.e.* Marxism). He added that they must treat the C.D.F. with respect because it acted in his name. It was tough talk for someone visiting a country for the first time. The Brazilians were not given time to explain that the charges did not stick.

This 1980 negative judgement on the Brazilians was passed from the outside. It was based on anonymous, hostile and selective reports. It assumed the worst. Its analysis presupposed that the most urgent problem facing the Brazilian Bishops was unorthodoxy, whereas they thought it was injustice and dire poverty. It reflected the judgement of Archbishop (now Cardinal) Alfonso Lopez Trujillo, President of C.E.L.A.M., the Latin American Bishops'

Council, who made no secret of his desire to root out liberation theology and 'smash' the Brazilian Bishops (see p. 86).

What has happened between 1980 and 1986 is simply that Pope John Paul has got to know the Brazilian Bishops better. He has exchanged second-hand reports for first-hand knowledge. Crucial was the encounter he had with representative Brazilian Bishops in the Vatican March 13-15 1986. It was not a formal meeting and not dignified as a particular Synod (the Dutch precedent of 1980 was not very encouraging, for it could not be made to work when the Bishops went back home to the Netherlands).

But the loosely-structured meeting enabled the Brazilians to say what they really thought about the Roman Curia, and the Roman Curia to say what it really thought about the Brazilian Bishops – all in the presence of the listening Pope who nodded encouragingly, if enigmatically, from time to time. One indication of the mood at this highly-secret meeting was that when Cardinal Bernadin Gantin, in the chair, proposed that the Brazilians should elect a spokesman, the Brazilians said they couldn't possibly do that because in their own meetings they continually interrupted each other. 'The right to interrupt' is the most fundamental human right. The ice was broken.

In the event they interrupted each other to such good effect that within two weeks John Paul wrote, or caused to be written, the letter that so moved them. The guilty suspects now became exemplary: 'You have performed an incomparable (*inestimável*) service for the Church of Brazil and, beyond that, for other Churches and the universal Church; a service which helps indirectly Brazilian society and, beyond that, the entire human family.' There could be no higher praise than that. They had found a new way of being 'Church'.

But it was not just the compliments which mattered to the Brazilians, gratifying though they were. It was the sense that what they had been trying to do was now properly understood. Their 'option for the poor' was now seen as they saw it themselves, and not as a cloak for political partisanship: 'As pastors you are extraordinarily close to your people, in solidarity with them in their joys and sufferings, as ready to educate them in faith and strengthen their Christian life as to succour their needs, have compassion on their afflictions and trials, and to bring them hope.' Then came the remark on liberation theology, which was further hailed as 'a new stage in theological reflection'. True, this 'new stage' was presented as in continuity with the apostolic tradition and the contemporary *magisterium* (including his own 'social encyclical', *Laborem Exercens*), but that did not worry the Brazilians. They had always believed that they were deepening and renewing tradition, not discarding or contradicting it.

So it would be truer to say that Pope John Paul has not so much changed his mind about liberation theology as changed his approach to the Brazilians. He remains deeply suspicious of liberation theology insofar as it is unpurged of 'Marxism', and while the Brazilians were being absolved, he was exhorting the Nicaraguan bishops to stand firm under the 'persecution' of the 'Marxist' Sandinistas.

For confirmation that there was a change of approach rather than of mind, one need only turn to the second Instruction *On Christian Freedom and Liberation* issued 5 April 1986 (though officially dated 22 March 1986). It did nothing to counter the negative emphasis of the September 1984 Instruction. Indeed, it explains that its warnings about 'deviations, or risks of deviations damaging to Christian faith . . . far from being outmoded, appear ever more timely and relevant' (p.1). The truth is that everyone was misled about the 'positive document' promised by the first Instruction. People assumed that, having disentangled the negative aspects of liberation theology, the positive document would redress the balance by saying what its merits were. But this was always a faulty assumption.

A more careful reading revealed that what was promised was a 'positive treatment of *the theme of liberation*'. This enabled John Paul, through the proxy of Ratzinger, to redefine the problem and turn liberation into a deeply spiritual experience rather in the manner of Alexander Solzhenitsyn. The prisoner is freer than his jailer. As the Pope says, 'Freedom is not the liberty to do anything whatsoever. It is the freedom to do good, and in this alone is happiness to be found. The good is thus the goal of freedom' (p.26). So he was rather upset that others had made off with this notion of 'liberation'.

What John Paul is most concerned with in this instruction – it bears his unmistakable personal stamp – is to denounce the myth of progress. In particular he warns against swallowing promises of paradise on earth that inevitably end in tyranny. So the second Instruction, though it makes some profound points, is not really about liberation theology at all. It is on another level of discourse. It ushers in another 'language-game' (Ludwig Wittgenstein). For that reason liberation theologian Jon Sobrino, a Basque Jesuit working in El Salvador, could describe it as 'a document without witnesses, without martyrs, without a home'.

Other liberation theologians gave the instruction a warmer welcome, and claimed that it had 'put an end to the debate'. That was tactically shrewd of them, no doubt. But no debate is ever finally 'resolved' in the Church, and the dialectic of primacy and collegiality, centre and periphery, authority and conscience, provides scenarios that have constantly to be replayed with a fresh cast and new hopes. That is what living in the Church means.

So what John Paul was signalling to the Brazilian Church was the urgent need for a truce. Now that he had got to know them better, he would fuss less and trust them more. He did not wish to go down in history exclusively as a Pope of bans and excommunications.

There was also a political factor whose importance emerged only gradually. In 1986 Brazil was at a delicate stage in the process of its 'return to democracy'. The nation was awash with schemes for a new constitution. The Church was deeply involved in these debates. As the bishops and Leonardo Boff always stress, 'formal democracy' – merely voting every now and again – is not enough. They need a *social* democracy which brings justice and fraternity. In the northeast of Brazil a young priest, Father Josimo Tavares, was shot in the back on 10 May 1986, by a hired assassin who justified his crime on the grounds that the priest's support for land-reform proved he was a 'Communist'. The Pope did not want to lend credence to that kind of propaganda. He wished to repudiate the idea that he was at odds with the Brazilian bishops.

Yet the whole protracted and bloody battle concerning liberation theology disclosed a curious feature of this pontificate. So many words are uttered and so many passions are aroused, and yet so little changes on the ground. Whether one thinks of the Jesuits, the Church in the Netherlands, or liberation theology, it almost seems as though, the Pope's victories are pyrrhic and exist on paper or the TV screen only.

The theory of Marshall McLuhan's disciple, Derrick de Kerckhove of the University of Toronto, who explains that Pope John Paul is the first 'bionic' Pope and a 'collective icon', simultaneously personal and planetary, would throw light on this. De Kerckhove also maintains that theological controversies count for little when the Pope arrives in his 'sequin-spangled helicopter' and 'persuades by his presence'. If that is true, I am not sure how desirable it is. For the basic cell of the Church is always a small group of people who know each other personally.

Back in the Vatican, there have been some changes at the top. Polish-born Cardinal Ladislaw Rubin has retired for health reasons and has been replaced as Prefect of the Congregation for the Oriental Churches by the Indian Cardinal, Simon Lourdasamy. Cardinal

Silvo Oddi duly retired on reaching 75 and was succeeded as Prefect of the Congregation for the Clergy by the like-minded Cardinal Antonio Innocenti. Among the diplomats, Archbishop Giorgio Zur has exchanged East Africa for Paraguay, billiards-playing Archbishop Luigi Barbarito has gone from parched Canberra, Australia, to leafy Wimbledon, London, while the first ever U.S. Ambassador to the Vatican, Knight of Malta, William Wilson, was hastily removed after an ill-timed business trip to Libya. His rumoured successor, at the time of writing, is Frank Shakespeare.

Ecumenical relations suffered a set-back when Orthodox bishops and theologians walked out of the fourth meeting of the Catholic-Orthodox theological commission at Bari in southern Italy on 8 June 1986. They complained that an exhibition of Macedonian icons in the Vatican was a *de facto* recognition of the Macedonian Church as 'autocephalous': most Orthodox think the Macedonians should remain under the Greek Patriarch. This quarrel made it less likely that Pope John Paul would be able to visit the Soviet Union in 1988 for the millennium of Christianity in Russia. Nor does he stand much chance of being able to visit Lithuania, for so long united with Poland, on his third visit home planned for 1987.

Anglican-Roman Catholic relations also suffered some rude buffeting. In September A.R.C.I.C.-II, meeting at Llandaff, officially 'brought the Reformation to an end' with a joint statement on that old bone of contention, 'justification' (by faith? or by works?). Whether this persuaded Evangelicals, who have the slogan 'justification' written on their banner, to look more benevolently on Rome, may be questioned. A.R.C.I.C.'s previous agreements on the Eucharist, and on Ministry and Authority, hitherto politely received, were dismissed by John Drury in *Theology* (July 1986) as 'loftily grandiloquent statements' which idealized the papacy and romanticized the Church.

Then there was the ordination of women. The Anglican Synod meeting at York in June 1986 had before it a scheme which would have resulted in a 'Church of England A' made up of traditionalists and an all-male clergy, and a 'Model B' which would accommodate doctrinal liberals and a mixed clergy. One or other would have to be 'disestablished'. This divisive, not to say ludicrous, plan was wisely abandoned. There will be more delay and another rethink. But out of it may come an enhanced sense of episcopal responsibility – what Vatican II called 'collegiality'. Are bishops, or are they not, the teachers (*doctores*) of the Church and the witnesses of faith (*testes fidei*)?

Women's ordination has been the subject of an exchange of letters between Canterbury and Rome. Dr Robert Runcie seized the initiative by saying very firmly that 'the context for the discussion' (of women's ordination), 'is the context of sacramental theology and the tradition of the Church'. In other words, it was not a matter of remedying an injustice or getting in the sociological swim of things or saying that if women can be Prime Ministers or work in the Stock Exchange then they can be priests. Ordination is not the Bastille the feminists have to conquer. It has a deep theological foundation. The primary meaning of the Incarnation is that Jesus is human, not that he is male. 'What is not taken up, is not saved', says an ancient maxim. If femininity is not included in Christ, then women are not saved. So Runcie, who met the Pope twice in 1986, in India in February and at Assisi in October, passes over to the attack: 'Because the humanity of Christ Our High Priest includes male and female, it is thus urged that the ministerial priesthood should now be opened to women in order to make it more perfectly represent Christ's inclusive High Priesthood.'

Pope John Paul left the task of answering this letter (said to have been drafted by Henry Chadwick) in detail to Willebrands. Though his reply held out little hope of a shift on the ordination of women, at least he agreed with Runcie in putting the question on the level of doctrine. But he argued that the idea of the priest as the *icon* or image of Christ precludes women from acting *in persona Christi*. However, the fantasy that the Roman Catholic Church was entering into serious discussion about women's ordination through the medium of ARCIC was scotched by the private understanding of the Roman Catholic members of the Commission. Their brief was to consider women's ordination *only* as an additional *obstacle* to future union, and if Anglican orders might eventually be recognized, a distinction would have to be made between those of men (possibly valid) and women (in no circumstances valid). This was a secret clause whose existence was not publicly revealed. It looks like a recipe for getting nowhere immensely slowly.

Little that is written in this new preface betrays a very sanguine view of the immediate future. The pontificate has settled down into a pattern. Its aim is to reassert control over the unruly provinces after the chaos allegedly caused and acquiesced in by Paul VI. But it may be too late. In 1975 I published a book called *The Runaway Church*. Lots of people have been running ever since. The fact is that if you say to lay people often enough, as Pope Pius XII did, 'You are the Church', they end up by believing it.

A word, penultimately, about the spirit in which this book is written. I am a card-carrying, active, believing and (I trust) loyal Roman Catholic. In his book on bishops Lord Longford was kind enough to describe me as 'devout'. I don't know about that. But I do know that one cannot write a single sentence about the Church without having some kind of implicit theology of the Church — without an ecclesiology. My theology is based four-square on that of Vatican II.

It leaves scope for freedom and that *parresia* – boldness in speaking out – mentioned in the *Acts of the Apostles*. To those who say 'Don't rock the boat', I can reply, 'But it is sometimes necessary to rock it to get it off the mud-flats.' I find two quotations helpful in this matter. Beaumarchais says in *The Marriage of Figaro* that 'without the freedom to criticise, no praise has any value'. It is a good rule for those whose business it is to write about the Vatican. And it echoes what Melchior Cano, a Spanish Dominican, said at the Council of Trent more than four centuries ago: 'Peter' [that is, the Pope], 'has no need of our lies or flattery. Those who blindly and indiscriminately defend every decision of the Supreme Pontiff are the very ones who do the most to undermine the authority of the Holy See instead of upholding it – they destroy instead of strengthening its foundations.'

It remains to thank Arthur Jones and Thomas C. Fox, past and present editors of *The National Catholic Reporter*, the only Catholic paper in the English-speaking world with the wit and the resources to employ a full-time Vatican Affairs writer. To John Wilkins, Editor of *The Tablet*, I owe a debt which only he can measure. I would also like to thank *The Universe*, now in the safe hands of the bishops, for help in picture research.

Oxford

8 September 1986.

Preface

This book was conceived at Knock in the West of Ireland on 30 September 1979, while waiting for Pope John Paul II to arrive. The confessional chapel had been turned into a hospitality room. There I met Lord Longford who proposed, not another book on the Pope, but a book on the Vatican. Within a few weeks I rashly signed a contract. But the project was delayed by the need to work on *John XXIII, Pope of the Council*, which took longer than I had expected. That's life. But the delay had the advantage that in the meantime the pontificate has acquired a definite shape, and this is reflected in the Roman Curia, the papal bureaucracy.

Some 'progressives' ('liberals' in the United States) will deplore this concentration on the Church at its most institutional. They say the Curia should be ignored as an irrelevance. In my view this is a mistake. For in the 'great tradition', represented for example by John Henry Newman and Friedrich von Hügel, there are always three elements in Catholicism that have to be held together in creative tension: theology, worship and government – or, if you prefer, thought, prayer and the institution. The structures, the organization, the apparatus are in principle at the service of the spiritual reality of *koinonia* or communion.

Once that point has been grasped, one can speak with great freedom, confident that the expression of mature faith will always be listened to in the Church. A few cherished maxims act as a lodestar. John Stuart Mill said: 'My love for an institution is in proportion to my desire to reform it.' That would be merely pompous unless one included oneself in the never-ending process of reform and conversion (*metanoia*). These are private matters for the *prie-dieu* or one's confessor. Even more relevant for a writer is Beaumarchais' remark in *The Marriage of Figaro* that 'without the freedom to criticize, no praise has any value'. In a curious way it echoes what the Spanish Dominican, Melchior Cano, said at the Council of Trent more than four centuries ago: 'Peter has no need of our lies or flattery. Those who blindly and indiscriminately defend every decision of the Supreme Pontiff are the very men who do most to undermine the authority of the Holy See instead of supporting it – they destroy instead of strengthening its foundations.' (Quoted in Adrian Hastings (ed.), *Bishops and Writers*.)

It should be clear by now that one cannot write or speak about the Vatican without some implicit theology of the Church. My theology of the Church stands foursquare on Vatican II. It can be seen at work everywhere in the book, but more expressly in the final chapter where I have allowed myself some prophetic license. True, I have not dealt directly with the squalid matter of Vatican finances. This is simply because I have nothing new to say on the subject. I defer in such matters to the expert, Rupert Cornwell of the *Financial Times* and John le Carré's brother (see Rupert Cornwell, *God's Banker*).

It remains to thank Arthur Jones and Thomas C. Fox, previous and present editors of the *National Catholic Reporter*, the only Catholic paper in the world with the wit and the resources to employ a full-time 'Vatican affairs writer'; also *The Universe* for their help providing pictures.

Castagnoli in Chianti
Feast of the Transfiguration, 6 August 1985

Postscript

Since completing this book there has been another 'earthquake', or at least near-miss, in the Roman Curia. There is yet another plan of reform. Its existence was just about admitted though its contents were not officially divulged. It was discussed at the meeting of the College of Cardinals, 20-23 November 1985. For a description of the proposals and a blow-by-blow account of what happened to them, see my *Synod Extraordinary* (Darton, Longman & Todd, 1986). The impression for the moment is that nothing much will happen very swiftly. Most of the features of the plan already appear in this book as dangerous trends. So it is quite possible that I have unwittingly written the epitaph of the Roman Curia of Paul VI, but also that 'preamble on the theological nature of the Curia' that the cardinals called for in November 1985. One is always happy to oblige.

8 December 1985

1

Of Bridges, Walls and Fountains

Most foreign visitors to Rome go there because of the Vatican and the Pope. In 1886 the poet and explorer Wilfrid Scawen Blunt decided to spend some time in Rome. Cardinal Manning, an old friend of his mother, encouraged the project. 'You will get back there,' said the Cardinal, 'into the rut of the centuries, and it will do you good.' (Elizabeth Longford, *Pilgrimage of Passion*.) Blunt, who was something of an old scamp, set off and duly had an audience with Pope Leo XIII. It didn't do him much good.

People have been going to Rome from the early Middle Ages, and 'Anglo-Saxons' were among the first to set up a 'college' on the banks of the Tiber. The very un-Latin word *Borgo* is a reminder of their presence. The college was only partly a school: it was also a hospice for visitors, an unofficial embassy to the popes, and a fortress to ward off the marauding Saracens (as the Muslims were locally known and still are in Italian puppet shows) who came sweeping up the Tiber in their longboats with distressing frequency. The name given to the quayside, *Lungotevere dei Sassoni*, is another memory of this Saxon presence, and the tower to the north of the tunnel under the Janiculum is all that remains of the French equivalent.

These earliest visitors, like those of today, were pilgrims. They went to Rome to venerate the relics of St Peter and St Paul and to see Peter's successor. They had the same motive, but they did not see what we see. On the Vatican Hill rose old St Peter's, conceived by Constantine after his conversion in 336. It was built in basilica style, modelled on the Roman courthouse – as indeed were all Roman churches at that date. The piazza in front of it was square in shape and nothing like as big as the area enclosed by Bernini's seventeenth-century colonnade. It lasted until the late fifteenth century. But the pilgrim in, say, the eighth century would also visit the church of St John Lateran, the Bishop of Rome's cathedral, St Mary Major and St Paul's without the Walls, which at this time was linked to the city by a magnificent marble colonnade, one of the wonders of the world. The modern pilgrim dodging through the traffic still makes the round of these same four basilicas.

But there are some very important differences. The word 'pope' was already in use, though at first it was applied to any priest (as it still is in some Orthodox churches today). But the preferred title for the Bishop of Rome was 'Vicar of Peter'. It was because he was held to be the successor of Peter, prince of the Apostles, that the Bishop of Rome acted as the final arbiter on the disputed questions that were put to him. At the Council of Chalcedon in 451 the 'tome' of Pope Leo the Great was hailed as an authentic account of the Incarnation with the cry: 'Peter has spoken through Leo.' Though there were tensions, there was at that time no break between East and West.

Yet the Pope had already acquired temporal power, and ruled over what later was called the Patrimony of Peter, simply because the Roman Emperor shifted his capital to the east, to Constantinople, and thus left 'Italy' undefended. The popes filled this power vacuum and became the sole defence against the barbarian hordes, the Goths and the Visigoths and other Germanic tribes, who intimidated and pillaged the north of the country until they were eventually repelled, bought off or, best of all, converted.

Christ made no promises of an earthly kingdom to St Peter, and the keys of the kingdom did not include or imply temporal power. But for a thousand years until 1870 it seemed natural that the Bishop of Rome should act as both temporal and spiritual leader. The tiara, a three-decker headpiece of Asiatic origin, was said to symbolize the pope's power over Heaven, Hell and Earth. (Bismark said he would gladly leave the first two realms to the Pope, provided he himself controlled the third.) The tiara was finally abandoned as inappropriate headgear for the 'servant of the servants of God' (Gregory the Great) as late as 1978. Its abandonment was John Paul I's contribution in his short reign of 33 days. But none of this would have worried the eighth-century pilgrim. He took it all in his stride.

If he were 'Saxon', he would also recall with pride that it was a pope, Gregory the Great, who had despatched the monk Augustine to England in 597. The fact that Gregory was in a hurry to convert the islanders before the year 600, when the end of the world was confidently predicted, was forgotten, as also was Augustine's letter, written from Gaul, to say that he had received such terrifying reports of the bloodthirsty habits of the inhabitants of Britain that he wanted to return home. The Pope ordered him to press on.

The mission to England, however, was important because it

showed the papacy to be a centre of missionary initiative. It was not evangelically passive. Other missions followed, notably that of St Cyril and St Methodius who worked among the Slav peoples, translating the Gospels and the liturgy into their languages. They even reached (it is said) the Vislani tribe of southern Poland. It was this atavistic memory that led Pope John Paul II to make Cyril and Methodius coequal patrons of Europe at the end of 1980. St Benedict, whose monks had evangelized Western Europe, had been assigned the post of patron of Europe in 1966, but John Paul wanted to make the contemporary point that there was a 'wider Europe' that included the Slavs. It was not suggested that St Benedict had fallen down on the job; but it was hinted that the present division of Europe was artificial and unhistorical.

Despite these examples of papal initiatives, it would be anachronistic to imagine that the Church at this time was anything like so dependent on the papacy as it later became. This was fortunate, for in the tenth century it went through the worst and most scandalous period of its history. Otto III, a successor of Charlemagne as Holy Roman Emperor (whom the Pope crowned in 800), visited Rome to see for himself Marozia. This remarkable lady was the mother of one pope, whom she conceived by another pope; the aunt of a third pope; and the grandmother of a fourth. As if this were not enough, with the aid of her mother she arranged for the election of nine popes in eight years, two of whom were strangled, one suffocated with a cushion, and the remainder were disposed of in ways unknown. By the time Otto visited her in 986 she had been in the Castel Sant'Angelo prison for fifty-four years. Otto had his cousin, Bruno, consecrated pope as Gregory V, and a synod ordered the execution of Marozia. A cushion was held firmly over her nose and mouth until she stopped breathing. There were no Lateran correspondents to report these appalling events. I think of Marozia every time I pass the grim Castel Sant'Angelo built on the mausoleum of the Emperor Hadrian.

In an article delightfully called 'The Ecclesiological Significance of Bad Popes', Edmund Hill O.P. points out that 'even when the Roman see suffered 200 years of scandalous degredation and decline . . . the other churches outside Italy were not seriously affected by this unfortunate state of affairs. It was, for example, a period of vigorous revival and reform in the Anglo-Saxon Church.' (*New Blackfriars*, March 1981.) The course of papal history is not so smooth as later apologetics claims. The ecclesiological significance of bad popes is that the Church can survive them.

I use these examples merely to show that, as Manning said, to go
to Rome is to 'get back into the rut of centuries'. History is inescapa-
ble in Rome. Everything that happens now reflects long-past events
in a bewildering kaleidoscope of continuity and change. The use of
the term 'Vatican', for example, would have been impossible in the
first millenium and for long after. Up to 1367, apart from their stay at
Avignon, the popes lived not in the Vatican but in the Lateran
Palace, next door to their cathedral church. St Peter's was always the
church of Christendom, and it had a unique role. But one could not
have said 'the Vatican' meaning the Pope and his Curia or civil service until the fifteenth century. Till then one would have had to say:
'The Lateran has just issued a decree forbidding clerical dress' (as
indeed happened).

So the Vatican that today's pilgrim sees is a very 'modern' creation when looked at in the long perspective of history. 'We think in
centuries here' is a favourite Roman saying. If we leave St Peter's out
of it for the moment, the most striking feature of the contemporary
Vatican is that it is almost entirely surrounded by high and formidable walls. I have twice walked round the walls of the Vatican, the first
time to see how long it took, the second to look at the monuments. ('If
you'd walked round seven times,' said a friend, 'they might have fallen down.') The total area occupied by the Vatican is 109 acres. It
took me about an hour to get round it.

'Something there is that doesn't love a wall,' sang Robert Frost,
and these walls are peculiarly forbidding. St Paul talks about knock-
ing walls down: 'For Christ is our peace . . . and has broken down
the dividing wall of hostility.' (Ephesians, 2:14.) Popes, one feels, as
pontiffs (*pontifices*), should be building bridges not walls. Inside the
Vatican St John's Tower remains as the last witness to the Saracen
threat. (Pope John XXIII turned it into a comfortable, four-storey
retreat, with a lift.) The Vatican walls, still solid and secure, zigzag
to provide enfilading fire according to the most advanced military
theories of the time they were built. They were designed to keep out
Christian princes. In 1527 Rome was sacked by mutinous Imperial
troops, with Benvenuto Cellini recording events from the Castel
Sant'Angelo. Most of Italy fell into the hands of the Spaniards.

The now highly decorative Swiss Guards date from this period.
They were merceneries. Niccolò Machiavelli, who died in the year
Rome was sacked, distrusted them. 'If a prince,' he wrote, 'bases the
defence of his state on mercenaries, he will never achieve stability or
security. For mercenaries are disunited, thirsty for power, undiscip-
lined, and disloyal.' (*The Prince*.)

Machiavelli also had thoughts on architecture that were antici-pated by Pope Nicholas V (another Niccolò). Of course a prince (that is a ruler) builds walls to keep enemies out, but they also serve to impress the inhabitants with the competence, glory and magnifi-cence of their ruler. So building big walls was a form of propaganda. On his death-bed Nicholas V gathered the cardinals to explain why he had devoted so much time to building and town planning. 'Mag-nificent buildings,' he explained, 'bring confidence to the people, and the splendour of quasi-eternal monuments strikes their imagina-tion as though they were works of God himself. Thus the veneration of the people is aroused, and in this way the idea of the divine origin of the Roman Church is enhanced and revived by religious admira-tion.' (Luigi Parpagliolo, *Roma*.) This does not sound very evangeli-cal. It was this same Nicholas V who ordered the demolition of the old St Peter's to make way for a new and magnificent pile.

This was a very Renaissance idea, and it was repugnant to Martin Luther who visited Rome and stayed with the Augustinians in their church on what is now the Piazza del Popolo. When one adds, as the late Archbishop 'Tommy' Roberts was fond of reminding everyone, that the new St Peter's was built on the proceeds of the sale of indulgences, then the Reformation as the rejection of Rome seems almost inevitable. The pure Gospel could not bear such extravagant magnificence.

Go to Rome, said Cardinal Manning, 'and it will do you good'. This has not been the invariable experience of pilgrims. There is a mediaeval Irish poem which warns that 'the trouble that you leave at home, you'll find in Rome, or not at all'. Dante thundered on about bad popes as did the English Franciscan William of Occam. But their 'bad popes' were not in Rome at all. They were in Avignon, and dependent on the favour of the French monarchs. Umberto Eco's novel, *The Name of the Rose*, vividly evokes this period of the papacy, when mystics like the Dominican Meister Eckhart were condemned (posthumously) and an earlier version of 'liberation theology' developed by the 'spiritual Franciscans' was harshly repressed. Pope John XXII thought it profoundly subversive to teach that 'Our Lord and Redeemer and his Apostles did not own anything either pri-vately or in common.' John XXII, the richest monarch in Europe, could hardly accept that. He made the name John unusable by the papacy for more than six centuries until Angelo Roncalli cheerfully revived it and began to speak of 'the Church of the poor'.

The new St Peter's was not an expression of the 'Church of the poor'. It was rather an example of that 'magnificence' of which

Nicholas V spoke. Four architects had already worked on it before Michelangelo was commissioned to complete it: the central piers and part of the surrounding walls were already built. Michelangelo's achievement was to stamp upon it his spiritual vision. He was not by profession an architect. Lord Clark says: 'It is the most sculptural of all his designs – a vast single unit that carries the eye round as if it were the carving of a torso.' (*Civilisation*.)

It was splendid indeed. But was it necessary? Mandel Creighton, the nineteenth-century Cambridge historian who later became Bishop of London, thought it was not:

> Even an age greedy of novelties and full of confidence in itself was startled at the demolition of the most venerable church in Christendom to·make way for something new. The basilica of St Peter's had been for ages the object of pilgrimages from every land. Outside, it gleamed with mosaics, of which the ship of Giotto is now the only survival; inside, its pavement was a marvel of mosaic art; its monuments told the history of the Roman Church for centuries. Men may praise the present day magnificence of St Peter's; they forget what was destroyed to make room for it. No more wanton or barbarous act of destruction was ever deliberately committed. (*A History of the Papacy from the Great Schism to the Sack of Rome*)

Creighton was speaking of Pope Julius II who made the fateful decision to pull down the old basilica. He attributed it to vanity and self-advertisement, and points out that from now on popes begin to show an indecent concern for their own funeral monuments.

One can grant all this and yet wonder whether the old St Peter's was all that solid on its foundations. Was it not about to tumble down? It is clear, however, that the St Peter's and the Vatican we see today were the product of a new vision, a new imagination. Titian's famous portrait of Pope Paul III makes him look like a crafty old fox, but the more one looks at it, the more it seems a wise old head. Paul III made the two decisions which transformed the Catholic Church: he called the Council of Trent and he sanctioned the 'Company of Jesus', a new religious order founded by a Basque called Inigo (or Ignatius in Latin). There was a new confidence and a new puritanism which reflected a desire not to give Protestants grounds for complaint. Subsequent popes were at least fairly respectable.

They also built the inner city of Rome we see today, according to Lord Clark 'the most grandiose piece of town planning ever attempted'. The new 'puritanism' of the Counter-Reformation did not extend to the arts. Baroque art expresses exuberance, joy, ecstasy and sheer fun. It loves *trompe l'oeil*, long vistas and above all fountains, the most insubstantial form of art. It is theatrical through and through. The new St Peter's Square is a magnificent stage set. Shakespeare was reminding his contemporaries:

> All the world's a stage
> And all the men and women merely players:
> They have their exits and their entrances . . .

Protestants of the more rigorous sort, persuaded that no civilization can be built on obedience and repression, might feel awkward in papal Rome, but (to quote Lord Clark for the last time):

> No one with an ounce of historical feeling or philosophic detachment can be blind to the great ideals, to the passionate belief in sanctity, to the expenditure of human genius in the service of God, which are made triumphantly visible to us with every step we take in Baroque Rome. Whatever it is, it isn't barbarian or provincial. Add to this that the Catholic revival was a popular movement, that it gave ordinary people a means of satisfying, through ritual, images and symbols, their deepest impulses, so that their minds were at peace; and I think one must agree to put off defining the word civilisation till we have looked at the Rome of the Popes.

We have been lured out of the Vatican, necessarily so, for at this date there was little distinction between the Vatican and the City of Rome. Back in the Sistine Chapel Michelangelo was painting his awesome *Last Judgement* which has looked down (save in exceptional circumstances) on all subsequent papal conclaves. It was originally conceived by Pope Clement VII as an act of atonement for the sack of Rome, the exorcism of a nightmare; but Paul III then transformed it into an assertion of the Church's power and a warning of the terrible fate that awaited all heretics and schismatics. It makes a powerful ideological statement that retains its force today despite the tourists who come to admire an artistic masterpiece.

The walls that surround the Vatican date from this same period. Popes, it seems, always signed their buildings with their coats of arms. The great wall builders were Pius IV (1559-65) and St Pius V (1556-72). (It was Pius V, incidentally, who continued to wear his Dominican habit after becoming Pope, thus starting the 'tradition' that popes wear white.) After these two sixteenth-century popes, the next spurt in wall building came in the nineteenth century and was the work of Gregory XVI (1830-46) and Pius IX (1846-78). This is symbolically significant. In the sixteenth century the Church built dogmatic walls against the threat of Protestantism at the Council of Trent. In the nineteenth century the popes, who had been humiliated by Napoleon and the French Revolution, denounced the indifferentism, democracy, secularism, socialism and the idea of progress – in short, the contemporary world – in the *Syllabus of Errors* (1864). Then Pio Nono tried to ward it off with the First Vatican Council (1869-70).

But in between the wall-building popes came those bewigged eighteenth-century popes who completed the urban landscape of the old city just at the time when the Grand Tour became fashionable. Their contribution has been described by Owen Chadwick:

> The Popes of the eighteenth century had a pleasant front to the world; like their city, dignified, aesthetic, ceremonious, baroque – with the new façade to Santa Maria Maggiore, which the Pope erected in the middle of the century . . . or with the most marvellous staircaise in Rome, the Spanish Steps erected in 1725 to commemoratee the Year of Jubilee; or with the gayest of the fountains of Rome, the Trevi, ordered by the Cossini Pope Clement XII and finished in 1762; or with the familiar Vatican museum itself, which in its main features was the work of the last Pope of the century, the Pope least able to afford the expense, but making the Vatican that which it is now . . . one of the artistic centres of the world. (*The Popes and European Revolution*)

Professor Chadwick makes eighteenth-century Rome sound like Trollope's Barchester, 'a sunlit countryside world without the rumblings of revolution; assured, stable-seeming, comfortable, archaic, well-paid, esteemed, kindly, courteous, and doing good by benevolence'. Even so, it was the century that saw fierce ecclesiastical battles with the Catholic monarchs of Europe (the quarrel over *Unigenitus* of 1725 has many features in common with that over *Humanae Vitae* of 1968); the suppression of the Jesuits; and, by the end of the century, the Pope carried off to France as a prisoner. Many good judges announced the end of the papacy as an institution.

Now we have assembled most of the elements that make up the Vatican and much of the Rome of today. Let us suppose we have a time machine available. A traveller from the eighth century would be utterly bewildered by eighteenth-century Rome, but using the Tiber and the outline of the hills as his guide, he might eventually work it out and find his way to the tomb of St Peter. The twentieth-century traveller could take with him a modern map which, intelligently used, would lead him to the familiar sights. Goethe leaned against the obelisk in the centre of St Peter's Square and ate a bunch of grapes, just as a modern pilgrim might.

But after this leisurely stroll through the centuries, the most fundamental question has still not been asked. Why is the Vatican there at all? Why is St Peter's here rather than in Antioch or Jerusalem? Part of the answer comes from the obelisk against which Goethe leaned. It was set up here only in 1586 and it took 900 men using 44 windlasses and 140 horses to haul it into position. It already had a long history. It was brought from Egypt in A.D. 60 in the biggest ship anyone had so far seen. In 64 the Emperor Nero had it installed in the circus he was building between the Janiculum and the Vatican Hill (about where Nervi's modern audience hall stands today). But this was a private circus, built for Nero's own pleasures. He liked chariot racing round the obelisk, which acted as a *stela* or marker.

On the night of 18-19 July 64, a fire broke out in the crowded, narrow streets of Rome, on the other side of the Tiber from Nero's circus. Fanned by violent winds, it lasted for just over a week. Most of the city was destroyed. Nero immediately embarked on extravagant and grandiose building projects. The homeless and foodless people of Rome thought this was not the most urgent priority. The rumour went round that Nero himself had started the fire in order to realize his dream of a magnificent Rome.

Nero got wind of these rumours. He determined to scotch them. A scapegoat would have to be found. A minor sect from Palestine of which little was known was conveniently to hand. And the mob would be appeased with a great show. On 13 October 64, anniversary of the day he became Emperor, Nero invited the Romans across the Tiber to see his new circus (all the others having been destroyed in the fire) and to join in the celebrations.

Tacitus described the scene in some detail. The Emperor himself took part in the games and drove his chariot careering wildly round the 300-yard track. Some of the Christians were dressed up in animal skins and then torn to pieces by enraged and hungry beasts. Others were used as human torches to light up the night sky and keep the spectators warm (for a Roman October can be very chilly after dusk). Yet others were crucified: on big feast days like this, the spectacle of an execution was the high point of the performance, the top of the bill. The work of Margherita Guarducci and other scholars has,

I believe, proved beyond reasonable doubt that Peter of Galilee, the leader of the Christians, was one of those who was crucified.

Once that is accepted, one can imaginatively reconstruct what happened next. There could obviously be no remains of those who were devoured by beasts or consumed by fire. But crucifixion at least left the dead man's friends and disciples with a body and the Romans, though they considered life cheap, were superstitious about death. It would be late at night when the body was recovered. From the Tiber up towards the Vatican Hill ran the Via Cornelia. It was lined with tombs, the grandest being nearest the Tiber. Halfway up the hill were the modest tombs of the less wealthy and, beyond that, a rocky wasteland. I believe that the broken body of Peter was brought to this place, buried and concealed beneath a rock. The secret was well kept until the conversion of Constantine when an altar was built over Peter's tomb: you can still see the remains of it in the recently excavated crypt (the *scavi*). I know of no place in Rome more moving. The basilica of St Peter's was then built over the tomb, in a great L-shaped space gouged out of the hill to accommodate it. From then on pilgrims have been going to Rome.

If this had not happened, the Vatican Hill would no doubt be covered like most of the other hills of Rome with vast apartment blocks. The key to the meaning of the Vatican and the Church is found here. It rests on these old bones which lie here awaiting the Resurrection. On this basis was subsequently built an enormous superstructure of theory and theology and speculation and faith and superstition and statecraft.

This chapter has been a walk around papal Rome. It must end with the last strictly papal contribution to the beauty of the city. On 10 September 1870, just ten days before the final collapse of the Papal States, Pius IX dejectedly blessed his forlorn troops – he expected them to put up merely token resistance – and went to inaugurate the fountain called *Acqua Pia* in his honour. It was near the Termini Station (which was already there) and is now in the square called Piazza Esedra. (The languid nudes were added later.)

One of the early witnesses in the beatification process of Pius IX (it began in 1907 and has made progress in the pontificate of Pope John Paul II) touchingly described this last appearance of the Pope as temporal sovereign. Giuseppe di Bisogno, Bishop of Urbani, told the tribunal:

The demonstration of affection by the people of Rome as he passed through the streets was indescribable. They pressed round his carriage crying, 'Holy Father, do not abandon us.' They said this because there had been a rumour that the Pope had fled Rome (as in 1848). The people had always loved him. This last demonstration was therefore most enthusiastic: it was his last public ceremony. (Pietro Pirri S.J. (ed.), *Pio IX e Vittorio Emanuele II*)

That was the end of the Papal States. From then on Pius IX complained that he was the 'prisoner of the Vatican' and did not emerge from his prison. An anti-clerical mob tried to throw his mortal remains into the Tiber in 1881 with raucous cries of 'Throw the old dolt into the river.' The Bishop of Rome was unable to set foot in the City of Rome until 1929. Rome had entered a new phase in its history: it became the capital city of a modern state.

It is surprising, in retrospect, how calmly and relatively painlessly this transition was achieved. Till then the received wisdom – for which Dutch, French and Irish Papal Zouaves had paid with their lives – was that the Papal States were essential to the independence of the Pope. As Lord Acton put it with his customary vigour:

> The conservation of the independence of the Holy See through the integrity of its territory has been an object of such importance as frequently to engage nearly the whole of Europe. . . . Empires have risen and fallen in its behalf, and it has been the paramount interest and motive in most of the greatest changes in the political arrangements of Europe. (From an article in *The Rambler*, 1880; quoted in Douglas Woodruff (ed.), *Essays on Church and State*, Hollis & Carter, 1952)

That was true. Yet how few mourned. The fact is that the loss of the Papal States was like getting rid of an embarrassing incubus. The deprivation of political power enabled the popes to concentrate on their spiritual authority. September 1870 marked the turning point. Rome was to change more in the next hundred years than it had in the previous three hundred. How it changed will be the theme of the next chapter.

2

From Sacred to Secular City

The novelist Henry James visited Rome in 1873, curious to know how the city had changed now that it had passed from papal to secular rule. The most striking change was on the newsstands: where once you could read only solemn and highly censored papers like the *Osservatore Romano* or *La Voce della Verità*, now there was a cheerful clutter of anti-clerical and irreverent newspapers as well. 'Rome reading unexpurgated news,' wrote James, 'is another Rome indeed.' The other difference he noted was the rapid increase in population: 'The Corso was always a well-filled street, but now it's a perpetual crush.' So James concluded: ' . . . by force of numbers, Rome has been secularized.' (Quoted in Bernard Wall, *Italy, A Personal Anthology*.) The process of secularization, then just begun, gathered pace in the next 115 years and transformed 'the sacred city' into the thoroughly secular city we know today.

When the Porta Pia was breached on 20 September 1870, Rome had a population of just over 200,000. It still had a rural air: oxen drank from the Triton fountain in the Piazza Barberini; the progress of His Eminence's carriage was often impeded by scuttling hens or obstinate goats. Giulio Andreotti, the durable Christian Democrat, had an old aunt who remembered Pope Pius IX driving slowly down the Via Giulia of an evening, pausing now and then to allow someone to kiss his ring or present a petition, as he recalls in his memoirs, *A Ogni Morte di Papa*.

But this cosy intimacy between the popes and Rome changed once it was decided that the city would become the capital of Italy. This was not an inevitable choice, and there was considerable debate about it in Florence, the first meeting place of the new Italian Parliament. But in the end history and the memory of the Roman Empire prevailed. By making Rome their capital, the new rulers of Italy were challenging the Pope on his home ground, and depriving him of the city of which he was bishop. If they had made Florence the capital, Rome might have continued to be a rather somnolent backwater where nothing much happened.

But the new rulers of Rome, for the most part anti-clericals and Freemasons, wanted a bustling and animated capital. Obviously they could not tear down the baroque Rome they had inherited. But they did their best to modify it with a series of architectural schemes that left a permanent mark. New public buildings arose along the Via Nazionale, and statues of statesmen in frock coats began to line the Corso Vittorio Emanuele. The 'Altar of the Nation' – official name for the monument to King Victor Emmanuel – was supposed to challenge the dome of St Peter's. The perceptive observer, Emile Zola, noted in his novel *Rome* that the whole area to the east of the Vatican from the Piazza del Risorgimento was so designed that no vistas opened on to St Peter's. The Palace of Justice on the Tiber, intended to embody the higher morality of the new state, began to sink into its foundations almost as soon as it was completed. It is still being shored up, like the justice it fallibly represents. What all this immense building activity proclaimed to the world was that Rome was now the capital of a modern state, rivalling Berlin, Vienna or Madrid.

The trouble was that few people outside Italy noticed this change of status. They continued to think of Rome as 'the capital of Catholicism' or 'the city of the Popes'. Whatever the superficial changes, Rome remained a centre of pilgrimage to the tombs of the Apostles, a place hallowed by the blood of the martyrs and the memory of the catacombs. Giulio Andreotti complains in his memoirs that everywhere he has gone to represent his country, government ministers, barbers and taxi drivers have all wanted to know how the Pope was getting on. They may have forgotten or never known the name of the Italian Prime Minister (there have been over forty since the war, though the rate of change is now slowing down), but they always knew the name of the Pope. Rome was indeed the capital of Italy, but in the minds of foreigners and the folk memory it remained 'the sacred city'.

'The sacred city': this term was actually used in the Lateran Treaties which finally solved 'the Roman Question' in 1929. After sulking at each other with occasional smiles for fifty-eight years, the Holy See and Italy were formally reconciled, and the Via della Conciliazione was opened up to symbolize the new-found harmony between both banks of the Tiber. This project dated back a long time: Montesquieu reports in 1729 that there was a plan to tear down the huddle of houses between St Peter's and the Tiber, but that it was not carried out because, paradoxically, it was believed that the smoke from so many fires 'purified the air'. The fact that Pope Pius XI (or rather his first Secretary of State, Pietro Gasparri) signed the treaties with Mussolini did not mean that he was a Fascist, and indeed they led to more, not fewer, Church–State conflicts in the 1930s. But Pius XI had let slip one incautious sentence as he celebrated the 'reconciliation': 'We should say that we have been nobly assisted by the other party. And perhaps there had to be someone like the man whom Providence put in our path, someone free from the obsessions of old and outmoded ways of thinking.' In the popular mind and in Fascist propaganda, that was simplified down to Pius XI having called Mussolini 'a man of Providence', a title the Duce was only too pleased to accept.

It was in the Fascist period that rhetoric about Rome was inflated beyond all reasonable bounds. Had not the Fascists come to power through their 'march on Rome'? They had indeed. Though historians (like Seton-Watson) have shown that it was really a very trivial affair, and that those marchers who did not get lost arrived prosaically by train, what mattered was the symbolism. The 'march on Rome' indicated vigour, energy, heroism. The Rome of the Fascists was simultaneously a restoration and a novelty: it was to become once more the 'Rome of the Caesars', capital not just of Italy but of a worldwide Empire (if one could be found). The new Fascist man would build a new Rome. It can still be seen at EUR, the Olympic Stadium, and other buildings dotted about the city (characterized by their plain, pedimentless rectangular windows).

There was intense debate and controversy about the origins of Rome and who its true heirs were. Mussolini had declared that, but for its encounter with the Roman Empire, Christianity would have remained 'a minor sect in the red-hot deserts of Palestine'. *Civiltà Cattolica* testily replied with its own account of the 'essentially Christian vocation' of Rome.

The 'Christian vocation' of Rome was the theme of a remarkable speech given by Eugenio Pacelli, Cardinal Secretary of State, on 24 February 1936. He presented the Pope and the Church as the true heirs of the *entire* history of Rome. He began grandly: 'Rome is a word of mystery, and the destiny of Rome is like a mystery; it is the eternal city, not so much because it can boast of bygone centuries but for the sake of centuries yet to come.' (Quoted in Luigi Parpagliolo, *Roma*.) The future Pius XII calls upon Livy, 'the city's greatest historian', who speaks of the fabulous origins of Rome which mingle divine realities with human realities (*miscendo humana divinis*). Even though Livy's account cannot be taken literally, Pacelli explained, it hints at the true vocation of Rome and prepares the day when the city will be 'ordered to a supernatural goal'. Thus by virtue of a 'divine election' Rome becomes unique among the cities of the world. It was to be the home of the Popes, 'the seat of the pastor of the one flock of Christ'.

Pacelli's prose becomes rhapsodic as he describes the present role of the Holy See:

> It is wonderful and consoling to think that the Vatican household of the common father (i.e. the Pope) is the household of all the sons of the Church, who come devotedly from the four corners of the earth to direct their gaze and their affection on the figure in white, the Supreme Pastor of Rome. . . . The Vatican is the goal of the believing pilgrim, the rock of unity of the flock, the fount of authority of pastors, the indefectible lighthouse of faith and moral truth which can illumine all the storms of error and passion so that poor humanity may arrive safely at the harbour of peace and salvation to which God has destined it.

That opening sentence is typical of one kind of Roman rhetoric which takes an aspiration for a reality: it was simply not true in 1936 and it is not true in 1986 that the sons (and daughters) of the Church feel at home in the Vatican. For the most part they cannot even get into it. What they can do, now as then, is what Pacelli envisages them doing: admiring, applauding, waving handkerchiefs, having a lump in the throat. But there is only one real actor on the scene, the Pope; the rest of the faithful are the grateful recipients of his advice and wisdom. The 'world' is still more remote: it is the dimly-perceived source of those errors and passions that only the beacon light of the Church (concentrated in the person of the Pope) can dissipate.

So to Pacelli's peroration:

> The destiny of Rome is subject to the Vicar of Christ; and through the Vicar of Christ it is directed towards and fixed upon a goal that is not of this world. No city anywhere in the world can surpass the destiny of Rome. Jerusalem and its people are no longer the city and the people of God; Rome is the new Sion, and every people which lives by the Roman faith is itself Roman. The world has larger cities of which people are justly proud; but Rome remains the city of God, the city of wisdom incarnate, the city that has the *magisterium* of truth and holiness.

Such rhetoric soon becomes wearisome; the triplets beat one about the head. But the verbiage contains a very steely claim that is not at all vague: this city *teaches* the world, its authority is supreme and unchallengeable, and it is the true heir of the Roman Empire (though in the spiritual sphere). Pascelli states in poetic terms what Vatican I put in abstractions.

Fascism collapsed in disgrace, leaving only architectural reminders of its aspiration to build a new Rome: the 'Rome of the Caesars' was not going to be reconstituted in the twentieth century. But by the same token the 'Rome of the Popes' gained in prestige. The 'sacred status' of Rome had saved it from destruction. Pius XII earned the title of 'defender of the city' (*defensor civitatis*). Enthusiastic mass audiences with Allied servicemen brought the papacy to a new level of popularity. The very existence of the Vatican as an independent enclave within Italy helped to make the distinction, needed by both victors and vanquished, between the Fascists and the Italians. There were some good Italians, including the Pope.

It is instructive to compare Pacelli's 'Roman' rhetoric nine years and a world war later. In 1945 he said in a general audience:

> It was not any narrow personal feeling which led Us to intervene so ardently for the safety of Rome. Our heart remains united by the dearest bonds with other cities, and we have worked to save them. On their ruins, on their sufferings and on the anguish of their inhabitants, We have wept. . . . But Rome is a 'unique city', unique by the greatness of its history and the predominant part it has played in the history of civilization. It is unique, above all, because its supernatural mission places it outside time and above distinctions of nationality. Rome is the homeland (*patria*) of all Catholics wherever they are.

That was a more measured statement of Roman claims, and it is more plausible to say that no Catholic is a stranger in Rome (*Roma patria communis*) than that they all belong to the household of the Vatican.

But of course Rome was not set 'outside time' as Pius XII suggested. The city and the country were changing rapidly. The emergence of a fundamentally Catholic party, the Christian Democrats, meant that for the first time since 1870 the Vatican had to deal with a government that was in broad sympathy with it. Although no one dreamed of restoring the Papal States, it was unnecessary to do so, for the papacy under Pius XII was in a very strong position: it could influence successive Italian governments from behind the scenes, yet could not be held responsible for any of the disasters or scandals that periodically afflicted them. And Rome could resume its interrupted role as 'sacred city'. The Holy Year of 1950 summed up and symbolized this restoration. All roads led to Rome once again. At the centre of the stage was the frail, aristocratic-looking Roman (Pius XII was the last Pope to be Roman-born). He blessed the whole world, *urbi et orbi*, first the city, and then the world.

Sacralization could scarcely be pushed any further than it was in the 1950s. The very word 'sacred' cropped up everywhere. It was used of the Vatican City State itself (the *sacra Città del Vaticano*) and that still provides the number plate on Vatican cars – SCV. 'Sacred' prefixed all the Roman Congregations. It could attach itself to anything the Pope did. According to the *Osservatore Romano* the Pope did not simply speak: no, 'inspired words fell from his sacred lips.' Irreverent journalists talked about the Pope's 'sacred sneeze'. The general atmosphere of 'sacredness' extended also to cardinals. When they went out in state they wore a long train that was carried by two pages while before them went two acolytes, walking hazardously backwards. This sight could still be seen in the Hotel Columbus in the Via della Conciliazione in the early 1960s. These individual signs of the sacred were tokens of the sacredness of the city itself. One could never forget where one was.

The irony was that at the very moment when the supreme sacralization of Rome was being proclaimed, the evidence that it was an increasingly secularized city was mounting. The 'sacredness' of Rome was like a Baroque façade: not only did it fail to tell you what the shape of the building was inside, it positively misled you about it. John XXIII had already realized this, and did his best to prune the rhetoric. He banned the 'sacred lips' and 'kissing the sacred purple'. He wrote in his diary on Sunday, 13 August 1961: 'It is commonly believed and considered fitting that the everyday language of the Pope should be full of mystery and awe. But the example of Jesus is most more closely following in appealing simplicity. . . . ' (*Journal of a Soul.*)

The whole of Pope John's 'revolution' is contained in that brief passage. To make evangelical simplicity the norm rather than impressing the populace (Nicholas V's principle) was a novel departure from papal precedent. Pope John also perceived, in consequence, another simple truth about the city of Rome. When one pushed aside the Pacellian rhetoric, looked at the facts and tried to 'discern the signs of the times', it became evident that Rome needed a bishop and needed one badly. It needed a bishop on theological and ecumenical grounds, for 'Bishop of Rome' was the foundation of

all the Pope's grander titles such as Patriarch of the West and Supreme Pastor. And Rome needed a bishop on practical and pastoral
grounds, for while no one was looking, the city of Rome had changed
its character and become 'missionary territory'. This explains why,
when Pope John announced the calling of the Ecumenical Council
on 25 January 1959, he also announced a Synod of the diocese of
Rome. The Synod was not, in fact, a great success. It was premature,
and would have made more sense *after* the Council than before it. But
that is the wisdom of hindsight. Pope John was an old man in a tear-
ing hurry.

As the Council assembled in October 1962, Cardinal Giovanni
Battista Montini, then Archbishop of Milan, gave an important
speech in the Campidoglio, the city hall of Rome. It makes a striking
contrast with Pacelli's speech in 1936. There is no more rhetoric
about the 'eternal mystery' of Rome. The ending of the Papal States
is presented as a liberation of the papacy for its spiritual mission.
Montini accepts that Camillo Cavour and the *Risorgimento* had been
right to insist on Rome as the capital of a united Italy, and he accepts
Cavour's slogan, 'A free Church in a free state', as a sound working
principle governing the relations between the Holy See and the
Republic of Italy. Naturally, he has not abandoned the central papal
claims. But they now become a *dimension* of Rome rather than a *definition* of the city. Characteristically, Montini puts his main point in the
form of a question: 'Can Rome be true to itself if it remains merely a
national capital? For there has survived another Rome, on another
level, the Rome of the Catholic faith.' (Quoted in Giancarlo Zizola,
Quale Papa?)

Montini, who became Paul VI, agonized about Rome as much as
he agonized about birth control. This can be seen in his hesitations
about whether to call another Holy Year in 1975. 'We have asked
Ourselves,' he noted on 9 May 1973, 'if such a tradition should be
maintained in an age which is so different from times gone by.' He
had helped prepare the 1950 Holy Year, which had been an exercise
in triumphalism and centralization. Where was collegiality? Where
was the local Church? But Paul VI swallowed his scruples and went
ahead. The Holy Year of 1975 may be said to have been a 'success' in
that crowds came, making the point that Rome was still the centre of
Catholicism. But one theme was absent from the rhetoric of the 1975
Holy Year. No one maintained any longer that the diocese of Rome
was *exemplary*. That was not a serious proposition. Instead, Rome
had become *typical*. All the problems of modern urban life were there,
so to speak, on the Pope's doorstep: terrorism; drugs; shanty towns;

refugees; uprooted peasants; inadequate housing, health care and education.

Objective studies were done which disclosed the reality concealed behind the façade of 'the sacred city'. Rome's population had increased tenfold in a hundred years. It had become difficult to discover anyone who was Roman-born in the new suburbs. True believers were even harder to find. In a survey published in the Holy Year of 1975, Emile Pin, then lecturer in sociology at the Gregorian University, reported that the doctrine of papal infallibility was rejected by 36 per cent of Romans and accepted by 38.7 per cent, while the rest were dubious about the whole thing. It was held by 81 per cent that it was 'inopportune' or 'wrong' for priests to intervene in politics. Only 50 per cent had any sympathy for cardinals, while 40 per cent had a good word for the Roman Curia. There were no concessions to gallantry: nuns came even lower in the estimation of Romans in 1975, probably because of the extensive properties they own in the city. Pin's book, *La Religiosità dei Romani*, was regarded as shocking at the time (only ten years ago) and rather rude: it was a bit like insulting one's grandmother in public.

These were – as Pin admitted – rather blunt instruments for measuring subtle shifts of religious feeling. But there was no arguing with the results of the Rome municipal elections of 20 June 1976. The Communists polled 690,262 votes (or 35.3 per cent) while the Christian Democrats ran them close with 652,744 votes (or 33.9 per cent). For the first time ever, the Communists were in power in the city of Rome. The nightmare that had haunted Pius XII – the red flag flying over the Campidoglio – was now realized. The Communists stayed in power in Rome until August 1985.

The consequences were not disastrous. Throughout this period the Italian Communist Party was intent on demonstrating its impartiality and respectability. It was the era of the 'historic compromise' and of Eurocommunism, which rejected the Soviet Union as the model of socialism. The Roman Communists proved to be good administrators. They improved the traffic flow and established pedestrian precincts. However, their municipal restaurants were not a success. They were in beautiful places and cheap but, as in Eastern Europe, they had the surliest of waiters.

Pius XII had seen every election, local or national, as a battle for the soul of Rome. The most important thing was to defeat the Communists. But in the 1960s the Romans ceased to think in these terms. They relaxed. Communist mayors did not usher in the revolution, cardinals did not swing from Roman lampposts, there were no tumbrils. Life went on much as before, but with a different gang dispensing patronage. But Communist rule was important in that it marked a further stage in the secularization of the city.

It was ironical that Pope John Paul II, 'the man from a far country' as he described himself on the day of his election, should find a Communist mayor in office on his arrival in Rome. Communists have never won a free election in Poland, nor are they foolish enough to attempt one. That Communists should win elections in the Western world is deeply worrying to Pope John Paul who believes that the process of secularization is not inevitable and that, with a little more resolution and energy, it could be rolled back.

The statistics are against him. In 1980 he was presented with the graph of decline. In 1960 89 per cent of Roman babies were baptized; by 1977 the figure had slumped to 81 per cent. In 1963 96.8 per cent of Roman marriages were celebrated in a church; by 1978 this figure had fallen to 73.9 per cent. So more than a quarter of Romans contented themselves with a civil marriage if, that is, they bothered to get married at all. None of these trends has been reversed or even dented in this pontificate. Describing Pope John Paul's impact in Italy in November 1982, Peter Nichols wrote: 'When the Pope travels outside Rome, he can normally expect large crowds and a good reception. Romans show less interest. He has himself curtailed his once frequent visits to parishes. The last was early in May, and there are no immediate plans for others.' (*The Times*, 13 October 1982.) Parish visitations were later resumed, but on a smaller scale and less frequently; the Pope had evidently concluded that they were time-consuming and not doing much good.

Meantime, all the statistical trends were downwards. At a meeting devoted to 'Religious and the Pastoral Challenge of Rome' in November 1984, Don Giovanni Battista Cappellaro declared that 80 per cent of *baptized* Roman Catholics 'are not in touch with the life of the Church'. More than one in three married couples are divorced or separated or contemplating such a solution. In Lazio, the province of Rome, there were in 1982 25,000 abortions compared with 55,000 live births. Those who worry about the Church in the Netherlands 'falling apart' could well devote a little more attention to the diocese of Rome.

But even post-Christian Rome remains culturally Catholic in the sense that it continues to understand the old symbols. On 14 May 1981, the day after the assassination attempt on John Paul II, a poster was rushed up on the walls and hoardings of Rome. This is an ancient tradition: posters do battle with each other and mark every triumph or tragedy. The poster was signed by Luigi Petroselli, the Communist mayor of Rome. Though sympathetic to the Pope whose life was still in danger, it also revealed how little remained of the tradition of Rome as a 'sacred city':

Citizens!

The drama that took place in St Peter's Square profoundly affects the whole city.

Rome is the capital of the republican state and the centre of Catholicism. Rome is also the city of the Popes, and the diocese of the Pope.

I was among the first to arrive at the Gemelli Hospital to express all our feelings, our hope and desire that John Paul II may return as soon as possible to the exercise of his mission.

This infamous act of violence in St Peter's Square is a challenge to all humanity. It shows that there are now no limits to violence. We should respond by transforming the disgust, horror and shock that we feel into a daily and ever stronger commitment to live together in peace (*convivenza*) and to remain united in resisting all the challenges of terrorism and violence.

Your Mayor

This could be considered as a piece of electioneering or a pre-emptive strike against the idea that the Bulgarian or Soviet Secret Service were involved in the shooting or – most accurately – as an expression of a concern for the common good of Rome that transcended party loyalties.

The process of which this chapter is the record can be traced in the two versions of the Concordat. Article I of the 1929 Concordat concluded: 'In consideration of the sacred character of the Eternal City, Bishopric of the Supreme Pontiff and goal of pilgrimages, the Italian government will engage to prevent in Rome all which may conflict with the said character.' (Translation in Eugene Cardinale, *The Holy See and the International Order*.)

The relevant passage in the revised 1985 Concordat, Article 2,4, says merely: 'The Italian Republic recognizes the particular significance that Rome, as the episcopal see of the Supreme Pontiff, has for Catholicism.' Italy, in other words, now accepts, as a matter of neutral fact, that the Holy See is there.

The annual meeting between Pope John Paul II and the Communist mayor of Rome became a ritual in which both sides combined politeness with little digs. In January 1985 Ugo Vetere stressed 'the fundamental values that are common to all the great cultural and ideological currents that run through our society', a sufficiently all-embracing claim. Antiphonally, John Paul took up the theme, noted that the social climate was less tense this year (i.e. terrorism was receding), and declared that the Church was ready to stimulate the commitment of everyone to the building of a better Rome, but 'without confusion of levels or functions or ideological positions'. (*Adista*, 24-26 January 1985.) There is always much talk on such occasions about *convivenza*, the common good, and the Graeco-Roman heritage is universally celebrated. These courteous exchanges mark the reluctant recognition on the part of the Bishop of Rome that he had perforce to accept the present administration of the city of Rome.

But that was largely window-dressing. There was much evidence in 1985 that Pope John Paul was trying to rouse Roman and Italian Catholics for a counter-attack. The Catholic press, especially the daily *L'Avvenire* and the weekly *Il Sabato*, both in the hands of *Communione e Liberazione*, a right-wing lay movement founded in 1956 by Mgr Luigi Guissani, gave the game away. In November 1984, for example, *L'Avvenire* printed a photograph of Cardinal Ugo Poletti, the Pope's Vicar for the diocese of Rome, alongside Nicola Signorello, leader of the Christian Democrats in the capital. That was the signal for the assault on Rome. An attempt was made to get parish priests and sisters to rally to the Christian Democratic cause. Few welcomed this return to the 1950s. But it worked, and eight months later Signorello was Mayor of Rome, thus ending nine years of Communist rule, and Poletti was President of the Italian Episcopal Conference (though he got no votes in the election for the post).

The *disimpegno* or detachment that marked John XXIII's attitude to Italian politics has been abandoned; abandoned, too, is the 'spiritual' rather than political concept of Catholic Action that Paul VI encouraged. The Pope is no longer seen as above the political *mêlée*. He joins in enthusiastically, and speaks clearly on divorce and abortion, which are political as well as moral problems in a pluralist society. In April 1985 he went to Loreto for a Convention of the Italian Church. He urged Italian Catholics to be 'united', and said that they had always displayed their unity in moments of grave national crisis. He praised 'the initiatives of the Church and the efforts that have formed the basis of Christian action in the social field'.

This was obscure and coded. The Italian press quickly cracked the code and concluded, no doubt correctly, that the Pope was urging Italian Catholics to vote for the Christian Democrats. *Post* but probably not *propter hoc* the Christian Democrats returned to power in

Rome, although Nicola Signorelle became mayor only as the head of a five-part coalition, based on the model of the national government, between Christian Democrats, Socialists, Republicans, Liberals and Social Democrats. Then, on 24 June 1985, Francesco Cossiga, a Christian Democrat, succeeded the much-loved Socialist, Sandro Pertini, as President of Italy. So the youngest post-war president, aged fifty-six, succeeded the oldest at eighty-eight. Cossiga is a Sardinian, like his late cousin, the former Communist leader Enrico Berlinguer; an Anglophile (he admires St Thomas More); and a pious Catholic who is said to be 'close to Opus Dei'. So both in Rome and in Italy in 1985 there was a process that could be called a 'restoration'. The old order reasserted itself.

It is too early to say whether this is a mere hiccup of history or a profound change in Roman society. It seems unlikely that it is a profound change, for Rome has become in the last twenty years an unquestionably secular city, over which the Pope has lost control. Rome still has more priests than any other city, 5,280 – bearing witness to its once sacred character. Pope John Paul has urged them to wear their soutanes all the time. But of this number of priests, only 1,153 are engaged in parish work for a population of over three million; and most of them are religious or volunteers from other dioceses who do their missionary stint in Rome and then gratefully go back home. This does not make for cohesion in the diocese or for clear pastoral policies. Throughout the century, in fact, Rome has failed to provide itself with priests. It must count among the least successful dioceses in the world. But in the end, what happens there depends on its bishop, the Pope. Rome provides the context for the work of the Roman Curia; but the popes provide the leadership. How they have differed among themselves will be the subject of the next chapter.

3.

Twentieth-Century Popes Revisited

From a distance, popes look much the same: tiny figures in white gesticulating on a remote balcony and uttering platitudes about peace. But come closer and their monotonous sameness soon vanishes. Each one has a personal history and an individual temperament. That this is so should be a truism; but it is commonly overlooked since the mythology decrees that the 'man' is swallowed up in his 'office'. Pope Pius XI once said to Angelo Roncalli, the future John XXIII: 'Achille Ratti (his family name) may apologize to you, but Pius XI cannot.' This ought not to have been so difficult: no one is demeaned by admitting that he was wrong or has behaved unjustly. But the exalted and almost superhuman concept of the office prevented this simple human and Christian act. My first point, then, is biographical: we will understand the popes who preceded John Paul II if we look at what they were like as human beings.

Moreover, once a pope is elected, he is there for life. The cardinals who elected him (or even those who carelessly omitted to) cannot change their minds later. They have to live with their choice. There are no mid-term nerves for a pope – and indeed we don't know until afterwards when mid-term was reached. Nor is there on hand a 'deputy pope' who, on the analogy of the Vice-President of the United States, is 'a heartbeat away from the papacy'. So it matters very much who is elected pope. He will leave his mark on the Church, perhaps on an era.

Add that the popes of this century have all tended to have very long lives (with the exception of John Paul I who, in the poetic phrase of Cardinal Carlo Confalonieri, merely 'flashed like a meteor across the sky'). St Pius X became Pope in 1903 at the age of sixty-eight and died in 1914, just before the outbreak of World War I, at seventy-nine. Benedict XV was a youthful sixty when elected in September 1914 and seventy-two when he died. Pius XI was sixty-five when elected in 1922 and lived to a vigorous eighty-two, though he did sometimes drop off to sleep during private audiences, shaking himself awake when it was a matter of appointments. 'No, no and no,' he would cry, 'not him.' Pius XII was sixty-two when elected and, despite a scare in 1954, clung to life and office until the age of eighty-two, allegedly kept alive by 'living cell therapy' – the regular injection of finely-ground tissues taken from freshly-slaughtered lambs – according to Paul Hoffmann. John XXIII was almost seventy-seven when elected and lived to call the Second Vatican Council and reach eighty-one. Paul VI died shortly before his eighty-first birthday. If John Paul II attains the eighty which seems to be par for twentieth-century popes, he will still be alive in the year 2000.

Popes differ from each other, and so do their papacies. This also makes a theological point. For if the way the popes actually exercise their office varies, then a theology of the papacy that would reduce them to bland uniformity will be unworkable in practice and wrong in theory. Not that there is such a thing as 'the theology of the papacy': Vatican I does not speak of 'the papacy' or 'the pope' (because these are conventional, not theological terms). Vatican I speaks of the Supreme Pontiff or, better, the Successor of St Peter. Modern theologians prefer to see the primacy of Peter as the 'ministry of Peter' to bring home the truth that the office is at the service of the Church, not an imposition on it.

Peter's ministry is to promote, safeguard and symbolize the unity of the Church. But Peter's successor is not the *cause* of the Church's unity. That would be a blasphemous suggestion. The source of Christian unity is the Holy Spirit poured out in our hearts whereby we are impelled to join together (Romans 5:5). The very diversity of popes makes this plain and *relativizes* them. It makes the point that the Petrine ministry has taken different forms in the past and so could take on a different form in the future. To use the language of the poet Sydney Carter: the Church does not have a blueprint, it has a greenprint.

There is, in other words, an element of indeterminacy about the papal office that has not sufficiently been remarked upon. However, if anyone had pointed that out in the pontificate of Pope Pius XII, he would probably have been gravely censured if not put on the *Index of Forbidden Books*. For Pius saw himself, and encouraged others to see him, as the very embodiment of the papacy (and this time it is *le mot juste*) who summed up in his person a development of nearly two thousand years. Malachi Martin got it right: 'Eugenio Pacelli, as Pius XII, was the Prince of Power and the last Pope in the traditional sense. . . . He was a model of what popes thought popes should be, a papal archetype towards which forty-one popes had striven since the middle of the sixteenth century.' (*Three Popes and a Cardinal.*)

Perhaps it was this sense of coming at the end of a line that led Pius XII to beatify his predecessor Pius X in 1950 and then to canonize him in 1954. He did not expect there to be a Pius XIII. He had become more interested in the past than the future and neglected to make new cardinals, so that the college that met to elect his successor was seriously over-age and undermanned.

Apart from such motives hidden deep in the psyche of Pius XII, it is difficult to think of any convincing ecclesial reason for canonizing Saint Pius X. Once the deed was done, of course, Catholic historians had to apply lashings of whitewash. The truth is that Pius X was difficult, suspicious, neurotic and simple-minded. True, he reformed the Roman Curia, embarked on the Herculean task of codifying canon law (not completed until Pentecost 1917), introduced useful liturgical reforms, simplified church music and admitted younger children to the Eucharist. These were all positive achievements. But they hardly justify the claim made in March 1985 by Pope John Paul II at Riese, the saint's home village in the Veneto, that 'in him one era of Church history came to an end, and another began that would lead to Vatican II'.

The notion that Saint Pius X was in any useful sense a pioneer of Vatican II is hard to sustain. For while John XXIII declared formally at the start of Vatican II that it was not called to condemn errors and that the Church today 'prefers to use the medicine of mercy rather than severity', condemning errors was the principal object of the pontificate of Pius X. He was obsessed with unorthodoxy. This comes through even in the historical study designed to promote his beatification. He saw perils everywhere. His 1907 encyclical *Pascendi* first invented 'Modernism' as a system and then condemned it with great vigour. Pius X carefully included in his encyclical a disciplinary section which meant commissions of enquiry in every diocese of Italy (at least) and wholesale sackings of seminary professors. Pius encouraged purges, witch-hunts and denunciations. The whole espionage system, organized by Mgr Umberto Benigni, was exposed thanks to the accidental discovery of a cache of documents in Ghent during World War I. The historical study (*Disquisitio*) pretends that Pius X had nothing directly to do with all these moves and blames over-zealous subordinates.

I want to quote two non-suspect contemporary judgements on Pius X. Fr Cyril Charles Martindale S.J., who became a Catholic during his schooldays at Harrow, had an audience with Pius X and found 'his hands inert and cold, and he gave the impression of being sulky and morose'. (Philip Caraman, *C.C. Martindale*, Longmans, 1967.) In the manuscript collection of St Andrews University in Scotland there is also a letter from Martindale to Wilfrid Ward, then Editor of the *Dublin Review*. He reports that an Italian Jesuit has been staying at Stonyhurst during the summer vacation of 1912 'to learn English'. The anonymous Jesuit, who was at the newly-founded Biblicum, said that Pius X had articles read aloud to him over lunch, but only until he found something incriminating. At this point he would instruct his secretary, Mgr Giambattista Bressan, to write an article denouncing the author, and to 'place' it in *L'Unità cattolica*, the Pope's favourite paper. The anonymous article would then provide grounds for the Holy Office to take action against the theologian in question. It was a reign of terror.

My second witness is Cardinal Désiré Mercier, Archbishop of Malines-Brussels, who became famous as the spokesman of 'gallant little Belgium' during World War I and later as the sponsor of the 'Malines Conversations' between Anglicans and Roman Catholics. He frankly could not stand Pius X, but dissimulated. In 1908 Wilfrid Ward wrote to the Duke of Norfolk: 'Cardinal Mercier thinks the Roman theology is quite impossible: yet though he is hand in glove with the Pope, he does not give him the least inkling of this view.' (Adrian Hastings (ed.), *Bishops and Writers*, Anthony Clarke, 1977.) The sixteen letters from Mercier to Ward in the St Andrews manuscript section confirm this judgement. Ward was in trouble because of his biography of Cardinal Wiseman. Nothing happened until the French translation came out with a final chapter entitled '*L'Esprit du siècle*' which, because Ward commended rather than abused 'the Spirit of the Age', sounded fearfully like 'Modernism'. Mercier consoles him as best he can, advising him to shut up and not try to defend himself, and above all, to desist for the time being from his project of a life of John Henry Newman. That would be like a red rag to a Roman bull.

Once Pius X was dead and Europe was in flames, Mercier could speak a little more freely. He wrote a pastoral letter called *From One Pope to the Next*. It remained somewhat ambiguous. 'Those who had the good fortune to come close to the heart of Pius X,' he wrote, 'know that an exquisite amalgam of melancholy and paternal gentleness reigned in his soul.' Though Mercier conceded that Pius X had acted vigorously to combat error, he adds that 'there have been worries, and legitimate ones, and souls have been hurt.' (*Per Crucem ad Lucem*.) That was as far as anyone dared to go in public in 1915.

But already there was another Pope, Benedict XV. He remains the most invisible and unappreciated Pope of this century, largely because his election came just after the outbreak of World War I. In August 1917 he pronounced it a 'useless slaughter' ('*inutile strage*' – often mistranslated as 'useless struggle'), a phrase which successfully united all the belligerents against him. The exception was the Italian survivors of the defeat of Caporetto in 1917 who eagerly retreated and 'gave the impression of people returning home after a long job of work, laughing and chattering'. (Christopher Seton-Watson, *Italy from Liberalism to Fascism*.) Alas, this impression was misleading. General Cadorno decimated them (that is, literally shot one in ten) and the shouts of 'for peace and the Pope' were soon silenced.

Benedict fared little better after the war. The Holy See was not allowed to take part in the Versailles conference. It had no recognized international status. Benedict busied himself with the reorganization of missionary work. This was much needed since the old patterns of colonialism were changing – the Germans had lost their colonial Empire – and the French hegemony needed challenging. He brought young Angelo Roncalli down from Bergamo to organize missionary funding in Italy.

Yet Benedict's pontificate was far from being a failure. He re-established diplomatic relations with France (broken off by Pius X) and established them in suitably discreet form with 'Protestant' Great Britain. He put an end in principle to witch-hunting in his encyclical *Ad Beatissimi*: 'There is no need to add epithets to the profession of Catholicism. It is enough for each to say, "*Christianus mihi nomen, Catholicus cognomen*" ("Christian is my name, and Catholic is my family name"). What matters is to live up to these names in one's life.'

That didn't stop the name-calling, but it was a start. Benedict also prepared the way for 'reconciliation' with the Italian state – whichever state. His approval of the foundation of an early version of the Christian Democratic Party (*Partito Popolare Italiano*) might have prevented the Fascists from coming to power, had it not been destroyed by his successor.

Achille Ratti, Pius XI, who reigned (the appropriate word for him) from 1923 to 1939, was the Pope with the mostest. He had the most canonizations, and the most Holy Years. He had the most concordats, including those with Benito Mussolini and Adolf Hitler (though the latter concordat is less sinister if one recalls that it was already being negotiated long before Hitler came to prominence or power). He wrote the most encyclicals, and it was in his pontificate that the notion of ordinary *magisterium* began to occupy a firm place in the theology manuals. It meant taking the Pope seriously as a teaching authority, whatever the occasion. Of course it never meant that everything he said was strictly infallible, but all his utterances acquired, as it were, an aura of infallibility. It was a case of 'creeping infallibility' as Sir Arnold Lunn, a famous convert of the 1930s, put it some years later.

Whatever one thinks about the encyclicals of Pius XI – and they are totally outdated by now – they had a sweep and a grandeur that compel a certain admiration. His natural form was the diatribe. In 1928 he put down the nascent ecumenical movement with heavy irony: 'Congresses and meetings are arranged, attended by a large concourse of hearers, where all without distinction, unbelievers as well as every kind of Christian, are invited to join in the discussion.' (*Mortalium Animos*.) It took more than thirty years to recover from that. With *Casti Connubii* in 1930 he castigated (implicitly) the Anglican Communion for its softness on artificial contraception, and pronounced that the woman's place was in the home. Again, it took another thirty years for people to enquire whether the Holy Spirit was not with the Lambeth Conference rather than with Pius XI.

Pius XI's literary activity was incessant. In 1931, taking advantage of the fact that it was forty years since Leo XIII's social encyclical *Rerum Novarum*, he 'brought Catholic social teaching up to date' on such elusive questions as 'the just wage' and 'socialism'. Whatever Pius meant by his condemnation of 'socialism', I learned in my youth, it did not include the British Labour Party. But John Pollard's thesis has shown that Pius XI was aiming his remarks at the Italian situation. *Quadragesimo Anno*, far from bringing comfort to the Fascists, on the contrary infuriated the Duce because it robbed him of what he thought was the only economic originality of Fascism, the corporate state.

Acrimony and police activity increased throughout the 1930s as Mussolini drew closer to Hitler. In 1937 Pius XI balanced his denunciation of Marxist atheism in *Divini Redemptoris* – Catholics were being murdered in Spain and Mexico – with an attack on the racist tendencies of National Socialism (*Mit brennender Sorge*). The latter was conveyed to Germany in cloak-and-dagger fashion, with the young Francis J. Spellman, later Archbishop of New York, acting as courier. Nothing became Pius XI in life so much as his leaving it. But no one has ever even remotely thought of beatifying him. He was too intolerant, ill-tempered, unjust, wayward. But he displayed remarkable energy and vigour. A fire smouldered in those aged eyes.

Pius XI broke the rules by clearly designating his Secretary of State, Eugenio Pacelli, as his successor. This probably did not have much influence on the conclave, for a Pope's wishes do not run beyond the grave. Indeed, though the myth was put about that Pius XII was elected unanimously minus one (his own vote), a substantial group of Italian cardinals opposed him because they thought he would be unable to cope with the upheavals and catastrophes that, in the spring of 1939, seemed imminent. They judged him too timid, too uncertain, too indecisive, too anxious.

But in the course of the next nineteen years, the image of Pius XII – thin, ascetic, aristocratic, eyes uplifted behind rimless spectacles, arms extended to embrace the world – imposed itself as the icon of the papacy itself. Or so it seemed at the time. Pius carried an intense awareness of the dignity of his office into the details of everyday life. He appointed his friend, Cardinal Luigi Maglione, former Nuncio to France, as his Secretary of State, but made it clear that this marked the end of their friendship: from now on the relationship would be that of superior to subordinate. (Andrea Riccardi, (ed.), *Pio XII*.) 'The Pope is always the Pope,' he told his confessor, the German Jesuit Augustin Bea, explaining why he always prepared his words so carefully even for private encounters. Pius XII was never relaxed, never off duty.

All of which makes him sound like a humourless monster or an insufferable prig. He had a touch of both. But it is not quite the whole story. One of those closest to him, Domenico Tardini, drew a portrait of Pius XII that helps to explain his attitudes and his 'silences'. Though unfairly considered 'hagiographical' when it appeared in 1960, the book repays a 'reading between the lines'. 'By temperament, Pius XII was gentle and rather shy. He did not have the temperament of a fighter (*lottatore*). . . . His great goodness impelled him to keep everyone happy and to annoy no one, to prefer the way of gentleness to that of severity, and persuasion to imposing his will.' (*Pio XII*.)

Tardini himself was the opposite, he was a *lottatore*, and he frankly explains how 'explosions' or losing his temper were part of his administrative technique. Tardini and Pacelli were both Romans, but Tardini was closer to the blunt, outspoken people of the Borgo than was Pius.

According to Tardini, Pius XII found reaching any decision a positive torture: 'Faced with contrary proposals and recommendations, he felt very uncomfortable, torn between his natural affability and the rigid demands of his conscience.' The result was that Pius preferred to leave controversial matters suspended in mid-air. He was the master of delay and postponement. Vacancies were left un-filled for months, sometimes years. Unable to decide on a successor to Maglione when his Secretary of State died in 1944, he simply left the post vacant and became his own Secretary of State. In practice, of course, it was the inability to chose between Tardini and Giovanni Battista Montini that hamstrung him. He kept them both working in tandem, knowing that they were quite likely to pedal off in different directions. That could be called 'pluralism' or 'indecisiveness'.

If Tardini is right that Pius XII was by temperament hesitant and unsure of himself, then the Pope's wartime behaviour becomes slightly more intelligible. It predisposed him to adopt a policy of the strictest impartiality between the belligerents: in that way, he would not have to commit himself. But his area of freedom was small. In a war sustained and fanned by ardent nationalisms, the 'suprana-tional' option of impartiality was bound to isolate the Holy See and cause misunderstandings on all sides. Moreover, since small nations were quite clearly being trampled upon and treated with monstrous injustice, papal even-handedness was experienced as papal weak-ness. Catholic Poland, in particular, felt let down. Pius XII 'seemed indifferent to their appalling fate'. So Pius was not merely 'silent' about Jews; he was 'silent' about his fellow Catholics.

Now that most of the relevant diplomatic documents have been published, one can see that the Americans, in the person of their rep-resentative, Myron Taylor, understood the 'isolation' of the Holy See better than their European allies who put constant pressure on the Pope to come down on their side. It would have been a great propaganda coup to have had a papal blessing for one's cause; yet one only has to state that to see why it was ruled out. However, even-handedness could have been combined with the denunciation of abuses of human rights: the concentration camps and the bombing of Dresden, though not morally identical, were both morally detesta-ble.

But it is easy to be right after the event. Apologists for Pius can make some good points in his defence. The first is that when human rights were flouted in Rome and the Jews were being herded off to Germany for extermination, Pius opened the religious houses of Rome to them so that 90 per cent of Roman Jews were saved. The Austrian historian F. Engel-Janosi claims that this 'success' was the direct result of Pius' 'diplomatic' approach to the Jewish question: silent in public, he could therefore be effective in private. He con-firms his theory by a comparison with the Netherlands, where the clergy were outspoken in defence of the Jews, but 79 per cent of Dutch Jews perished. (Riccardi, *Pio XII.*) On this horrifying statistical body count, the Dutch stand condemned for their imprudence, while Pius XII is vindicated. Thus a virtue is made out of his temperamental inability to make up his mind.

But if Pius XII's insecure temperament helps to explain his war-time silences on international issues, his government of the Church at this same time was marked by decisiveness and vigour. He made peace with the right-wing *Action Française*, thus appearing to repudiate his predecessor who had condemned it. And in 1942 he despatched Angelicum Professor Réginald Garrigou-Lagrange to occupied France where he wrought havoc among the Dominicans as visitor. The editors of *La Vie Intellectuelle* and *La Vie Spirituelle* were sacked. (Riccardi.) Where it really mattered to him Pius XII, far from being hesitant, acted swiftly and with authority. Everything depended on what his priorities were.

Like Pius X, the man he canonized, Pius XII was preoccupied with orthodoxy. The mission of Garrigou-Lagrange to France in 1942 was only the first skirmish in a long-drawn out battle against what was called '*la théologie nouvelle*', which in practice meant whatever the Jesuits at Fourvière, Lyons, and the Dominicans at Le Saulchoir, were doing. They were renewing theology through biblical and patristic studies and through an *historical* approach to questions that was infinitely more satisfying and spiritually enriching than the timeless abstractions propounded by a Garrigou-Lagrange.

Yet Pius XII, despite a popular legend to the contrary, was not theologically very well educated. Having spent most of his life in diplomacy and worked with Cardinal Pietro Gasparri on the codification of canon law, his knowledge of theology proper was 'slight' – '*scarsa*', says Riccardi. As a theologian he was a *terrible simplificateur*: whatever appeared to depart from 'the deposit of faith' was anathema. It was enough for Garrigou-Lagrange (whom we will meet again in the next chapter as supervisor of Karol Wojtyla's thesis) to assure him that the deposit of faith was being gnawed away by French theologians for him to act. They were condemned in *Humani Generis* in 1950. Once again professors were sacked, silenced and, in the case of Yves Congar, exiled to Cambridge.

Perhaps there is no contradiction between feeling unsure of oneself and being despotic: the insecure are the most inclined to authoritarianism. Show them an abyss of uncertainty and they recoil in horror. Pius XII detested the 'theology' of risk that was fashionable in post-war France. (God, the French pointed out, had taken a considerable risk in creating the world.) 'Given a choice,' Pius declared, 'between apostolic efficacy and the integrity of the priesthood, I would always choose the integrity of the priesthood.' (Riccardi.) That question-begging disjunction spelt the doom of the priest-worker experiment.

One last feature of Pius XII's outlook must be mentioned: he had an apocalyptic sense that the world was getting worse and that nothing much could be done about it. How far the message of Fátima contributed to this mood, one cannot say: but by a curious coincidence Pius XII had been ordained Archbishop on 13 May 1917, the very day on which Our Lady began her series of appearances to the peasant children in Portugal. His apocalyptic vision meant that he was unable to find much good in the contemporary world. The definition of the Assumption of Our Lady into heaven – the sole instance so far of the exercise of papal infallibility – was said to be both 'necessary for salvation' and 'likely greatly to help the advance of society': a somewhat puzzling claim. According to Cardinal Giuseppe Siri, Pius XII's dauphin, the Assumption was defined in such a way as to throw down a challenge 'to a world that preferred cinema stars and sports heroes to true teachers'. In other words it was a piece of world-defying ecclesiastical *machismo*, and the fact that other Christians were shocked or appalled merely proved its wisdom: they would learn what a real teacher was. Pius XII's apocalyptic pessimism dispensed him from thinking too much about the consequences of his actions. Whether he really said to the French Ambassador, '*Après moi, le déluge*' may be doubted. But he certainly behaved as though he did not care what happened after his much-postponed death. In death, said Benny Lai, he looked human for the first time: till then, no one had ever seen him without his spectacles.

Having published a full biography of Pope John XXIII, I can be brief about him here. Quite clearly he transformed the image of the papacy more than any other pope of this century. He did it by goodness. Goodness can only be experienced, it cannot be explained. For a public figure who reaches people only through the distorting lens of the media, John's ability to communicate even with those he had never met was remarkable. On his death in 1963 the Union Jack fluttered at half-mast in Belfast – a sight that had never before been seen in that divided city. We can put it down to his charisma, a word that had a religious habitat before it was used of politicians (it means simply the gift of grace), but then we have merely substituted one word for another.

There is, however, one key for understanding John's impact on the world. His predecessors, as we have seen, had led people to think of popes as above common humanity. Occasionally they descended from the solitude of their Olympian heights and condemned something. But when John wrote *Mater et Magistra* and *Pacem in Terris*, he was concerned with things ordinary people cared about, such as peace, justice and living harmoniously together (*convivenza* was one of his favourite words). No one was in any doubt about John's humanity, but it was not so much opposed to spirituality as the fulfilment of it. He 'made the supernatural seem natural', said Cardinal Léon-Joseph Suenens. Instead of maintaining the remote aristocratic presence cultivated by Pius XII on public occasions, John was fraternal and friendly. One of his favourite texts was from Genesis: 'I am Joseph, your brother.' He meant it. He used it to welcome Socialists in Venice, and the American Jews who came to visit him in Rome, and even with journalists. Blaise Pascal wrote in his *Pensées*: 'When we see a natural style we are quite amazed and delighted, because we expected to see an author and find a man.' People were amazed and delighted by Pope John because previous office-holders led them to expect to meet an autocrat imbued with a sense of his own dignity, and instead they met a brother.

But Pope John was not just a kind-hearted old boy with big ears who radiated love and charm. He was a serious Church historian who told the Council that 'history is the teacher of life' (*magistra veritatis*). This gave him a sense of perspective, and an awareness that Christian doctrine had developed in the course of time and tried to answer different questions at different periods; it was not frozen for ever in once-for-all, timeless statements. John saw tradition as a flowing river to which many streams had contributed. His sense of history made him keenly aware of the *kairos*, the right moment, the time when God acts in the world or the Holy Spirit calls. He did not want to miss the *kairos*. That was why he called Vatican II. The Roman Curia and the local churches were drifting apart. So let the bishops of the world meet not to condemn errors, but to renew the Church and get the relationship between the bishops and the Bishop of Rome working effectively again.

The technical name for this was 'collegiality', or the sharing of all the world's bishops in 'the solicitude of all the churches'. Interrupted by the Franco-Prussian War, Vatican I had dealt only with the papal office. John wanted his Council to correct this imbalance by seeing the Bishop of Rome not as above the Church but as the one who 'presides over the assembly of charity'. (St Irenaeus.) Of course we are free to say that this definition of the Petrine ministry also suited his temperament; but then we must also say that his temperament permitted the rediscovery of a style of papal ministry that released fresh energies in the Church. Pope John was not an initiator so much as an enabler. He knew from experience that bans, anathemas, excommunications and condemnations merely poisoned the atmosphere of the Church and left a trail of human havoc. He had seen it in Bergamo in the pontificate of Pius X; he saw it again in 1950 as Nuncio to Paris. In his pontificate Jesuits such as Henri de Lubac and Karl Rahner, and Dominicans like Yves-Marie Congar and Marie-Dominique Chenu, began to emerge from the shadows of disapproval. Silenced and censored under Pius XII, they returned to make an important contribution to Vatican II.

No one was more pleased with this reversal of fortune than Giovanni Battista Montini, who succeeded Pope John in July 1963. He was the best-read and best-informed Pope of the century. He took the name Paul VI as a sign that he would be a missionary to the modern world. He had long kept up with theological developments in France and Germany. When in the 1930s Karl Adam's book *The Spirit of Catholicism* was banned in Rome, Montini kept the remaining stock in his apartment and gave copies to trusted visitors. In 1934 he visited abbeys in England and Scotland. When theologians were being condemned in the early 1950s, they would always get a friendly reception from him in the Vatican and a shrug of the shoulders at the latest Ottaviani incident. He was himself demoted to Milan in 1954 and was pointedly denied the cardinal's hat that 'went with the job'. So prepared to suffer 'for the Church', Montini had also suffered 'at the hands of the Church' (to use the distinction of the French Dominican, Père Clérissac). But he did not repine in Milan and in 1955 met the doughty Bishop George Bell of Chichester, who reported him as saying: 'Although the Holy Father has often urged collaboration between Catholics and separated brethren, he has never indicated how this should be done.' Bell comments: 'He was like a curate being discreetly critical of his Vicar.' (Bernard and Margaret Pawley, *Rome and Canterbury through the Centuries*.) The next year Archbishop Montini invited a group of Anglicans to Milan for a ten-day study session.

Undoubtedly, of all the popes of the twentieth century he was the best prepared for the office. He had lived through the pontificates of Pius XI and Pius XII from the inside. He knew exactly what needed to be done about the Roman Curia, and he went ahead and did it in 1967. He became Pope at a time when, thanks to Pope John, the prestige of the papacy stood higher than it had for centuries. Why is it, then, that his pontificate, though so full of splendid gestures and sentiments, seemed in the end to falter? A number of reasons may be suggested.

First, he was temperamentally a second-in-command. In the photographs of the Pius XI and Pius XII period that is how we see him: a slim, youthful shadow at the Pope's elbow as he signs some important document. The fact that Montini might have drafted the document himself is beside the point. What he felt about his election as Pope can be seen in a 'personal note' that he revealed nine years later: 'Perhaps the Lord called me to this service not because I have any aptitude for it, or so that I can govern and save the Church in its present difficulties, but so that I can suffer something for the Church so that it will be clear that it is the Lord, and not anyone else, who guides it and saves it.' (*Insegnamenti.*) This, I believe, is more than a merely conventional expression of humility: it is a real confession that he feels the task to be beyond him and that, humanly speaking, he will fail. Not all popes see their office in this way. Pope John Paul II feels that his election made up for all the centuries in which the ravaged and martyred Polish Church was neglected; and the fact that he survived Mehmet Ali Agca's assassination attempt confirmed the divine blessing. Paul VI had no such reassurance about his mission.

One of the reasons for Paul's discouragement was that he inherited from John XXIII a Council he would never have called. We know this because, on the day it was announced, he spoke on the telephone to his mentor, Fr Giulio Bevilacqua, and said: 'This holy old boy doesn't seem to realize what a hornet's nest he's stirring up.' (Fappani-Molinari.) Bevilacqua told him to have confidence that the Holy Spirit was still at work in the Church. Montini soon came round to this view, and became the chief Italian advocate of a Council conducted in the spirit of Pope John. That, indeed, is why he succeeded him as Pope: he was committed to the Council, and knew where it ought to be heading. No one has questioned my judgement that Montini's letter of 18 October 1962 provided the only practical plan for the Council and is 'the single most important document' for understanding it. (Hebblethwaite, *John XXIII, Pope of the Council.*)

But precisely because he was a prudent and farsighted man, Paul VI guessed what would happen in the post-conciliar period when the parties who had confronted each other in St Peter's would continue to argue about exactly who had won. So Paul strove for as large a consensus as possible in the Council, and some of his amendments were designed as potions to soothe the bruised. His aim was that there should be '*des convaincus, pas de vaincus*': no one should feel defeated, everyone should be persuaded. Much of Paul's behaviour both during and after the Council can be explained by his desire to respect the feelings of the defeated minority who were mostly in the Roman Curia. He was accused of having surrendered to them – a nonsensical charge that the conservatives themselves certainly never believed.

Thus Paul VI was in what is now called a no-win situation. The Petrine ministry was for him a perpetual cross. He could not go back to the autocratic simplicities of Pius XII; but neither could he emulate the winning directness of John XXIII. So he was left with his own tortured self, his agony, his doubts, the intellectual's sense of complexity. When Arrigo Levi remarked to him in an interview that it was only in the Soviet Union that the principle of authority remained intact, Paul VI murmured: 'Is that a good or a bad thing?'

People said that he couldn't make up his mind; but when he did, as for example on clerical celibacy and birth control, he was accused of behaving arbitrarily and without proper consultation. 'How easy it is to study,' he said of birth control, 'how hard to decide.' He could so easily have continued to sit on the fence. Yet his condemnation of artificial birth control in *Humanae Vitae* was far milder and more pastorally sensitive to the rights of conscience and the action of the Holy Spirit in the faithful than the fierce draft prepared for him by Cardinal Alfredo Ottaviani's Holy Office. It has never been recognized that Paul VI was closer in tone to the 'majority report' of the birth-control commission (which gave qualified approval) than to that of the minority (which rejected the whole idea out of hand in the name of tradition and authority). This is, admittedly, a matter of nuances and fine print; but unlike John Paul II, Paul VI did not allege that contraceptive users were 'denying the sovereignty of God'. Paul VI took the long view. He is due for rehabilitation.

Historians argue endlessly about 'periodization', that is about how to divide up Paul VI's fifteen-year pontificate. Did it begin to go downhill with *Humanae Vitae* in 1968 or earlier still? Did his magnificent document, *Evangelii Nuntiandi*, of 1975 in response to the Synod on Evangelization, represent a fresh and belated burst of energy? Did Paul end more optimistically than he began? Whatever the answer may be to these questions, Paul VI's pontificate ended strongly.

In 1978, the year of his death, tragedy struck. Aldo Moro, Secretary of the Christian Democratic Party (in practice its leader) had been a friend of Montini's since the time he was chaplain to F.U.C.I.

the Federation of Italian Catholic Students. Montini, under Fascism, may be said to have prepared the democratic future of post-war Italy. But now Moro was captured by the Red Brigades, tortured, kept in suspense for several weeks and finally brutally murdered and dumped not far from the Piazza del Gesù, his headquarters. Paul VI broke with protocol and went down to St John Lateran to unbraid the Lord for allowing this terrible event. It was like the book of Job. The eighty-year-old whose querulous lamentations (he couldn't do much about his voice) had seemed so irrelevant, suddenly spoke for Italy and became the voice of the whole nation.

Then he could die.

Yves Congar wrote of his death:

Paul died with the words 'Our Father who art in heaven' on his lips. It was the death he had always prayed for. 'What is the greatest misfortune here below?' he had asked, and answered, 'to be unable to say "Our Father".' (16 April 1965) 'What is the Church doing in this world?' he asked on another occasion, and replied, 'Making it possible for us to say "Our Father".' (23 March 1966) Paul, who had such a wonderful sense of the meaningful gesture, planned his funeral with an eye to making it sum up his life. His coffin was on ground level. It was surmounted not by the tiara that he had given away (and that no future Pope would use), not even by a mitre or a stole, but by the open book of the Gospels, its pages riffled by the light breeze. (*Modernité*)

Pope Paul died on 6 August 1978, feast of the Transfiguration. On this same day in 1945 the atomic bomb had been dropped for the first time with devastating results.

Even in thirty-three days, Albino Luciani left his mark on the papal office. He abolished the coronation ceremony, thus finally dispensing with the tiara. The Vatican Press Office lied about the circumstances of his death for reasons of edification, thus giving rise to suspicions that were exploited by popular writers. Finally, he invented the first double-barrelled name in the history of the papacy, hoping in this way to express his debt to his two predecessors, John and Paul. But Pope John Paul's unexpected death meant that his successor was virtually obliged to take the same name. How justified that was will appear in the next chapter.

4

The Mind of Karol Wojtyla

Among the conclusions one could draw from the previous chapter is that popes often come in contrasting pairs. After the aristocratic, remote, 'angelic' Pius XII came the peasant, loveable, fraternal John XXIII. John, indeed, used to play on this. He is supposed to have said to a newly appointed Archbishop of Le Mans in France, worried that he could not possibly succeed the learned, saintly and oh-so-good Cardinal Georges Grente: 'Just do what I do – exactly the opposite of my predecessor.'

The contrast between successive popes is not really surprising. For the question facing every conclave is always that of continuity or change. Since there is not really much room for substantial change, they usually opt for continuity but with a different style. This is what happened in 1978. The early death of Albino Luciani after only 33 days as Pope made the issues more dramatic. There was a smell of crisis in the air. What the Church now needed was a strong man who would stand up on the battlements and proclaim the faith without hesitation to the whole world. That was why Cardinal Karol Wojtyla was elected. The principal Italian runners, Giovanni Benelli, Archbishop of Florence, and Giuseppe Siri, Archbishop of Genoa, succeeded in cancelling each other out, and so opened the way for the Cardinal Archbishop of Kraków, Karol Wojtyla, the first non-Italian since the Dutchman Adrian VI, who died – poisoned by his physician, it was rumoured – in 1523.

There was obviously continuity between Montini and Wojtyla, and even a certain affinity. It was not for nothing that Pope Paul had made him the second Polish cardinal in 1967 (when foolish commentators said Paul was dividing the Polish Church). Nor was it by chance that Cardinal Wojtyla was chosen to give the retreat to the Roman Curia in Lent 1976 (the conferences were published under the title *Sign of Contradiction*). And Wojtyla may be said to have anticipated and contributed to *Humanae Vitae* with his lectures in the Catholic University of Lublin in 1960 (published in English as *Love and Responsibility*).

So one could go on, demonstrating the deep harmony of views between Paul VI and John Paul II. It really existed, but it was deceptive. There is a difference of style that is so marked that one can read much of what John Paul does as a critique of his predecessor's feebleness. Where Paul VI agonized and dithered, John Paul plunges courageously in. He proclaims without hesitation or ambiguity 'the joy of faith in a troubled world', as he declared in his first encyclical, *Redemptor Hominis* (1979). Here are two examples of this contrast of style.

Though Pope Paul began travelling the entire world as 'the pilgrim pope', his journeys were limited in duration, conformed to a systematic and symbolic plan (beginning in the Holy Land, where Christianity started), and ended altogether after his Far Eastern journey in 1970. During his last eight years he stayed put. When Paul VI went to Uganda in 1969, he stayed for only three days and gave three important sermons or addresses. John Paul's first visit to Africa took him to six countries in ten days and he made over 70 speeches. Not unconnected with this passion for travel – John Paul's third visit to Africa in August 1985 was his twenty-seventh international journey – is the present Pope's undoubted skill in handling the medium of television. Like President Ronald Reagan but to an even greater extent, John Paul may be called a 'great communicator'. Paul VI, by contrast, was a private person who could not project himself well when faced by crowds or cameras.

In what one must perforce call their 'Dutch policy', there was little to choose between Paul VI and John Paul II in the perception of the problem. They agreed broadly on both the analysis and the solution: Vatican II had gone to the heads of the Dutch, who interpreted it in a reckless manner. Paul VI tackled the problem by censoring the *New Catechism*, halting the Dutch Pastoral Council in 1970, and appointing 'conservative' bishops such as Adrianus Simonis to Rotterdam, and Jan Gijsen to Roermond. John Paul has endorsed this policy but pursued it with greater vigour and determination. He got the Dutch Bishops to Rome in January 1980 for a 'Special Synod' where, cut off from their people and outvoted by the Roman Curia, they in effect rejected the pastoral policies which had been in vogue for the previous fifteen years. They went home and naturally could not make the changed policies stick. More and more conservative bishops were appointed (see Chapter 8). Finally, John Paul himself, like Daniel in the lion's den, boldly went to Holland in May 1985 to put the message across in person. If he failed, it was a magnificent, heroic failure.

Another aspect of the contrast between the two popes is in their conversation and the way they see their office. Paul VI talked frankly to a few close friends, among them Jean Guitton. In 1967 he described the pressures on the Pope, and his *métier*, thus:

> In the pope's life there are no times of rest or respite. Fatherhood is never suspended. And since what he is dealing with always goes beyond the bounds of possibility, the only solution he has is to abandon himself to the present moment, which is the Lord. A pope lives from crisis to crisis, from moment to moment. He goes, like the Hebrews in the desert, from manna to manna. And he has not much time to look back on the road he has travelled, or forward to the way that lies ahead. (*Dialogues avec Paul VI*)

That suggests that Paul VI saw his pontificate as a perpetual improvisation, as though his daily agenda came from elsewhere and was supplied by events. When he woke up in the morning and wondered what to do, he would find the answer somewhere in the press summaries provided by the Secretariat of State. This approach was very characteristic of Montini and takes us to the heart of his papal spirituality: most of the time he had to wait on God, and let himself be guided by the surprising Holy Spirit.

Pope John Paul II would not disagree with this as theology. But his practice is very different, and for the reason given by Paul VI: 'In a Pope's life there are no times of rest or respite.' There is little time to think, to read, to assimilate the new. Pope John Paul II, therefore, has to live off the capital he acquired and built up before he became Pope – for now that he is Pope, it is too late to learn new things.

If Paul VI's conversation revealed both his anguish and his faith, John Paul II gives little away. For a man so loquacious in public, he is surprisingly reticent and mysterious in private. To some who asked him whether on his visit to France he would refer to the French Church as 'the eldest daughter of the Church', he replied with a punch on the shoulder and '*Pourquoi pas, mon vieux?*' An English Monsignor was invited to lunch to explain what happened at the National Pastoral Conference held in Liverpool in 1980. The Pope listened in silence and at the end said merely: '*Deo Gratias*'. Cardinal Léon-Joseph Suenens only knew that his resignation as Archbishop of Malines-Brussels had been accepted and that he had been confirmed as guide to the charismatic movement as the lift doors closed and he was borne ineluctably away. There are many similar tales. John Paul's conversation is cryptic and enigmatic.

It boils down to this. The Pope is a most courteous listener, but his interlocutors sometimes feel that what they are saying is being slotted into predetermined boxes. I have had three conversations with Pope John Paul and the most I can claim is that each time I made him laugh. On the way to Africa in 1980 Fr Romeo Panciroli, then Vatican press officer, introduced me as the correspondent of the *National Catholic Register*, a right-wing magazine which contrasts with my own *National Catholic Reporter*. I asked the Holy Father whether, when he met the new Archbishop of Canterbury, Robert Runcie, in Accra, Ghana, he would refer to the Anglican Communion as a 'sister church'. 'Re-read *Lumen Gentium*' (the Council's constitution on the Church), he advised, holding firmly on to my hand, 'there you will see that in Christ we are all brothers and sisters.' Had he misunderstood the question? Not altogether, for he went on to say, 'Sister church is only an analogy.' In the event he did not use the term 'sister church' when speaking with Runcie. He used it instead for the Roman Catholic 'young churches' of Africa which were now sufficiently 'grown up' to merit this title.

On the way back from Africa I noted that the only two Presidents we had met who had any claim to be Catholics – Mobutu of Zaire and Houphouet-Boigny of Ivory Coast – had married, despite their advanced ages, just before the Pope arrived. What was the explanation, I ingenuously enquired, of this sudden passion for matrimony? The truth was that the local papal nuncios had advised the Presidents concerned to regularize their marriages before John Paul arrived. He answered my question: 'You will understand that I cannot enter into personal details?' I nodded my respect for the secrets of the confessional. 'Let us simply say,' John Paul concluded, 'that this is the first fruits of my pastoral visit to Africa.' Shrewd and yet somewhat evasive.

For an even better example of papal banter – no other word seems appropriate – one cannot do better than take the exchanges on the way to Canada in autumn 1984. John Paul, looking bronzed and fit after a stay at his summer palace at Castelgandolfo, came down into the rear of the plane as is his wont. Most of the questions concerned the Instruction issued by the Congregation for the Doctrine of Faith (the former Holy Office) just a month before on 3 September. This document (we'll meet it again) condemned liberation theology at least in its 'Marxist' versions. Here is how the discussion went:

'How can you expect to continue the dialogue with Marxist governments after the recent Instruction of the Congregation for the Doctrine of Faith?'

John Paul: 'Why do you ask? Does it say anything against Marxists?'

'It looks as though it does, and also against Marxist governments.'

John Paul: 'And is what it says directed *only* against Marxist governments?'

'So it's directed against others too?'

John Paul: 'It's all set down very clearly, and naturally some governments will recognize themselves in what is written there. But the document says nothing which attacks directly Marxists or Marxist governments.'

(Honesty compels me to interject that the Instruction does actually describe certain 'totalitarian and atheistic regimes' – not, it is true, identified as 'Marxist' – in the following terms: 'This shame of our time cannot be ignored: while claiming to bring them freedom, these regimes keep whole nations in conditions of servitude that are unworthy of mankind' (11,10).)

'So the dialogue continues?'

John Paul: 'We're trying to do just that. But you need two to dialogue. Dialogue can never be manipulation.'

'When you go to Santo Domingo, you will be very close to Cuba. Would you like to go to Cuba?'

John Paul: 'Oh yes, I'd love to go there. But perhaps the Cubans are not . . . '

'Perhaps the Cubans would be happy to receive you?'

John Paul: 'Oh yes, the Cubans, they are good people.'

'What will be the fate of the priests who are government ministers in Nicaragua?'

John Paul: 'They will be dealt with according to canon law.'

'What do you think about the feminists who are preparing to challenge you in Canada?'

John Paul: 'I love everyone, including these ladies. But to love everyone does not mean not loving truth. As the ancients said: *Amicus Plato, sed magis amica veritatis* (Plato is a friend, but truth is a greater friend).'

This is not exactly as scintillating as Boswell on Johnson or Eckermann on Goethe. Perhaps modern journalists get what they deserve. The last remark about women's ordination illustrates the danger of these impromptu press conferences in the plane.

For once the Pope descends from his *cathedra* (or *sedes*, the Holy See) and joins in a current controversy, his arguments have as much weight as anyone else's, and no more. In his lengthy conversation with André Frossard, the only writer to have had almost unlimited access to him, John Paul rejects the ordination of women on the grounds that 'Our Lady was not present at the last Supper.' (*Be not Afraid!*) It is possible to find this argument less than wholly convincing. Before the papal visit to Holland in May 1985, Cardinal Simonis said that awkward questions should not be addressed to the Holy Father because he had not sufficient command of Dutch to improvise his answers. He had to speak for centuries. He could not ad lib the *magisterium*.

All of which is true. Yet the off-the-cuff remarks take us closer to the mind of John Paul than do his more carefully crafted formal utterances. They reveal him in his humanity. The key to his thinking is to be found in the historical experience of Poland. This is not the same as saying that he is 'conservative' or whatever because he is Polish. That is too simplistic and perhaps 'racist'. In any case, he is not a 'typical Polish priest'. Not many Polish priests ski and practise philosophy. No others have become Pope. Yet being Polish is the most important fact about him. Apart from two years at the Belgian College in Rome from 1946 to 1948, he spent his first fifty-eight years in Poland.

The Wojtyla family situation was interesting. Born on 18 May 1920, just as Poland regained independence, Karol lost his mother when he was nine years old and his elder brother shortly afterwards. Though he is very reluctant to speak of his family, he told Frossard:

> At twenty, I had already lost all the people I loved and even the ones that I might have loved, such as the big sister who had died, so I was told, six years before my birth. I was not old enough to make my first communion when I lost my mother, who did not have the happiness of seeing the day to which she looked forward as a great day. She wanted two sons, one a doctor, and one a priest; my brother was a doctor and, in spite of everything, I have become a priest. (*Be Not Afraid!*)

It would be easy to over-interpret here. But a few things may be safely said. The lack of any feminine presence in the household helped towards the idealization of Our Lady, who becomes the type of 'the eternal feminine' (as well as the alternative to Eve, the temptress). And did he feel some impulse to, as it were, 'make his mother happy' by becoming a priest? I don't know. But what is certainly true, as Peter Nichols perceptively wrote, is this: 'The family means to him something natural, but which he never had. (*The Times*, 1 June 1982.) By the age of twenty he was an orphan, with no possibility even of nephews and nieces; he appears as a sort of Methuselah.

Then on top of this personal tragedy came national catastrophe, with the Nazi occupation of Poland. The Poles were to be worked to death and, when they could no longer work, exterminated. Poland would be first *Judenrein* and then *Polenrein*. The killing of priests, academics, and cultural leaders began at once in 1939 in Karol Wojtyla's own Jagiellonian University in Kraków. It aroused great indignation in the Western press but, after the collapse of France, the governor, Hans Frank, correctly guessed that his 'pacification programme' would arouse less foreign interest. 'I have to admit,' he minuted, 'that several thousand Poles, particularly those who are the spiritual leaders of society, will have to die.' This is quoted by Jan Tomasz Gross in his *Polish Society under German Occupation*. Gross, a Yale sociology professor, describes how hope was systematically destroyed. It little mattered whether you tried to bribe the occupiers or defied them: you met the same fate in the end. It was a situation of *anomia*, of lawlessness, a topsy-turvy world in which nothing made sense any more.

In spiritual terms the occupation was like the 'dark night of the soul' as described by the sixteenth-century Spanish mystic St John of the Cross. This phrase was used on the tombstone of Cardinal Adam Sapieha, Archbishop of Kraków and the young Wojtyla's mentor. 'He sustained the faith of Poles,' says his epitaph in the Franciscan church, 'during their dark night of the soul.' There are only two responses to such an experience: despair or faith.

Karol Wojtyla was just on the eve of his twentieth birthday when he wrote his first play, *Job*. It was written very quickly (according to his poet friend Marek Skwarnicki) during Holy Week 1940. No wonder he turned to the book of Job. Here was a man who had lost everything. Not only that, but the very basis of rationality was subverted: the wicked prosper while goodness is mocked. Hans Frank had installed himself in Wavel Castle by the Vistula. Polish kings were buried in the crypt of the cathedral which is within the castle walls. Frank's presence there was insult, injury and blasphemy.

Karol Wojtyla's play faces up to the tragedy of Poland but in the end transforms it. At the end of the play Job, the man of the Old Testament, has a vision of Christ who is dispossessed of everything, humiliated, mocked, hung on a cross of shame. But the Lord raises him up and vindicates him. The last word will be not defeat but resurrection. (Bodeslaw Taborski, who has edited and translated Karol Wojtyla's plays and writings on the theatre, tells me in a letter that he hopes they will be published in 1986 by the University of California Press.) It was a question that had been much discussed by Catholic literary critics in the 1930s: can there, ultimately, be a Christian tragedy? The answer was no, because life ultimately will turn out to be a Divine Comedy in the sense of Dante – that is, God will reveal himself as all in all.

It has been said that most people have their mind-set formed by the age of twenty-five, and that afterwards new ideas work their way in only with difficulty. By the age of twenty-five Karol Wojtyla had experienced the twentieth century at its most devastating. Close to Kraków was the murder camp of Auschwitz to which the Jews of the ghetto were consigned. The 'liberation' of Poland by the Red Army turned out to be a sham: it left Wojtyla permanently sceptical about political slogans and the way they exploited people. Then the atomic bombs were dropped on Hiroshima and Nagasaki.

All these events crowding together gave Karol Wojtyla a strong sense that civilization, whether in the East or the West, was only a thin veneer painted over barbarism. A force for evil stalked the world. A cosmic struggle was going on between God and Satan. This gave, and gives, an eschatological edge to all the thinking of Pope John Paul. The vast cosmic drama is being played out in the events of this world. So Mehmet Ali Agca's murder attempt is another episode in the eternal struggle between good and evil. In this apocalyptic sense he sees Our Lady as she is hinted at in Genesis as 'the woman who will crush the head of the serpent'. The date of the assassination attempt, 13 May 1981, was the feast of Our Lady of Fátima. A year later John Paul went to Fátima to thank Mary for saving his life.

This sense of living on the edge of doom may explain why all the items on the agenda of the Western churches since Vatican II – typically birth control, women's ordination, due process, collegiality, even ecumenism – do not really engage his attention. His apocalyptic faith is concerned with life or death issues. 'Faith begins on the other side of despair.'

The quotation is from Georges Bernanos, the French novelist, who belongs to the same 'spiritual family' as the Pope. For Karol Wojtyla the priest is an heroic figure like the Abbé Donissan in *Sous le Soleil de Satan*, Bernanos' first novel. He stands alone on the battlements, the champion of his people, locked in single-handed combat with the evil one. This was how John Paul addressed West German priests at Altötting in 1980:

You are called to share in a special way in the spiritual struggle.

You are called to this constant combat that Mother Church is engaged upon and which fashions it into the image of the Woman, the Mother of the Lord. At the heart of your vocation is the adoration of holy God; but by the same token you are particularly exposed to the temptations of the Evil One, as is evident in the temptations of the Lord.

It is very dramatic, not to say melodramatic; and most of us are not used to thinking in this way.

But if you start from this conception of the priest as engaged in a spiritual battle, you will not take kindly towards those who wish to slink off from the battlefield to seek a more comfortable billet. John Paul regards them simply as cowards and deserters. That is why he withdrew Paul VI's compassionate norms on laicization and substituted savage norms that few can understand and hardly anyone can fulfil. They mean in effect that marriage and priestly ordination have been assimilated to each other: the only way out of either state is by an annulment – that is by a declaration, with antecedent proof, that there never really was a marriage and never really was an ordination. That's tough: but in the apocalyptic vision I have sketched out, a few individual casualties are of no consequence. For he believes, quoting Bernanos again, that 'the Church does not need reformers so much as saints', as he said in a sermon on St Charles Borromeo. (*Osservatore Romano*, English, 3 December 1984.) Bernanos also said, 'There is only one sadness – not to be a saint.'

Moreover – and this is something we in the West have no conception of – a priest in Poland who leaves the ministry is almost obliged to enter the service of the Communist Party, join its propaganda outfit, and vilify what he once loved, or at least seek to divide it by making 'progressive' noises. (See Maciej Pomian-Srzednicki, *Religious Change in Contemporary Poland*, for ex-priests working in anti-religious propaganda.) What else can he do? The *todo o nada* or all or nothing of St John of the Cross is reflected in Karol Wojtyla. It makes him a man of decisive choices, if you like it; or of uncompassionate extremes, if you don't.

That was for the future. But Karol Wojtyla knew what he was taking on when he was ordained priest on 1 November 1946, in Sapieha's private chapel. He pledged his word, and that was that. So he said his first three Masses on All Souls' Day, a feast that has special importance both in Poland and Italy. Interestingly, on All Souls' Day 1984 he found himself in a Milan cemetery and drew a parallel between his own life and that of his patron, St Charles Borromeo:

It is worth remarking that he made the final decision to dedicate himself to the service of God on the occasion of the death of his brother Frederico. Becoming the only son in his family, many people insisted that he marry in order to continue the Borromeo line. Instead, the death of his brother opened his eyes to the poverty of human realities. (*Osservatore Romano*, English, 2 December 1984)

That sounds like thinly veiled autobiography.

His ordination in 1946 had been brought forward because Sapieha had already decided to send him to Rome. A rapid post-war visit revealed to the aged Cardinal that he hardly knew a soul there. He decided to put that right by sending his best and brightest seminarians to Rome. That was how his own career had begun forty years before. So Karol Wojtyla left Poland for the first time and studied at the Angelicum, the Dominican University in Rome. The reason why he chose as the subject of his thesis 'The Act of Faith in St John of the Cross' has already been hinted at. Nothing less would do.

There were other contributing factors. He knew the Carmelites from his home town of Wadowice and was later to beatify one of them, Fr Rafal Kalinowski, known as 'the martyr of the confessional', on 22 June 1983 during his second visit to Poland. Again, St John of Cross was a poet and was included in his underground poetry readings in Kraków. In March 1946, the year he left for Rome, Karol Wojtyla published his first poems, *Songs of the Hidden God*, in a Carmelite publication, *Glos Karmelu*. He could easily have become a Carmelite himself. But Bishop Julian Groblicki said that he was turned down because 'you are born for greater things' ('*Ad majores res natus es*').

But the either-or, all-or-nothing, *todo o nada* attitude remained with him. Other forms of spirituality, though just as austere, have greater respect for creation, can say 'both-and', are less absolutist.

Having been ordained and done his doctorate on St John of the Cross, Wojtyla returned to Kraków. Though he was curate in a parish, he also began to teach philosophy at Kraków and at the Catholic University of Lublin, the only independent university between the River Elbe and the Pacific. But what sort of philosophy? At the Angelicum his thesis had been directed by the Dominican, Fr Garrigou-Lagrange, leader of the opposition to the 'new theology', sworn enemy of the 'historical school' of the French Jesuits and Dominicans. But Wojtyla, though disposed to welcome such a brand of 'eternal-verities' Thomism, had already had a metaphysical experience that changed his life. Frossard, who himself had a dramatic conversion, calls it 'miraculous' and 'a Copernican revolution'. Pope John Paul described to him how he began his clandestine philosophy studies in October 1942:

> Straightaway I found myself up against an obstacle. My literary training, centred round the humanities, had not prepared me at all for the scholastic theses and formulas with which the manual was filled. I had to cut a path through a thick undergrowth of concepts, analyses and axioms without even being able to identify the ground over which I was moving. After two months of hacking through this vegetation I came to a clearing, to the discovery of the deep reasons for what until then I had only lived and felt. When I passed the examination I told my examiner that in my view the new vision of the world which I had acquired in my struggle with that metaphysics manual was more valuable than the mark which I had obtained. I was not exaggerating. What intuition and sensibility had until then taught me about the world found solid confirmation. (*Be not Afraid!*)

It is obviously difficult to communicate this kind of experience to those who have never had it. It doesn't sound like a mystical experience in the strict sense. It could be called a metaphysical conversion. What really matters is its effect on Karol Wojtyla's style of thinking.

It led him to temper his Thomism with a thesis on the work of Max Scheler, the aberrant disciple of Edmund Husserl, founding father of phenomenology. He asked, 'Can a Christian ethic be based on the philosophy of Max Scheler?' His answer was 'no'. But according to Oxford Professor Michael Dummett, Wojtyla picked up a philosophical style that is reminiscent of late Husserl (*spät-Husserl*). It has three features. The thinker simply utters: he does not set out his own view in contradistinction to other possible positions, giving reasons why his own is superior. He is not required to produce arguments in its favour: he simply states it, and if challenged, restates it. Nor does he give examples of how what he is saying might be 'cashed'. Dummett, invariably (and accurately) described in the media as 'a devout Roman Catholic', assured me that he made this criticism not, as some might suppose, from the point of view of 'Oxford philosophy', but from the point of view of St Thomas Aquinas who always sets out rival positions clearly, gives his reasons and offers – not very good – examples. All these comments were made concerning *The Acting Person*, Wojtyla's major philosophical work.

The philosophical style learned in Lublin can be seen at work in his pontificate. He frequently answers one question with another (as in the plane on the way back from Canada). He is firmly convinced that one can penetrate through to the essence of the thing – of priesthood or religious life or marriage, for example – simply by thinking about it. As a result, he sometimes seems to ignore altogether the dimension of time, and so to dispense with history and the development of doctrine. Visiting Pope John's Bergamo, he tried to console priests and nuns allegedly worried by 'all these changes' by reminding them that 'We are what we have always been – and by that I mean we must remain as Christ the Lord intended.'

But is it really possible to make this leap in seven-league boots from the first to the twentieth century? Religious and priestly life have a history, and have taken many forms. To make an absolute out of the present discipline is abusive. Canonizing the present makes life difficult. To be fair to John Paul, he does not claim to be any sort of historian. He told Frossard candidly: 'Circumstances have never left me much time for study. By temperament I prefer thought to erudition.' Introspection and meditation are his path to truth.

All Pope John Paul's reservations about what is happening in the contemporary Church stem from this lack of any real sense of history. It works in two ways. When someone like Edward Schillebeeckx O.P. shows from the history of the ministry that the Church has always given itself the priests it needed, and that the way is theoretically open to the ordination of married men and women, moves are made against him. When Leonardo Boff tries to respond to the Spirit speaking in the 'signs of the times', he is very firmly squashed. So the methods are not very different from those of Garrigou-Lagrange in the pontificate of Pius XII, and the conflict is about the same issue: what is the place of history, both as a sense of the past and a response to the present, in Catholic thinking?

It is interesting that in *The Acting Person* he should quote the Council only once. Strictly speaking, it had no place in a philosophical work, but he was a Bishop and was happy to discover that he had been vindicated by Vatican II. The text he quotes is this:

The role and competence of the Church being what it is, she must in no way be confused with the political community, nor bound to any political system. For she is at once the sign and safeguard of the transcendence of the human person (*Gaudium et Spes*, No. 76, quoted in *The Acting Person*)

So while theologians elsewhere were discovering 'new insights' and 'fresh emphases' in the Council, Wojtyla experienced it as confirming what he already knew about the central role of the human person. This is certainly the key to his thinking. The 'dignity of the human person' is a philosophical premise from which he can draw endless conclusions about the proper conditions of work, the iniquity of torture, the defence of human rights, the errors of Marxist collectivism, and so on. But it underpins a theological concept, given that it is Christ, the Second Adam, who 'reveals man to man himself, and so reveals his true vocation'. (*Gaudium et Spes*, No.22.)

Thus, by the time he was elected Pope in October 1978, Karol Wojtyla was a well-rounded, chunky personality with clear views on all the problems of the Church. His lonely childhood, his wartime experiences, his apocalyptic vision, his literary ambitions, his philosophical work and the constant experience of being in opposition made him the Pope he would become. He was unlikely to change much subsequently. Though it did not become clear immediately, his pontificate would be first a holding operation, designed to correct the mistakes of Paul VI, and then one of 'restoration' of pre-conciliar values. I first used the term 'restoration' in October 1979 after the visit to the United States. No one took it seriously. But when Cardinal Joseph Ratzinger, chief theologian of the Vatican, used it late in 1984 it became, so to speak, the official watchword of the pontificate.

But if there was to be a restoration, an essential instrument for carrying it though would be the Roman Curia, the papal bureaucracy. To that we now turn, first in general, then in more detail.

5

Peter's Secretaries

The Roman Curia is at the service of the Pope. It is in effect the papal secretariat. The first Benedictine monk to be Pope, Gregory the Great, had been a Roman senator with the habit of command and administration at his fingertips. He used his fellow monks to help him with his correspondence. He sent one of them, Augustine, to England.

The modern Curia does not resemble Gregory's monastic community except in the requirement of celibacy. It does not invariably do what the pope wants. 'Outsider' popes (that is, those who were not trained in the Curia) like John XXIII have to learn how to handle these independent-minded prelates. 'Insider' popes like Paul VI, who worked for twenty-nine years in the Secretariat of State, know how the system works and have more chance of licking it into shape – especially if they have a Giovanni Benelli in charge. As a residential bishop and a foreigner, Karol Wojtyla was doubly an outsider. Yet this does not seem to have caused him any special difficulties.

I once asked a friend of his whether Cardinal Wojtyla was a good administrator as Archbishop of Kraków. There was a long pause. Then Stefan (let's call him that) said, 'I don't think he was very interested in administration. He preferred to bypass difficult questions. He left some people who were no good in important positions. His own role was to inspire: he thought that if he did that, then situations would change.' Stefan added, after an even longer pause, 'I think he was really a one-man band.' Another witness, Janusz said his regime in Kraków was one of 'efficient chaos'. Hanna said, 'He really wasn't very good at talking to the laity, but now he's pope we all have to rally round.' All these remarks throw light on the present pontificate. Administration is not John Paul's strong suit. He is content to inspire. He leaves more humdrum and hand-dirtying tasks to others.

There are occasional complaints about a 'Polish Mafia' in the Curia. It was said of Pius X that he had 'turned the barque of Peter into a gondola' by bringing so many Venetians down with him. John Paul II has not introduced all that many new Poles into the Curia. Ladislaw Rubin, now Prefect of the Oriental Churches Congregation, was already in Rome, as was the incapacitated André Deskur, President Emeritus of the Pontifical Commission for Social Communications. Both are now cardinals.

Mgr Jacques Martin, Prefect of the Pontifical Household, is a Frenchman who regulates private audiences and therefore access to the Pope. A witty historian who wrote a thesis on nineteenth-century papal nuncios to France, he has an unrivalled knowledge of the Vatican and can be seen, looking rather awkward, on all papal trips. He confessed: 'I am the link with the Pope, the lift (or elevator, if you are American). Everyone has to pass through my hands. But besides the lift there is also a back staircase and that is packed with Poles.'

Access to the back staircase is controlled by Mgr Stanislaw Dziwisz whose name is linked with the root *dziw*, which means 'wonder'. He was already the Pope's secretary in Kraków. You saw him cradle John Paul after Mehmet Ali Agca's murder attempt. He is the man who always hands the Pope his manuscript just before, after testing the microphone, he begins to speak. Present at most meals, he sometimes looks bored, since he does not have his chief's command of languages. He takes most papal telephone calls, and sometimes seems abrupt. Some says he throws his weight about. But this has been said of most papal secretaries. There is a mediaeval saying: '*Timeo non Petrum, sed secretarium eius*' ('I don't mind Peter, it's his secretary who scares me').

Besides Dziwisz, there are a few Poles placed in strategic positions where they can keep an eye on things. So Bishop Kazamierz Majdanski of Szczecin-Kamien is on the Pontifical Council for the Family; Marek Skwarnicki is a member of the Laity Council; Halina Bortnowska, a lay theologian, is a member of the Secretariat for Christian Unity, but having been imprisoned for a week after martial law, she dare not leave Poland for fear of never returning. They do not add up to a 'Polish Mafia'.

What is probably true is that the Poles, with 30 million Catholics, were previously under-represented in the Curia and are now making up for it. But they do have one great perk: they tend to get invited more regularly to the papal Mass at 7 a.m., followed by a hearty papal breakfast. But that is understandable: most people, however good they are at languages, prefer to speak their own language at breakfast, if they speak at all.

But the Curia remains predominantly Italian, and Italian is its everyday language (with exceptions that I will note). Its work remains largely invisible to the Catholic world. Even well-informed Catholics can seldom name more than two or three members of the Roman Curia – which is as it should be. The Curia is not as important as it sometimes thinks it is. But it deserves to be better known. Bishops are better informed than priests because they have to deal with the Curia on their *ad limina* (to the threshold of Peter) visits every five years. Religious superiors – provincials and their consultors – also need to know which way the wind is blowing. If only to set up their windshelters. What is astonishing is the smallness of the central administrative team compared with the vast number of those they theoretically administer.

At the last count there were 810,464,000 Catholics forming 18.4 per cent of the world's population. They are grouped in 359,000 parishes and 2,456 dioceses. (*Osservatore Romano*, English, 29 October 1984.) Yet the Curia has only 1,800 active members on its payroll, which works out at one bureaucrat for every 450,000 Catholics. As Arthur Jones remarked in a study of the business efficiency of the Vatican, 'If the central bureaucracy of the U.S. boasted the same *per capita* ratio, there would be but 511 federal employees in Washington instead of 300,000.' (*Forbes*, 14 January 1985.) The Vatican has a lean team. It provides fantastic value for money.

On these grounds some observers have therefore congratulated it on its efficiency. Peter F. Drucker of the American Institute of Management (AIM) said it was one of the three most efficiently administered organizations in history. The fact that the other two were General Motors and the Prussian Army should perhaps put us on our guard. The object of General Motors is to produce and sell as many cars as possible. The object of the Prussian Army was to deter enemies or, if that failed, to defeat them in battle. Whatever the object of the Roman Curia, it overlaps neither with that of General Motors nor with that of the Prussian Army.

The *raison d'être* of the Roman Curia is to help the Pope do his work. The Bishop of Rome has to announce that Christ is risen, is truly risen, indeed. He has to proclaim 'the joy of faith in a troubled world' – a phrase from *Redemptor Hominis*, John Paul II's first encyclical. So that is what his 'bureaucrats' have to do as well. They may lose sight of this vision. They may become 'burnt-out cases' like the Monsignor in Morris West's novel *The Devil's Advocate*. They may slump into what Max Weber called 'the routinization of charisma'. These are all possible dangers. But most of them know that they have no business substituting themselves for the Pope or the local churches.

This holds – or ought to hold – at every level of the Roman Curia. But of course it is inevitably the top cardinals who have the glamour and whatever power is going. The chief Vatican congregations (or dicasteries as they are known, following the terminology of the Roman Empire from which they derive) are often thought of as government 'ministries' or 'departments'. But this analogy is misleading. For curial offices have very little power – and what little they have can always be contested.

The Congregation for Religious, for example, can only give advice to the nearly 1 million nuns and 154,148 religious priests theoretically in its charge. It has to check out changes in constitutions, but otherwise the superiors of the countless religious orders remain ultimately responsible for what happens. And they may find the Congregation for Religious, under its new Prefect, Cardinal Jérôme Hamer O.P., making extravagant and preposterous demands on them such as that all political statements made by any religious anywhere must first have the approval of the Sacred Congregation or, failing that, of the local papal nuncio. That was the rather ludicrous or, to put it more kindly, unworkable suggestion put to the Swiss religious in May 1985. The Curia can always, of course, claim to be acting 'on Higher Authority' (capital letters are mandatory), but that has to be demonstrated. It cannot be assumed that when the Congregation for Religious pronounces on nuns' hemlines it is speaking 'in the name of the Holy Father'. But this ambivalence bedevils much of the work of the Curia.

However, this picture of a relatively impotent 'ministry' or dicastery, with little real authority, has to be qualified by including another characteristic feature of the Curia. At the top level cardinals not only run their own departments but are on the 'boards' (usually called 'councils') of other congregations. There is, in short, a system of interlocking directorates which means that a well-placed cardinal in theory knows what is going on in a number of other departments. Using this criterion, the top cardinal in 1984 was Bernadin Gantin who was on the boards of the Congregations for the Doctrine of the Faith, Bishops, Oriental Churches, Religious, Evangelization, Saints, Catholic Education, not to mention the Secretariats for Non-Christian Religions and Non-Believers. Cardinal Joseph Ratzinger came second in this pecking order, and Cardinal William Wakefield Baum, formerly Archbishop of Washington, third. This does not, however, mean that they can influence policies outside their own departments, but at least they know, usually, what is going on. However, there is no real sense of 'cabinet' government in the Curia, still

less a notion of collective responsibility. Everything in the end is
determined by the 'prince' to whom the cardinals are indebted. 'You
feel a greater bond of loyalty to the Pope who made you a cardinal,'
one of them enigmatically told me, 'than to his successor who did not
appoint you.' I have been puzzling out that remark ever since.

All the objections to the Roman Curia – and there have been a
great many in the course of history – boil down to this: its members
claim to act in the name of the Pope when in fact they are usurping
his authority. Here is a classical statement from a moderate Benedictine, Patrick Granfield:

> The Vatican bureaucracy is often linked to the imperialistic con-
> ception of the papacy. The cumbersome machinery of the Roman
> Curia, despite recent improvements, is still far from efficient.
> Excessive paperwork – someone called it a *Papierkrieg* – unreason-
> able delays, and a reluctance to recognize the principle of subsid-
> iarity characterize the Church's central administration. These
> flaws are, of course, endemic to any large social institution but in
> Rome, through centuries of practice, they have been honed to per-
> fection. (*The Papacy in Transition*)

The reason Granfield sees inefficiency where Drucker saw efficiency
is that they are using different yardsticks. Drucker was thinking in
terms of institutional durability: 'No profit-seeking corporation has
ever impressed us so much as the Roman Catholic Church. The
hierarchy moves quickly on administrative measures, slowly in alter-
ation of its social customs, and not at all where dogma is concerned'.
(Jones, in *Forbes*.) Granfield, as a monk and a theologian, wants to
subordinate the institution – in this case the Roman Curia – to the
goals of the Church as communion or *koinonia*. That is the right
criterion to apply. The Curia should never be allowed to become an
end in itself. As much as possible should be left to the local Churches.
That is what the principle of 'subsidiarity', discussed in papal social
encyclicals, means.

At the same time Granfield's detailed comments are rather unfair.
The Roman Curia is not a cumbersome machine: it is as slim as it can
possibly be. The Secretariat of State, for example, has a staff of just
over 150 to deal with relations and Churches throughout most of the
world. Cardinal Joseph Ratzinger complained that he had only
about ten officials to examine theologians denounced to his Congregation. Everyone in the Curia is overworked. Just after the Schillebeeckx 'conversation' in Rome in 1980, Archbishop (as he then

was) Jérôme Hamer was asked how he was. He replied that he was feeling rather harassed; there was so much to do; unorthodoxy was pressing in from all sides. He sounded for all the world like a worried doctor in the midst of a 'flu epidemic. He should have been advised to relax. But he was driven by what he saw as a sense of duty. Ever vigilant, he stood on the bridge, scanning the horizon for possible errors.

Onlookers can easily be deceived by appearances. The Anglican Bishop of Taunton, Peter Nott, who spent two weeks studying the Curia in the spring of 1985, felt able to report that 'centralization seemed less oppressive than expected', 'the staff of each congregation was relatively small' and – clinching point – 'the Vatican exists to promote unity through co-ordination not domination.' (*The Tablet*, 8 June 1985.) So it does. The test, however, is not what the Vatican says of itself, but what it actually does. And the small staff and slimness of which the Curia boasts also mean that it does not have enough people or resources to engage in much travel or widespread consultation. Seen from the centre, the centralization may not seem oppressive; experienced, at the sharp end, the same decisions can look very different.

Granfield's complaint about 'excessive paperwork' is too vague. Excessive in relation to what? Most curial officials manage to keep their desks tidy and move paper about with fair speed. Anyway, 'paperwork' is what the Curia is mostly concerned with. It provides judgements (from the Sacred Penitentiary, the Apostolic Signatura, and the Rota, a sort of appeal court in marriage cases); answers letters (in principle by the next day); prepares documents; does a *potpourri* of views on, say, women's ordination; drafts reports; approves of this or censures that. All these diverse activities involve setting words down on paper – or, more recently and in the Secretariat of State at least, setting words down on word processors. This last aid is a great help, I was told, because even documents destined for a vast audience can now be 'personalized'.

Ask a curialist what he is doing and he will almost invariably reply (if he agrees to answer) that he is working on a particularly difficult case or 'preparing a document' on 'the spirituality of the diocesan priest' or 'the future of the urban parish'. Both these examples come from the Congregation for the Clergy. Each curial department has an annual plenary meeting when the outside members and consultors come along. Preparing for this meeting and making sure nothing goes wrong at it is one of the principal tasks of the curialist. It is a relatively unstrenuous form of accountability. 'Getting past the plenary' can become the main aim in curial life. The foreigners – *questa gente da fuori* – can usually be sent bamboozled home. Bureaucrats, as Henry Kissinger noted, pretend to be studying options when they in fact are seeking a quiet life.

Granfield also complains of 'unreasonable delays'. Everyone who has dealt with the Roman Curia will be able to give examples of horrendous delay that causes great human suffering. But this arises almost invariably in juridical questions – annulments of marriages or dispensations from the priesthood, for example – where evidence has to be gathered and weighed. To receive a curt note three years later saying 'negative, insufficient reasons' does tend to make people angry. One undispensed priest and his family have called their cat 'Cardinal Insufficient Reasons' after Ratzinger. But pettifogging and the law's delays are not peculiar to the Vatican.

Granfield's final charge, that the incompetence of the Curia is the result of long practice over the centuries, is if true the gravest of all. In the eighteenth century masterly inactivity was certainly a way of life. An Ambassador reported to his government: 'In Rome everyone gives orders and no one obeys them and really things work well enough.' (Maurice Andrieux, *Daily Life in Papal Rome in the Eighteenth Century*.) Pope Benedict XIV, the most popular Pope before John XXIII, informed by a crazed Fanciscan that Antichrist had been born in an Abruzzi village, asked how old he was. On being told three, Benedict said, 'Very well, then it will be for my successor to deal with him.' (Andrieux.) But that story illustrates not incompetence so much as prudence, the only virtue that can be learned from experience.

Much criticism of the Curia is the result of a reflex action. The men in the trenches resent the remoteness of the staff officers in their comfortable billets at H.Q. That is only natural. For Fr Leonardo Boff O.F.M., Cardinal Joseph Ratzinger's view from the window of the Piazza di Sant'Uffizio is bound to be wrong because he is in the wrong place or the wrong palace. The right place is with the poor. Be with them and then reread the *Magnificat*, which speaks of the mighty being toppled from their thrones.

Since Catholics do not like to tackle their popes directly, they prefer to criticize the Curia. It provides a magnificent scapegoat. It is distant and faceless. Moreover, there was one historical moment when the Curia fulfilled all the worst expectations one might have of it: throughout the Council, but especially during its first session in 1962, it was on the defensive. The story had the simplicity of a mediaeval morality play in which noble-hearted bishops from outside Rome were pitted against incompetent and mean-minded curialists. The young Joseph Ratzinger was then a poacher rather than a gamekeeper. He supplied arguments and ammunition to Cardinal Joseph Frings of Cologne, who launched a celebrated attack on the Holy Office (as it then was) and its iniquitous methods. It was vigorously applauded. Twenty years later, Ratzinger became the Prefect of this same department, now rebaptized Congregation for the Doctrine of Faith.

My point is that the Curia provides a splendid lightning conductor. It performs the useful function of diverting attacks on the Pope. This made a good deal of sense in the pontificate of Pope John XXIII, when the myth of the 'good guy pope hamstrung by inept curial officials' was a reasonable approximation to the truth. It no longer makes any sense at all, yet the myth continues to flourish. Here is Fr Francis Xavier Murphy C.S.S.R. (alias 'Xavier Rynne') on Pope John Paul II's first encyclical, *Redemptor Hominis*:

> Replete with extravagant terminology and idiosyncratic doctrinal turns, it gushed forth in vigorous waves of language that gave the Vatican Congregations for the Doctrine of Faith fits, as its scriveners endeavoured to pull it into shape and cope with its theological content. (Francis Xavier Murphy, *The Papacy Today*)

The key word is 'scriveners'. We know exactly what to think about these petty pen-pushers who never had an original thought in their lives and cannot understand this energumen, this overflowing fountain, of a Polish Pope. He is bold and unconventional. They are small-minded and parasitical. This is in fact a grotesque parody of the situation. A myth devised for one situation cannot be bodily shifted to another. It ignores two facts. The Curia is in the main in broad agreement with the policies of John Paul II. But that does not prevent it from thinking that he talks too much.

The Roman Curia, like the city of Rome itself, is essentially a product of the baroque age and the Counter-Reformation. It was largely the creation of the Franciscan Pope Sixtus V in 1588. It was not designed for dialogue but for mission. It did not enter into discussion with local Churches: it gave them orders about seminaries and catechisms (both Council of Trent innovations). It was not ecumenical since its highest priority was to defend Catholic orthodoxy and beat the Protestants to the mission fields which, thanks to the religious orders, it very largely did. What is now known as the Congregation for the Clergy was previously called, with admirable simplicity, the Congregation for the Council, and it dates back to 1564. Between the sixteenth century and 1870 'the Council' meant the Council of Trent.

After 1870 'the Council' meant Vatican I (which wasn't called that because no one at the time dreamt of another Council). The idea that the Successor of Peter was 'endowed with that infallibility which the Church possesses' consoled the popes for the loss of the Papal States. Spiritual power made up for the absence of temporal power. It also led to increasing and hitherto unheard-of centralization. Railways made travel to Rome easier. The telegraph meant that Rome could intervene more swiftly. The communication was two-way: the national colleges in Rome were greatly expanded, and a bath of *romanità* was advised for anyone who wanted to become a bishop. The Latin American College was opened in 1858 and the North American College in 1859.

By 1965 'the Council' had come to mean Vatican II, and a new theology of the Church as the people of God entailed inevitably the reform of the Curia. This came about in two ways: through the creation of new offices such as the Secretariats for Christian Unity, Non-Christian Religions and Non-Believers which, placed alongside the 'old Curia', exercised a healthy influence on it; and secondly through the apostolic constitution *Regimini Sanctae Ecclesiae* promulgated by Paul VI in 1967.

Cardinal Agostino Casaroli, now Secretary of State, has said that Paul VI's treatment of the Curia was radical, 'comparable to the reforms of Sixtus V in 1588 and Pius X in 1908'. Certainly it was an attempt to graft upon a Curia designed for other purposes a dialogue-minded team that would put itself at the pastoral service of the Pope for the good of the whole Church.

Regimini Sanctae Ecclesiae was certainly an epoch-making document. It provided that modern languages could be used in official letters and documents; previously documents were written in Latin. It made diocesan bishops members of all curial departments. It required retirement (or the offer of it) at seventy-five; this struck a blow at gerontocracy, though the fact that it did not apply to popes disgruntled some. I suspect that when Paul VI made this regulation he did not expect to live beyond seventy-five. But he surprised himself and knew that cardinals were muttering in their sleeves: 'If I'm too old to be Prefect of the Congregation of Bishops at seventy-five, why should the Pope continue beyond this age?' 'You cannot resign from paternity', was Paul VI's riposte. But retirement at seventy-five put an end to the system in which curial cardinals were like mediaeval barons running independent fiefdoms.

Paul VI also changed the names of Curial offices. This may seem trivial or merely cosmetic, but in effect it was an attempt to push the Curia into a new age and involve it in the enterprise of Vatican II. The once feared Holy Office became the Congregation for the Doctrine of Faith. It was assigned the positive task of encouraging sound theology. The International Theological Commission of thirty members was set up to 'continue the spirit of the Council' and give the Congregation for the Doctrine of Faith a wider range of advisers than the Roman theological colleges could provide. After Dr Joseph Goebbels, 'Propaganda' clearly would not do as the name of the Missions dicastery. It was given the unwieldly title of the Congregation for the Evangelization of Peoples. But these old names are still used for the squares they inhabit. Ring the Vatican telephone exchange, 698, and it is still wiser to ask to be put through to the Holy Office or Propaganda.

This does not mean that the reforms of Paul VI failed, merely that old habits die hard. In the rest of this book we will see how the 'new Curia', the product of Vatican II, modified or failed to modify the 'old Curia', inherited from the Counter-Reformation. The most important structural change – unnoticed by Peter Drucker – was that Paul VI gave the Secretariat of State a 'co-ordinating role' and named Mgr Giovanni Benelli 'substitute', with the task of implementing it. In practice, there is not a lot of difference between 'co-ordination' and 'control', and Benelli, though not the ogre I depicted in the *Observer* in March 1973, certainly knew all about control. So the next chapter, which starts the study of curial departments, will begin with the Secretariat of State. Then I will deal with the 'old Curia', and finally with the 'new Curia'.

This chapter began with the question: is it appropriate to call the Curia a bureaucracy and are its dicasteries like government ministries? One last consideration will suggest that the Curia is totally unlike secular governments. What is the method of entry? Could a layman or laywoman say: 'I would like to work in the Curia'? Is there any career structure? The short answer is that there is none. Working for the Lord is not a 'career'. Do not expect to get rich in his service: in fact the rare laypeople who work in the Vatican, in the Library or the radio station for instance, can only survive by moonlighting. Moreover, they know that they will never get to the top administrative posts, since these are a clerical preserve.

How, then, *does* anyone enter the Roman Curia? Having discussed this with many curialists over the years, the only satisfactory answer is: the old-boy network and sheer chance. You are, for example, a

Dominican and a canon lawyer of modest reputation – good thesis
and one or two important articles. One day you have lunch with
someone from the Congregation for the Doctrine of Faith who says,
over *grappa*, 'We need people like you. It won't be for very long. You
can begin with a five-year stint.' But Dominican canon lawyers are
not exactly queueing up to join the C.D.F. – or even to teach in the
Angelicum. The best curialists are always the most reluctant; keen-
ness is a bad sign. Italians and a certain sort of Spaniard, of course,
have no such inhibitions.

To illustrate the chancy nature of curial appointments, I will consider the career of Giovanni Coppa, titular Archbishop of Serta. He
has never been to his notional diocese in the land of the unbelievers
(*in partibus infidelium*), which probably means somewhere in Asia
Minor. He is an Archbishop without any people. Never mind, he has
a more important role.

His title is 'the Delegate for the pontifical representatives to the
Holy See', which suggests a diplomatic function. But that is fictional.
In practice, Coppa is in overall charge of the Pope's speech-writing
team. He looks after the Italian translations (which are crucial).
Born on 9 November 1925, Mgr Coppa is now sixty, and he had to
wait until his fifty-fourth year to reach his present post. How did he
get there?

He was born in Alba near Turin in Northern Italy, attended the
local seminary, and was ordained in January 1949. So far, so unre-
markable. Then he went to the Catholic University of the Sacred
Heart in Milan where he did a doctorate on the iconography of the
Trinity from Christian origins to the beginning of the fourteenth century.

His next move was crucial, and it defies explanation. His thesis
completed, he was 'called' to the Apostolic Chancery in 1952. Six
years later he was again 'called', this time to the Secretariat of State,
and from here his career was properly launched. His skill as a
Latinist came in useful during the Council. In his spare time he has
worked mostly on St Ambrose, the layman who was prevailed upon
to become Bishop of Milan. He has produced scholarly editions of
Ambrose's treatises *De Mysteriis* (on the Sacraments) and *Expositio
Evangelii secundum Lucam* (on St Luke's Gospel). Who 'called' him in
the first place when he was twenty-six? Who, in short, was his patron? He was unusual in not having been to a Roman university. So
someone spotted him as a man of talent, a high flyer, and brought
him to Rome to work as a canonist although his thesis had been in
quite another field. My guess is that his patron was Giovanni Bat-

tista Montini, who would certainly have appreciated Coppa's work on St Ambrose; but such matters are rarely discussed publicly. If all goes well, one day Archbishop Coppa will become Cardinal Coppa.

I use the example of Coppa merely to show that there is no regular procedure for entry into the Roman Curia. The exception is the Secretariat of State, which normally expects its men to have studied at the Accademia Pontificia, the school for Vatican diplomats opposite the elephant in Piazza Minerva. There the future Paul VI lectured in diplomatic history, subjecting a single year to intense scrutiny each semester. The Italians have signally failed to supply a stream of students; in 1985 it was provided with its first non-Italian rector, the Californian Mgr Justin Rigali. But even the Secretariat of State does not insist on this mode of entry, as the example of Coppa shows. For the rest, there is no equivalent of the civil service examination. Of course in practice there are some minimum requirements without which the curialist would be a burden: an ability to speak at least three languages; and a doctorate in theology or canon law (though ecclesiastical doctorates are not necessarily evidence of scholarly ability).

Italians still form the majority in the Curia, and their presence does not require much explanation: they are simply following in the tradition. Non-Italians seem to be there by accident: they have been at a Roman university and appear to flourish in Rome (some people do); or one of their professors, who is also a consultor of a Roman Congregation, remembers old So-and-so and puts his name forward; or a religious order thinks it might be prudent to 'second' some of its members of the Curia so that, while serving the Pope, it may also know what is going on. The Secretariat for Christian Unity behaves more sensibly than other departments: Mgr Basil Meeking, a New Zealander, is there because he had written a thesis on the laity in the documents of the World Council of Churches (WCC). But that is a rare case. More typical is the curialist who is there because his bishop saw in this a Heaven-sent opportunity to remove a difficult man from the diocese and at the same time 'internationalize the Curia'. In this way the bishop can kill two birds with one stone.

But if getting into the Roman Curia is a matter of chance, getting on in it is largely a matter of keeping the paper moving and one's head down. There is an ecclesiastical equivalent of Buggins' turn. Perhaps we should call it Mgr Bugnini's turn. In the eighteenth century the best way to get on (*camminare*) was 'to stick to the rules while making skilful use of the slightest incident that came along'. (Andrieux, *Daily Life* . . .) Cardinal Agostino Casaroli, now Secretary of

State, once joked of his own career: 'Promotion to the rank of under-secretary came by the natural process of being there and growing older.' This was, of course, unduly self-deprecating. But civil servants all the world over will see its point. When in doubt, bureaucrats play for safety.

In the end, the principal difference between other international bureaucracies and the Roman Curia is that besides being a secretariat it is also a court, like a royal court. That is what the word Curia means, though it also carries associations with a court of law. One eighteenth-century cardinal put it very brutally when he admitted: 'I know neither theology nor church history, but I know how to live in a court.' The pope is more like an absolute monarch than anything else. True, he is constrained by the Word of God, the deposit of faith, the tradition of the Church, and so on. But he is not judged by anyone from below, and there is no court of appeal against his judgements. The Church is not a democracy. And in spite of all the brave talk of 'consultation', 'collegiality' and 'co-responsibility' in the twenty years since the Council, in practice they are difficult to achieve. The natural tendency is to fall back into the old habits of direct intervention. This is especially so if one has an apocalyptic vision of the Church elsewhere as 'falling apart' with the Pope as its energetic saviour. Not everyone in the Curia sees the world in such lurid hues, but loyal critics of the papal style would not feel very comfortable working there. Besides, there is another factor not found in other bureaucracies. The reason the Curia is efficient, one top archbishop told me, is that 'these men are ecclesiastics: we can depend on their obedience'.

6

Papal Diplomacy

Somewhat astonishingly, the new Code of Canon Law, promulgated in 1983, has only two paragraphs about the Roman Curia. The first of them brings out the importance of the Secretariat of State:

> The Supreme Pontiff usually conducts the business of the universal Church through the Roman Curia, which acts in his name and with his authority for the good and for the service of the Churches. The Curia is composed of the Secretariat of State or Papal Secretariat, the Council for the Public Affairs of the Church, the Congregations, the Tribunals and other Institutes. (No. 360)

Since the Secretariat of State includes the Council for the Public Affairs of the Church, its pre-eminence is very clearly asserted. It is the dynamo of the Curia, the nerve and communications centre. It is worth looking at the Latin here. To say that 'the Supreme Pontiff usually conducts the business of the Universal Church' in this way is not to say that he must necessarily do so. The Latin says: *'Curia Romana, qua negotia ecclesiae universae Summus Pontifex expedire solet . . .'* That means simply that the Supreme Pontiff habitually does business in this way. No one, I think, has ever claimed that the Curia is of divine institution, that is, willed or instituted by Christ himself. The Curia could wither away. Canon Law recognizes that it is a human institution.

Yet the late Giovanni Benelli claimed to detect a foreshadowing of the papal diplomatic service in the way Titus and Timothy were sent by Paul 'on missions'. No one found this very convincing. Too extravagant claims about the Curia are inevitably refuted by history. For the central role played by the Secretariat of State is a very modern phenomenon. It was only in 1605 that the Secretariat was able to demand weekly reports from its nuncios or envoys; and only in 1721 that the Cardinal Secretary of State became automatically Prime Minister of the Papal States and at the same time Foreign Minister. And it was not until 1967 that the Secretariat of State came first in the *Annuario Pontifico* and was assigned the all-embracing task of 'co-ordination'. Mgr Paul Poupard, who should know, claims it is the 'eye, the heart and the arm of the pope'.

It is certainly closest to him physically. The Secretariat of State is on the third floor of the Apostolic Palace which rises to the right of St Peter's Square. It occupies a series of interconnecting rooms around the inner courtyard of San Damaso. Just before passing through the door where the words '*Segretario di Stato*' are inscribed on the stained-glass transom, one finds a sixteenth-century map painted on the wall. North America is called '*terra incognita*', Russia is '*Salmatia*' and there is simply no Australia. Another map in the reception area brings things slightly more up to date by showing where papal diplomats were in the pontificate of Pius XII. Washington, which then had an apostolic delegate, appears as *Vashingtonensis* and Warsaw as *Varsaviensis*. By 1986, of course, *Vashingtonensis* has a pro-nuncio, and *Varsaviensis* has not had a papal diplomat since the Communists took over. But the maps are never altered. The visual aid of one period becomes another era's treasure.

It was in the pontificate of Pius XII that the Secretariat of State expanded most rapidly. This was paradoxical, because Pius XII never appointed a successor to his only Secretary of State, Cardinal Luigi Maglione, who died in 1944. Henceforward Pius became 'his own Secretary of State', the post he had occupied under Pius XI. In practice, the two departments were run by the fiery Roman, Domenico Tardini, in charge of Extraordinary Affairs (the first section), and the Brescian intellectual Giovanni Battista Montini, who looked after Ordinary Affairs (the second section). This distinction has now happily been abolished. It was never very easy to grasp. It began after the Napoleonic wars when Pope Pius VI created a special advisory body of cardinals to examine the special problems involved in dealing with the new or restored regimes that had emerged. So 'extraordinary affairs' in principle meant dealing with states rather than with inner-Church matters. But as Robert Graham S.J. remarks of Pius XII: 'Even the Pope did not take the distinction too literally and often enough, by consigning a particular problem to one of his aides, he automatically decided whether it was, respectively, "extraordinary" or "ordinary".' (*Paul VI et la Modernité dans l'Église.*) The confusion was well reflected in a story told by Fr Graham. One day a *minutante* (official) of the first section reported breathlessly to Tardini: '*Monsignore*, his eminence Cardinal X has run off with his housekeeper!' Without looking up from his papers, Tardini is supposed to have replied: 'Tell that to Montini – he deals with ordinary affairs.'

No doubt it was experiences like these that led Montini, when he became Pope, to clarify the different functions within the Secretariat of State and to create the Council for the Public Affairs of the Church to deal with diplomatic matters, international relations and the international organizations. The Vatican has 'observer' status at the United Nations, Unesco (culture), the F.A.O. (Food and Agriculture), the E.E.C. (European Community) and the O.A.S. (Organization of American States).

But once again one has to pinch oneself to remember how small all these offices were in comparison with the magnitude of the tasks they were embarked upon. Tardini's department of Extraordinary Affairs went from sixteen in 1944 to seventy- two in 1955, while Montini's staff at Ordinary Affairs leaped from thirty-four to seventy-four, according to Andrea Riccardi. (*Pio XII.*)

Since Cardinal Agostino Casaroli, the present Secretary of State, learned his diplomatic skills under these two very different men, it will be useful to contrast them here, for they represent two different traditions in the Secretariat of State. Tardini was in the mould of Pietro Gasparri, Secretary of State in the 1920s, and principal author of the 1917 Code of Canon Law. His main concern was not to compromise the Church with any political forces that might try to exploit it. Ironic and detached, Tardini accepted the maxim of Mgr Francesco Borgongini Duca, Pope John's old classmate, as Riccardi recounts: 'When we extract from a government some concessions in favour of the freedom of the Church in the nomination of bishops, Catholic schools, influence over youth, we save far more souls than when we preach or hear confessions.' That made some sense in the time of Fascism and Nazism. But it implied that the principal aim of Vatican diplomacy was the defence of the Church as institution. The only 'rights' which counted were the 'rights of the Church'. It did not take into account the 'pastoral' nature of the Church or the fact that its mission is to all mankind.

Montini, by contrast, was a very un-Roman figure. His education had not been overly clerical. His father was a politican and newspaper editor of sound anti-Fascist instincts. As chaplain to F.U.C.I., the Union of Catholic Students in the Fascist period, Montini helped to prepare the generation of Christian Democratic politicans who emerged after the war. Very roughly one can say that in the Secretariat of State Tardini represented tradition, while Montini played the card of modernity and dialogue. That is why he was exiled to Milan in 1954. But when he came back as Pope in 1963, he did his best to implement the reforms he had brooded over during his twenty-nine years of service in the Secretariat of State.

The present Secretary of State, Cardinal Agostino Casaroli, son of a tailor from Piacenza, follows the Montini rather than the Tardini line. Pope John XXIII recognized his ability and sent him to international conferences on diplomatic and consular relations. This brought him into contact with Communist diplomats, and he became the first Vatican diplomat to travel extensively in Eastern Europe. 'The Church has no enemies,' Pope John told him; and Casaroli noted how Pope John's goodness had melted away the ideological ice-floes. That was how Casaroli's association with the *Ostpolitik* (or Eastern European policy) began. From 1969 he was head of the newly created Council for the Public Affairs of the Church. In the 1960s and 1970s he became known as 'the Henry Kissinger of the Vatican'.

He once described with exemplary frankness his aim in negotiations with Communist governments. First secure the *esse* of the Church – its very existence – by making sure, for example, that bishops were not merely government stooges. Then one could move on to a second stage of *bene esse* in which certain rights would be legally guaranteed. Typically they would include the right of assembly, the right to maintain and build churches, the right of children to attend catechism classes, the right of the Church to have some sort of access to the media. Beyond that lay the shimmering horizon of the *plene esse* where the Church would be fully free within a Communist regime. Casaroli would be the first to admit that this delectable state of things has nowhere been achieved. It is no doubt an unattainable horizon. But horizons exist to stretch the mind and imagination. Casaroli likes to quote Dante: 'He does not fail whose gaze is fixed on a star.'

During this period, Casaroli had many other problems to deal with. He renegotiated the Concordats with Spain and with Italy, the latter taking over ten years. He is no stickler for concordats. 'The ideal,' he says, 'is concord, not concordat.' He doesn't much mind what form it takes, provided there is agreement. Thus he was happy with the 'protocol' signed with Yugoslavia in 1966. Casaroli's methods have not changed. He is essentially a backroom man, a boffin, the master of the dossier. Though he gives an occasional well thought-out lecture, most of his work is done in private. He does not get flustered or angry. He is revered by his staff and has done for his generation what Tardini did for his.

Pope John Paul II inherited his Secretary of State, Cardinal Jean Villot, from Pope Paul VI. Villot, depicted in David Yallop's *In God's Name* as prepared to murder in order to cling to office, was in fact anxious to leave and go home. But he was kept on until his death in April 1979. Casaroli then became Secretary of State. This was a surprise, for the Polish bishops were known to be mistrustful of his *Ostpolitik*. They feared that the Vatican diplomats might negotiate with the Polish government over their heads. They thought they knew the Polish situation better than Italians who merely dropped in from time to time. However, these objections were set aside. Casaroli was known to be a man of great loyalty who had already served four popes with great skill. And positively, there was a lot to be said for having an experienced Italian alongside the first non-Italian Pope for 457 years.

Villot had been a 'pastor' rather than a 'diplomat', and he saw his principal work as fostering contact with the local churches. Casaroli does not neglect this aspect of his task, but by training and habit he is more concerned with the traditional diplomatic and political role of the Secretariat of State. In addition, he has been given a number of other special assignments which have enhanced the importance of his office even more. He was given full powers to sort out the affairs of the *Istituto di Opere di Religione* (I.O.R.), popularly known as 'the Vatican Bank'. He attended the Special Session of the United Nations on Disarmament in July 1982, and in January 1983 chaired the 'consultation' among American and European bishops that preceded the US bishops' peace pastoral. One may be sure that he is well briefed on the implications of the S.D.I. (Strategic Defence Initiative, commonly called 'Star Wars'), which the Pontifical Academy of Science, which includes Russians and Americans, began to study in January 1985.

But the main additional duty in this pontificate is that of accompanying the Pope on his international travels. There is not a great deal for him to do, on these occasions, and to deprive a man like Casaroli of his desk and his dossiers is rather cruel – though contact with the office is maintained through Vatican Radio. I once met him as we waited for Mass to begin outside the Chinese-built People's Palace of Culture in Kinshasa, Zaire. At eight o'clock in the morning the heat was already intense, and a mitre makes a very inadequate sun-hat. We knew we were going to have to sweat it out until midday at least. 'Are you still interested in the *Ostpolitik?*' Casaroli asked, referring to our previous conversations. I said that I was. 'Well,' he said, 'Now I feel I belong to the Church of Silence. I can't get on with my work and yet I have to be here.'

Casaroli goes on papal journeys in case something untoward happens: an assassination attempt or a diplomatic blunder or an upset

President. He can also play a useful dogsbody role as papal surrogate. It was obviously impossible for the Pope to visit political prisoners on the journey to the Philippines in February 1981, but Casaroli could go along discreetly without television cameras and bring the Pope's blessing. These Far Eastern visits also gave him a chance to have a closer look at China, which fascinates him. Sometimes Casaroli uses the occasion of a papal journey to deliver a lecture on international affairs. His lecture to the Empire Club of Canada in Toronto on 14 September 1984 was on 'The Papacy and the Challenges of the Modern World'.

It was interesting as a revelation of how Casaroli understands the role of the Holy See on the international scene as a 'transnational actor'. (See R.O. Keohane and J.S. Nye (eds.), *Transactional Relations in World Politics*, especially L. Vallier's chapter, 'The Roman Catholic Church as a Transnational Actor'.) Here Casaroli both makes a claim and admits a temptation:

> In relation to the matters in question here, the Holy See, in some ways, holds a privileged position. Not having any political, territorial or military interests of its own to defend, it is in a position to see with greater objectivity the reality and implications of the problems that arise on the international scene. At the same time, however, it has to be careful of the temptation to judge and evaluate concrete situations, which are sometimes very complex, from a point of view that is too theoretical or which oversimplifies things. The Holy See must also endeavour to maintain complete independence and the greatest balance of judgement, even when its *rapport* with the various parties involved is not always of the same quality: with some its relations are friendly; with others, unsatisfactory; or even not good at all. It must be ready to examine and evaluate with equal objectivity the motives and behaviour of one and the other side, and be prepared to keep open the channels of dialogue with all: at least with all those willing to listen.

If we translate this rather dry language into practical terms, Casaroli was saying among other things that the Holy See must remain as even-handed as possible and does not have to choose between East and West, for example. It may know where its friends are, but it must not shut the door on anyone.

Curiously enough, it was precisely at this time that rumours began to circulate in Rome about an earthquake or *terremoto* in the Vatican.

This is the usual Vatican term for a shake-up or reshuffle. (The most spectacular was in 1954 when Montini was despatched to Milan without a cardinal's hat.) Casaroli was going to resign, it was said, because he did not like the tone of Cardinal Joseph Ratzinger's Instruction 'On Certain Aspects of Liberation Theology', made public on 3 September 1984. Moreover, although he is a member of the Congregation for the Doctrine of Faith, he had not been properly informed about the meeting which approved the offending text. The passage which, in Casaroli's view, went over the top states:

> A major fact of our time ought to evoke the reflection of all those who would sincerely work for the true liberation of their brothers: millions of our own contemporaries legitimately yearn to recover those basic freedoms of which they were deprived by totalitarian and atheistic regimes which came to power by violent and revolutionary means, precisely in the name of liberation of the people. This shame of our time cannot be ignored: while claiming to bring them freedom, these regimes keep whole nations in conditions of servitude which are unworthy of mankind. Those who, perhaps inadvertently, make themselves accomplices of similar enslavements betray the very poor they mean to help.

One member of the Secretariat of State said, 'We are not accustomed to such brutal and offensive language.' It put in jeopardy all Casaroli's patient diplomatic work in Eastern Europe which had been directed largely by Archbishop Achille Silvestrini, his successor as head of the Council for the Public Affairs of the Church, and carried out on the ground by Archbishop Luigi Pozzi. It was not that any of them thought the content false: it was just that this sweeping political judgement had no place in a document allegedly of a theological nature. One immediate consequence was that Cardinal Josef Glemp could not get a meeting with General Wojiech Jaruzelski. The Instruction poisoned the atmosphere. It also seemed to echo Reagan's denunciations of the Soviet Union as 'this evil empire'. It did not display 'even-handedness'. The C.D.F. could say what it liked about theology, that was its field of competence; but it had no business straying into international politics. This time Ratzinger had over-reached himself. The Secretariat of State sees him as a blundering Bavarian with little experience of international affairs.

Casaroli did not resign. Instead he did something unprecedented in the annals of the Roman Curia. He publicly disagreed with Ratzinger. He disassociated himself from the Instruction. It was subtly done. He pointed out that the Instruction itself mentions some future 'positive' document, and suggested that it would have been better to have produced the 'positive' document first. He also revealed that he had missed the crucial meeting. He was signalling to the East Europeans and anyone else who cared to take note that the policy of dialogue begun by John XXIII and developed by Paul VI had not been abandoned in this pontificate.

Casaroli made other moves to preserve his area of freedom. The Toronto speech referred to above can now be read as a defence of Paul VI. In it Casaroli mentioned *Populorum Progressio*, the 1967 encyclical which begins with the remark, 'Development is the new name for peace': 'His encyclical, which remains in a sense the *Magna Carta* of papal teaching in this matter, appears as an echo of the Gospel saying, "I have compassion on these multitudes".' He pointedly did not refer to *Laborem Exercens*, John Paul II's 'social encyclical', which covers some of the same ground. That was in Toronto on 14 September. On 26 September in Brescia, Pope Paul VI's home town, Casaroli unveiled a statue to his former mentor in the cathedral. He praised Pope Paul as a man of dialogue and compassion and said, 'Man is made for dialogue . . . and the man who does not talk to others, who is not open to reality, does not listen, does not answer, is like a plant denied nourishment from the soil.' The Italian press said this was an 'attack' on Pope John Paul. Even if it was too cryptic to reach that conclusion, it is undeniable that Casaroli, as he approached his seventieth birthday on 24 November 1984, served notice that the pontificate of Paul VI could not be written off so easily and that Vatican II's emphasis on dialogue remained an abiding part of the Catholic tradition. That Casaroli should be allowed to display such freedom of spirit was no doubt a condition of him staying at his post. So in the end there was no earthquake. One was reminded of the dullest headline *The Times* ever had: 'Small earthquake in Chile. No casualties'.

After such dramatic near- or non-events, it is a relief to turn to the more bread-and-butter issues of the day-to-day operations of the Secretariat. It has just over 150 members divided into eight language 'desks': French, Italian, English, German, Spanish, Portuguese, Latin and Polish. Their principal task is to deal with the Pope's correspondence, whether the writer is President Ronald Reagan or Anon from Bootle. The Secretariat of State is also responsible for the papal honours list: who is worthy of becoming a Knight of St Gregory or who gets a *Bene Merenti* medal for 50 years of bravery before the organ. (Archbishop Bruno Heim has written an expensive book about papal gongs.)

It also tells the Vatican Press Office and Vatican Radio what to say and, conversely, keeps a weather eye on the world press: each day Pope John Paul II receives a single thick volume of press cuttings plus 'certain newspapers'. No one will say which. If they don't include *Le Monde*, *El Pais*, *The Times*, the *Corriere della Sera*, the *Frankfurter Allgemeine* and the *New York Times*, then I'm a Dutchman.

The diplomatic bags through which papal representatives communicate with the Secretariat of State also bulge with press cuttings from theologians deemed unorthodox. The Holy See is now represented in 122 countries – though there is much doubling up. Pio Laghi is Pro-Nuncio to the United States and observer at the O.A.S. (Organization of American States). In Africa and the Middle East papal envoys are expected to 'cover' three or four countries. They are called nuncios where they are *ex-officio* dean of the diplomatic corps (this happens mostly in Europe and certain Latin American countries); pro-nuncios where they are not automatically deans; and apostolic delegates where they represent the Pope to the local Church and have no official diplomatic functions *vis-à-vis* the state.

Diplomatic relations are reciprocal, which simply means that if the Vatican has 122 missions abroad then there are in theory 122 missions in Rome. Again there is much doubling up. Dr Chiang Hai Ding is the Ambassador of Singapore to the Holy See; but he is also Ambassador to the European Economic Community and Benelux, which naturally takes up most of his time. He goes to Rome at least four times a year, however, and is exceptionally well informed. Riccardo Peter has the difficult task of representing Nicaragua. Exiled by the Somoza dictatorship, he eked out a living by working for Vatican Radio while writing a thesis at the Gregorian University After the fall of Somoza in 1979 he became at thirty-five the youngest Ambassador to the Vatican. His brief was obvious. He would be the first to confess that he has not been very successful in persuading the Holy See that the Nicaraguan revolution had an important Christian component. He feels better understood in the Secretariat of State than anywhere else in the Vatican.

I mention Chiang Hai Ding and Riccardo Peter to illustrate the rich range of Roman diplomatic life. A British minister (as he then was) to the Holy See, finding the Foreign Office briefing inadequate, sought advice from the late Sir Alec Randall who had been number two there. 'The first thing you have to remember, old boy,' said Sir Alec, 'is that you have absolutely nothing to do. And the second is that the Vatican is a first-rate listening post. So you keep your ear to the ground. You'll learn a lot.' So the dips keep their ears to the ground.

Vatican diplomats keep their ears to the ground in foreign parts. Mgr Alberto Giovanetti claims that Vatican diplomats are better informed than others because parish priests supply them with information not available to secular diplomats who never leave the capital and have to rely on the local press. He also maintains that celibacy permits Vatican diplomats to work longer hours. Giovanetti, who worked in the Vatican delegation to the United Nations in New York, wrote a splendid novel which reflects his experiences as in a distorting mirror, *Requiem for a Spy*. The K.G.B. substitute their own man for the latest Vatican representative, with fairly predictable results. I won't spoil the story. Read it.

But the Vatican diplomatic service has often been criticized: in 1969 Cardinal Léon-Joseph Suenens said its representatives were 'spies on the local churches'. During the Allende regime in Chile the nunciature was daubed with slogans proclaiming 'The Church is the Church of the poor.' The main charge is that diplomatic considerations inhibit prophecy. More bluntly: it may seem diplomatically preferable to support the *status quo* by propping up an unjust regime, typically a military dictatorship, rather than listen to the local bishops who denounce it as tyrannical. This happened scandalously in the last days of Somoza in Nicaragua.

That is not to deny the usefulness of the Vatican diplomatic service. It can act as a buffer between the local bishops and a threatened regime. If the regime falls, it is easier to remove the pro-nuncio than to replace the bishops. And the Vatican mediation in the Beagle Channel dispute between Chile and Argentina resolved a problem that had taken these two supposedly 'Catholic' countries to the brink of war. Guided by Casaroli, Pope John Paul has carefully spoken of reconciliation between two 'peoples', thus avoiding any value judgement on their current regimes.

The Vatican diplomatic service was reformed by Pope Paul VI with his *motu proprio* of 24 June 1969, *Sollicitudo Omnium Ecclesiarum*. Paul tried to bring a 'pastoral' dimension to the work of his representatives. What he was trying to do was better expressed in an address to papal envoys gathered in Manila on 28 November 1970:

The nuncio's role is also evolving. Until now the nuncio was little more than the Pope's representative to Governments and Churches. Above all his activity was of an hierarchical and administrative nature; in a certain sense he remained a stranger to the local Church. . . . Today the nuncio must give a more pronounced pastoral emphasis to his work. He too is at the service of the Kingdom of God as it goes forward in this land. (Cardinale, *The Holy See and the International Order*)

Despite these brave words which Archbishop Cardinale himself certainly took to heart as Apostolic Delegate to England, Wales and Scotland, it was difficult to detect any notable change. At the 1974 Synod on 'Evangelization' Bishop James Sangu of Tanzania boldly grasped the nettle:

> Following the signs of the times and thinking of most of Africa, we humbly ask the Holy See to see to it that the image of the Vatican diplomatic corps takes on a more universal or 'Catholic' character than the present one which is seen as 'mostly Italian'. It is painful to hear the accusation that the Holy See is practising nationalism in the Catholic Church.

All these and other objections to the Vatican diplomatic service were considered and unceremoniously dismissed in a curious book published in 1981. Its author was Mgr Mario Oliveri, at that time a youthful thirty-five and secretary at the Apostolic Delegation in London. He has since been moved to Brussels. Its title was *The Representatives: The Real Nature and Function of Papal Legates*. Oliveri sportingly sums up the objections to the papal diplomatic service:

* Nunciatures suggest to the world that the Church is analogous to a political power.
* Their duties could be entrusted to Presidents of Episcopal Conferences who, anyway, are better informed about local situations.
* Their functions could be assigned to competent laypeople.

Oliveri puts forward these objections only in order to refute them. But they make a strong case: the plain fact is that the Council didn't know what to do with the whole panoply of nuncios, inter-nuncios, apostolic delegates, *chargés d'affaires* and the rest.

They appeared all the more anomalous after Vatican II emphasized the importance of the local Church and collegiality. They are a ghostly relic of the defunct Papal States.

This is not to say they should be abolished. But they *could* be abolished. It was the question raised at the start of this chapter. Are the Secretariat of State and the Vatican diplomatic service 'of divine institution'? Even Oliveri does not go quite that far. He concedes that 'diplomatic representation is not absolutely essential to the basic nature of the Bishop of Rome's particular office or that there could not be at any time an alternative to it'. But he later informs us that pontifical representatives 'are an integral part of the Church's life', which makes them sound pretty indispensable. And the late Giovanni Benelli contributes a preface in which he claims that papal diplomacy is 'an irreplaceable instrument', which falls just short of stating its necessity.

Casaroli wisely does not involve himself in such theoretical questions. As long as the Vatican diplomatic service is there, he says, let us use it, pragmatically, for the cause of justice and peace. Casaroli also knows that Pope John Paul is in a weak position to insist on its necessity or even its usefulness, since the Polish bishops have got on perfectly well without benefit of nuncio or apostolic delegate since the war. They would resent the imposition of such an individual. So Casaroli simply raises his eyes to heaven, sighs a little, remembers the great tradition of Tardini and Montini, and goes back to his files. He is the sort of man, said Desmond O'Grady, who gives the Curia a good name. (*Catholic Herald*, 30 November 1984.) I once told him that my articles about his *Ostpolitik* in the *Observer* had made far less stir than comparable articles about Giovanni Benelli. 'The reason is obvious,' said Casaroli: 'you were much too kind to me. That doesn't interest anyone.'

7

Watchdogs of Orthodoxy

With the Congregation for the Doctrine of Faith (henceforward
C.D.F.) we enter the department of the Vatican that staunch Protestants and sturdy Englishmen love to hate. Founded by Paul III in
1542, as 'the Sacred Congregation of the Universal Inquisition', its
function was to defend the Church against the threat of heresy, real
or supposed. Its most celebrated victims were Giordano Bruno,
burned at the stake in the Campo dei Fiori in 1600, and Galileo
Galilei who, in the circumstances, got off lightly. But apart from
these famous names, lives were wrecked, theologians were silenced
and books were banned during the next four centuries. The Inquisition inspired feelings of dread and horror. It encouraged the habit of
delation. It changed its name in 1908 to 'the Holy Office' but there
was no change in practice. Of all the curial offices, it was the one that
was the least loved and had most to live down. If one looked for a secular equivalent, one had to turn to George Orwell's Ministry of
Truth in *1984*, for it too was concerned with 'thought-crime'.

During the second Vatican Council there were many demands
that something should be done about the scandal. Cardinal Alfredo
Ottaviani, at that time Pro-Prefect of the Holy Office, led the conservatives at the Council and claimed, predictably enough, that any
attack on the Holy Office was an attack on the Pope. That did not
inhibit Cardinal Joseph Frings, Archbishop of Cologne, who said in
a dramatic session on 8 November 1963:

> The distinction between administrative and judicial matters must
> apply to all Congregations, including the Holy Office. The way
> the Holy Office proceeds is not adapted to our age, harms the
> Church and is an occasion of scandal for non-Catholics. I know
> how difficult is the task of those who for many years have worked
> in the Holy Office for the defence of revealed truth. But one must
> insist that the Holy Office should accept that no one should be
> accused and condemned without first being heard, that his bishop
> should be informed at the same time, and that the accused should

know the charges against him and be given a chance to correct what he said or wrote.

This protest against arbitrariness was enthusiastically applauded. Fring's theological adviser, who had a hand in this speech, was Joseph Ratzinger, then thirty-six-years old. Nineteen years later he became Prefect of the reformed Holy Office.

Pope Paul VI responded to this widespread desire for reform by abolishing the Index of Forbidden Books and publishing his *motu proprio, Integrae Servandae*, on 7 December 1965, the crowded last-but-one day of the Council. It gave the office its present title, Congregation for the Doctrine of Faith, which was intended to express a different function. Quoting I John 4:18, which says that 'perfect love casts out fear', he said that 'the defence of faith today is better provided for by encouraging good theology.' So the C.D.F. was to stress the positive rather than the negative, to encourage rather than to bully, to open wellsprings rather than to close them down. It was to hold conferences and study sessions on disputed questions, a total novelty. Its procedure was revised. There remained as the last resort the role of 'fraternally correcting errors', but that was not its main aim. The trouble with all these reforms was that they were meant to be implemented by the very people who had resisted change all along. Ottaviani lingered on as Prefect, increasingly blind and out of sorts.

But he made a significant admission in 1966:

> The procedure has been changed. . . . The accused has a greater chance to defend himself, to express his own opinion and have it discussed. We have returned to the procedure envisaged by Benedict XIV. We have to admit that in the course of centuries the Holy Office had departed from that procedure and substituted an authoritarian approach. It was unfortunate that this happened. (Interview in *La Gente*, 13 April 1966)

Since Benedict XIV had reigned from 1740 to 1756, one may say that it had taken an unconscionably long time to implement the procedure so wisely 'envisaged' in the age of Enlightenment.

The pace of reform quickened a little when Ottaviani gave way to Cardinal Franjo Seper, formerly Archbishop of Zagreb. He had talked sense at the 1968 Synod, and earned a modest international reputation. Above all, he was not as entrenched as Ottaviani, who always gave the impression of fighting the last battle in the wrong ditch. So Seper was able to accept without demur the setting up of an international Theological Commission (I.T.C.) in April 1969. Thirty theologians (all male, all clerical or religious) from various parts of the world would happily complement the consultors who were habitually available in Rome. The I.T.C. would correct an imbalance, and keep green the memory of the Council, where non-Roman theologians had provided most of the intellectual input.

So by the early 1970s, the reform of the C.D.F. was beginning to bite. Karl Rahner, previously a victim of the Holy Office, was a member of the I.T.C. (though he resigned in 1974). In 1973 the C.D.F. published a declaration, *Mysterium Ecclesiae*, which to some extent exemplified the 'positive approach' Paul VI had demanded. In the background was Hans Küng's disturbing book *Infallible?*, which called into question Vatican I's definition of infallibility. But instead of simply refuting him, as the Holy Office would have done, *Mysterium Ecclesiae* meets Küng at least halfway in that it recognizes the time-conditioned nature of conciliar statements. This would not be regarded as a great advance by most literary critics, but for the C.D.F., it was a notable step forwards:

> It sometimes happens that some dogmatic truth is first expressed incompletely (but not falsely), and at a later date, when considered in a broader context of faith or human knowledge, it receives a fuller and more perfect expression. . . . Even though the truths which the Church intends to teach through her dogmatic formulations are distinct from the changeable conceptions of a given epoch and can be expressed without them, nevertheless, it can sometimes happen that these truths may be enunciated by the Magisterium in terms that bear the traces of such conceptions. . . . (quoted after Raymond E. Brown, *Crises Facing the Church*)

For Protestants biblical fundamentalism is the greatest threat. Catholics are more inclined to be tempted by 'conciliar fundamentalism'. It was officially abandoned in 1973 in this C.D.F. declaration. Pope John's lapidary statement at the opening of Vatican II was now 'cashed': 'The substance of the ancient deposit of faith is one thing, the way it is presented is another.' (See Hebblethwaite, *John XXIII, Pope of the Council*, for the complicated history of this phrase.) The C.D.F. was now doing what Paul VI hoped it would do.

But not everyone was happy about these changes. In 1971 Cardinal Karol Wojtyla addressed the Polish Congress of Theology on the theme 'Theology and Theologians in the Post-Conciliar Church' (*Teologia theologowie w Kosciele*). Wojtyla's lecture was entirely concerned with the relationship between theologians and the *magisterium*. The Council, he explained, had been the model of fruitful and harmonious collaboration between theologians and bishops. But it had been over for six years. Since then the relationship had been soured. The proper task of theologians is to 'guard, defend and teach the sacred deposit of revelation' in close association with the bishops but in strict subordination to them. The function of theologians is 'purely consultative' (Roman jargon for saying they may not decide anything). Wojtyla then quoted with approval a remark of Cardinal Franjo Seper who had warned against 'making the Word of God an instrument for forcing one's own opinions'. It is not unreasonable to suppose that if Cardinal Wojtyla had these thoughts in 1971, they would have been reinforced by the time he was elected Pope in 1978. Most people become more like themselves as they grow older.

Meantime the man who would succeed Seper as Prefect of the C.D.F. on 29 November 1981, Joseph Ratzinger, was also having doubts about where post-conciliar theology was heading. He was greatly disturbed by the revolutionary and anti-authoritarian mood of 1968. His theology students began to read Herbert Marcuse, Theodore Adorno, Hans-Georg Gadamer and other neo-Marxists. Among them was the young Brazilian Franciscan, Leonardo Boff. Their paths would cross. Ratzinger later explained this fatal attraction to Marxism in terms of transferred guilt: the youth of Europe and America, embarrassed by its wealth in a world of poverty and oppression, romantically took the side of 'the wretched of the earth'. (See his lecture on liberation theology in *Il Sabato*.) Ratzinger believed this movement was well intentioned but fundamentally misguided. He moved to the right in theology and in politics. Rival professors accused him of conforming for the sake of his career. 'If you want to be a cardinal in Germany today,' Hans Küng tartly remarked, 'you have to start practising early.' Not surprisingly, this remark rankled. It was remembered when Ratzinger became Archbishop of Munich in 1977.

So already in the 1970s Catholic theology was beginning to be polarized. There were those like Cardinals Karol Wojtyla and Joseph Höffner, of Cologne, who believed that obedience to the *magisterium*, the Church's teaching authority, was paramount. Few theologians saw things in quite such simplistic terms. For the *magisterium* itself is dependent on theologians who provide it with arguments and evidence. It does not exist in isolation from their work. Of course, some theologians eluded the problem by getting on with humble scholarly tasks like determining the transmission of manuscripts of St Cyprian (as did Fr Maurice Bévenot S.J.). But there were others who felt that the 'insights of Vatican II' had not yet been fully exploited. That could mean almost anything. I will mention four theologians whose work later drew down the fire of the C.D.F.

In 1971 Hans Küng produced a slim volume called *Wozu Priester?* (published in English as *Why Priests?*) which startled the unhistorically-minded almost as much as *Infallible?* had. For Küng declared that although the idea of priestly ordination was a 'legitimate development', one could not say that it was 'instituted by Christ', 'since everyone knows that it is neither mentioned nor implicit in any Pauline text'. Even worse, Küng denied that priestly ordination carried with it any 'divine right of leadership in the Church'. The power to pronounce the words of consecration – which was all that was left to define the priest – 'may offer a kind of global superiority in relation to the other faithful, but there is no longer anything in that that would induce a gifted man to enter into the ecclesial ministry'. Whatever was true historically, it was clear that Küng's doctrine of ministry was institutionally suicidal. Who would become an ordained priest on that discouraging basis?

The Flemish Dominican, Edward Schillebeeckx, joined in this discussion and said that ministry came from below, not from above. In one sense, this was a truism: every minister must necessarily emerge from a Christian community, and then, in a second stage, the Church recognizes, accepts and blesses this call. But it seemed to hostile critics that Schillebeeckx was trying to justify the practice of 'basic communities' or 'critical groups' who appointed their own eucharistic ministers or made use of suspended, married priests. Schillebeeckx, in fact, was careful not to expose his flank by arguing in this crude way. But in a polemical atmosphere, nuances and protestations of good intentions went by the board.

The *annus mirabilis* of 1971 also saw the publication of Gustavo Gutierrez's *A Theology of Liberation* (Lima, 1971, trans. Orbis, New York, 1973). Much of it was ponderous and rather dull. It read like an anthology of pastoral letters from bishops in various parts of Latin America. But what they had in common was that they accepted the verdict of the Latin American Bishops' Conference (C.E.L.A.M.) at Medellín in September, 1968. There the bishops said that the best way to translate the Christian doctrine of salvation was as '*liberación*'. 'God has sent his Son,' they declared, 'so that in the flesh he may liberate all men from the slavery which holds them in thrall, from sin,

ignorance, hunger, wretchedness and oppression – in a word from
the injustice and hate which stem from human egoism.' (*La Iglesia en
la actual transformación de América Latina a la luz del Concilio*,
C.E.L.A.M., 1959.) Gutierrez, a Peruvian Indian, simply developed
this idea. His greatest success lay in his title. He is called the 'father
of liberation theology' not because he invented it, but because he
named the thing.

Meanwhile, in this same year 1971, the Brazilian Franciscan
Leonardo Boff was studying in Germany. In his dissertation, first
published in German in 1972, he discusses a question that had been
worrying German theologians since Adolf Harnack at the beginning
of the century. What is the true nature of Catholicism? Is it a 'corrup-
tion of the Gospel', as classical Protestants believed, or a legitimate
development? Boff replied that 'Catholicism' was not some falling
away from a primitive ideal, but on the contrary, the only way to
embody the Gospel in society. Catholicism is the 'incarnation' of the
Gospel. (*Church: Charism and Power*.) No one could complain about
that. But then Boff concedes part of the Protestant case when he
suggests that the Catholic temptation (or 'pathology' as he calls it) is
to surrender to the values of contemporary society and so to be
authoritarian in an authoritarian age.

In 1972 Boff wrote the following words, which provided the rope
with which he was to be hanged in 1985. Which historical period he
is writing about remains unclear, but it sounds vaguely like the
Counter-Reformation and he seems to have the Holy Office in his
sights:

> All decisions were centralized in a small hierarchical *élite* through
> the absolutizing of doctrine, cultural forms and the distribution of
> power within the community. The absolutizing of one form of the
> Church's presence in society led to the oppression of the faithful.
> Institutional arthritis led to a lack of imagination and an absence
> of critical spirit and creativity. Anything new was immediately
> under suspicion. . . . The drive for security was stronger than that
> for truth and authenticity. Tensions were, and often are, suffo-
> cated by means of a repression that often violates the basic human
> rights that are proclaimed even by atheistic societies. (*Church:
> Charism and Power*)

But no conclusive action was undertaken against either Küng or
Schillebeeckx in the pontificate of Paul VI. None was even attempted against Gutierrez or Boff, who had the immunity of being from

the 'third world'. Was this another instance of Paul's feebleness and fecklessness? There was some who thought so, including Wojtyla and Ratzinger.

The grounds for saying this are simply that when Karol Wojtyla became Pope in 1978 and Joseph Ratzinger his Prefect of the C.D.F. in January 1982, vigorous action was taken against these four theologians. The disagreements of the early 1970s became the *'colloquia'* (conversations) of the 1980s. It was also noticed that the four incriminated theologians (not to mention others who for the time being lay in the penumbra of condemnation) were all associated with the multi-language review *Concilium*. Founded in 1965 to continue the spirit of the Council, it has somehow survived. A proposal for a Polish edition was turned down on the grounds that 'Polish theologians all read foreign languages' and consequently did not need it. But this was less innocent than it sounds. A rival review, *Communio*, founded in 1972, was supported by all those who had been disappointed by the Council. Among them were Karol Wojtyla, Joseph Ratzinger, Swiss theologian Hans Urs von Balthasar and Henri de Lubac (whom John Paul II would make a cardinal). So the story of the C.D.F. in this pontificate may be read most simply as the temporary victory of *Communio* over *Concilium*.

The only English member of the board of *Concilium* is Nicholas Lash, Norris-Hulse Professor of Theology in Cambridge. He says of this experience:

We are a mixed bunch, none of us unscarred by the fearfulness and egotism that are the marks of original sin (but then the same is probably true of some of the officials in Cardinal Ratzinger's Congregation). We have all in our time said silly things – some sillier than others! Nevertheless I am continually impressed, not just by my colleagues' erudition and intelligence, but by their passionate and loyal devotion to the Catholic Church. And precisely in a context of 'post-classicist' cultural and theological pluralism, so extensive a network of contributors and editorial consultants, serving a journal published in seven languages, and directed by a board drawn from eleven nationalities has, I believe, an indispensable service to render to the Church – even if it is a service in permanent need of fraternal correction (correction which is frequently applied in the proper manner by the journal *Communio* with which Cardinal Ratzinger is, of course, closely associated). (*New Blackfriars*, June 1985, p.286)

Ratzinger had been a founder member of *Concilium* in 1964. Unembarrassed by this early association, he now says:

> I have not changed; it is the others who have. . . . Right from our first meetings in 1964, I made two points to my colleagues. *First*, that our group should never fall into any sectarianism and arrogance, as if we alone were doing the correct theology and could, as a kind of progressive *magisterium*, decide what in time to come progressive theology was to teach. *Secondly*, that we have to face up to the letter and spirit of Vatican II – then still in progress – without any idiosyncratic flights ahead.

The implication is that the dangerous trends Ratzinger farsightedly warned against in 1964 have all been realized some twenty years later.

Ratzinger has been placed in an awkward and unenviable position. From being one theologian among others, he has become the judge of his peers. Where once he had to produce arguments to back up his personal theological positions, he now can use the full weight of his authority against his former colleagues and students. In the 1970s he could 'refute' Leonardo Boff, should the need arise, in a learned article or an acidulous book review. Now he deals with Boff simply by 'silencing' him. Even then he cannot discover 'errors', still less 'heresies', in Boff's writings. The letter conveying the sad news concludes: 'The Congregation feels . . . obliged to declare that L. Boff's options, here analysed, are such as to endanger the sound doctrine of the faith, to promote and safeguard which is the task of the same Congregation.' (*Osservatore Romano*, English, 9 April 1985.) This is the first instance of someone being silenced for his 'options' (*opzioni* is the Italian word). Boff claims his 'option' is for the poorest. One might be tempted to think that the silencing of Boff is a greater danger to faith than anything Boff might have said.

Ratzinger seems to reserve his legendary charm these days for ecumenical visitors. Martin Conway, who went to the Vatican in spring 1983 with the British Council of Churches delegation in response to Pope John Paul's invitation issued at Canterbury to 'come and see', said of him:

> This is a man who is not only extremely intelligent, but who delights in being with other intelligent people, and who was excited by this rare chance of a discussion with equals who had a different point of view. He clearly had a real sense of eagerness, of

preparing for this conversation with zest, because it was so rare.

It was rare, of course, because when Ratzinger has a 'conversation' or *colloquium* with a Catholic theologian, they do not meet as equals. Ratzinger acts as both judge and jury. His object is to catch the theologian out. There is fear in the air. Schillebeeckx told me that the worst part of his *colloquium* in December 1980 (it was pre-Ratzinger) was having to make amiable small talk during the coffee break. Boff said that Ratzinger welcomed him with a smile.

It is worth while giving another Anglican judgement simply to show that there is a real problem about the limits of theological discourse. Theologians can go astray and fall into error. The question is whether that point has actually been reached and whether the bounds of legitimate pluralism have been transgressed. No Roman Catholic theologian, happily, has gone as far as Don Cupitt, Dean of Emmanuel College, Cambridge, who has denied not only the divinity of Christ but the personal nature of God. Howard Root, the Director of the Anglican Centre in Rome and therefore the informal Anglican Ambassador to the Vatican, while admitting that the Anglicans are frightened by anything resembling the Inquisition, nevertheless thinks that there is something to be learned from the rigour of the C.D.F.:

> I wonder whether Anglicans might not like from time to time to have the work of some theologians at least looked at by a body which – drawn from the many strands in its own communion – could at least say after serious study and discussion that e.g. 'We are terribly sorry, but it seems to us that Professor X, or Canon Z, seems rather to have departed from Anglican understanding and expression of the Christian faith. We feel an obligation to tell people that this is our considered judgement. We suggest no punitive action, and claim no desire or power to inflict any penalty; but we should be grateful if Anglicans everywhere would look at these works and then tell us whether they think our judgement is right.'
> (*Newsletter of the Friends of the Anglican Centre in Rome*, Autumn 1984)

But one only has to set down this delightfully understated text with its sense of pluralism and respect for the work of individual scholars to grasp the contrast with the more robust style of Rome. Ratzinger is perfectly prepared to take on all comers, to create a desert and call it peace.

Moreover, Ratzinger is not the most tactful of men. Having set the

Brazilian Church by the ears, he then coolly explained that he wouldn't really call the silencing of Boff 'a punishment'. It was much more like 'a sabbatical year' or 'a period of reflection'. That had been suggested to Boff before. A spell of *romanità* would help to sort out his problems. Boff replied that he would feel closer to Christ among the Indians of the Amazon than in Rome. And off he went. The Brazilian Bishops know perfectly well that Cardinals Alfonso Lopez Trujillo, Archbishop of Medellín, Colombia, and Joseph Höffner of Cologne, are members of the board of the C.D.F. and are determined to 'smash' liberation theology. Ratzinger is all the more ready to join in this enterprise in that he thinks that his old student, Boff, is 'no longer a serious theologian, is in fact a theological showman'. (Reported by Brazilian Bishop Bonaventura Kloppenburg in *Verja*, São Paulo, 9 January 1985.) This is a small world. Boff was once secretary to Kloppenburg, a fellow Franciscan. Kloppenburg is a leading member of the International Theological Commission. It was he who launched the first serious attack on Boff's book *Church: Charism and Power* in the review – you guessed – *Communio*. Emotions of disappointment and *odium theologicum* play their part. All these personal factors count.

Of course they are not normally detectable. The public story is that C.D.F., alarmed by various dangerous tendencies, is courageously intervening to save the Church from disaster. But invariably the theologians concerned do not recognize themselves in the portrait Ratzinger draws of them. This was particularly true of the Instruction 'On Certain Forms of Liberation Theology'. Its main worry was that liberation theologians have become Marxist. They deny this.

Gustavo Gutierrez had already been over this ground in his lengthy reply to Ratzinger's May 1983 critique of *A Theology of Liberation*. (Text in *Paginas*, Lima, September 1984.) The first 'dialogue' of liberation theology was with the 'human sciences', necessarily so, since it was impossible to describe the contemporary scene in Latin America without some recourse to sociology. Of course, he admits, 'the human sciences' do not provide an established 'body of knowledge', tidily packaged and ready for instant use. To call them 'scientific' does not mean that their conclusions are unassailable; on the contrary they have to be constantly checked and rechecked against experience. Ratzinger brushes aside this important point, and says with heavy irony:

But the term 'scientific' exerts an almost mythical fascination even though not everything called 'scientific' is necessarily scientific at all. That is why the borrowing of a method of approach to reality should be preceded by a careful epistemological critique. This preliminary critical study is missing from more than one theology of liberation. ('On Certain Forms of Liberation Theology')

Gutierrez replies that liberation theology has remained 'critical', critical of the conceptual tools it uses, critical of the elements of Marxism that are sometimes found in the social sciences, and critical of the actual 'liberation movements' in their countries. Gutierrez has opposed the Maoist *Sendero Luminoso* in Peru, for example. So he can put his hand on his heart and make this solemn statement:

In no case has anyone suggested that the atheistic ideology of Marxism should be accepted: if that happened, we would be outside the realm of Christian faith altogether and no longer talking about theology. Nor has there been any agreement with the totalitarian interpretation of history as the negation of human liberty. These two aspects – the atheistic ideology and totalitarian vision – are clearly excluded from our faith, and from a sound social analysis. (Full text in *Il Regno*, Bologna, 1 November 1984)

But this was not enough for Ratzinger, who continued to hound Gutierrez through the agency of the Peruvian bishops (who were and still are divided on the issue). But the central question is whether one can use elements of Marxism without becoming a Marxist. Fr Pedro Arrupe, General of the Jesuits, had argued this in his letter 'On Marxist Analysis' of 8 December 1980. That may have sealed his fate, for in the Instruction 'On Certain Forms of Liberation Theology' Ratzinger writes:

The ideological principles come prior to the study of social reality and are presupposed by it. Thus no separation of the parts of this epistemologically unique complex is possible. If one tries to take only one part, say the analysis, one ends up having to accept the entire ideology.

Marxism, in other words, is a complete system. In for a penny, in for a pound. Buy one element, and all the others tumble into your shopping basket. This is one possible view of Marxism. I defended it myself in *Christian Marxist Dialogue and Beyond* (1977). One can certainly say that this danger exists, and that some fall into the trap.

But it is not a *necessary* truth, and certainly not a theological truth contained in the deposit of faith. It is difficult, therefore, to see how a theological condemnation with such devastating human and political consequences can be based on so contingent, flimsy and unverifiable a judgement.

But, of course, it is very characteristic of the inquisitor to know your own mind better than you know it yourself. 'You may think you are not a Marxist,' says the inquisitor, 'but I happen to know that you are because the inner logic of your position carries you there despite your protestations of loyalty and faith. I am only concerned for your good. *Anathema sit.* Let it be anathema.'

Apart from using dubious and inconclusive arguments, Ratzinger distorts the theologians he wishes to denounce. It is interesting, for example, that Boff was attacked not as a 'liberation theologian' or a neo-Marxist but for his views on the Church (formulated, as we have seen, in Germany in the 1970s). Ratzinger alleges that Boff has a 'relativizing concept of the Church': in other words, he does not know where 'the one true Church of Christ' really is to be found. Much is made of *Lumen Gentium*, the Council's constitution on the Church, where *subsistit in* replaced *est* in the sentence 'This Church (i.e. the sole Church of Christ) subsists in the Roman Catholic Church'. This was not to deny that other 'ecclesial elements' (*elementa ecclesiae*) could be found in other churches. This emendation made ecumenism possible. Ratzinger totally misunderstands Boff on this point. In his account of their *colloquium* Boff explains the change in the way solid theologians like Bishop Christopher Butler and Avery Dulles have done:

> The unity between the Church of Christ and the Catholic Church is not static but dynamic. The church of Christ is realized in the Catholic Church in a manner which corresponds to the dynamic and sacramental nature of the Church. I never said that 'the Catholic Church does not anywhere exist'. ('Cronica eclesiastica' in *Revista Eclesiastica Brasiliera*, December 1984 – this was one of the last numbers to be edited by Boff before he was sacked)

It would be interesting to ask Ratzinger how many people have actually become Protestant as a result of reading Boff.

Ratzinger differs from his predecessors in being ready to give interviews and write articles in which he speaks in his own name. His most famous interview was in the Italian magazine, *Jesus* (November

1984), and it was worked up into a book, *Rapporto sulla Fede* (Report on Faith). Somewhat disarmingly Ratzinger claims that the views he expresses are 'purely personal' and 'do not commit the institutions of the Holy See'. One can understand his reluctance to 'commit the Holy See' every time he opens his mouth. But he can hardly expect people to believe that there is no inner connection between what he says when wearing his Prefect of the C.D.F. hat and when not wearing it.

In the event these unofficial utterances were immensely valuable because they revealed the general *Weltanschauung* that lies behind the individual, official pronouncements and bans. They show a Ratzinger deeply pessimistic about the way the Church has gone in the twenty years since the end of the Council in 1965. He sees the Church as 'collapsing'. He thinks Karl Rahner did immense harm with 'his catch-phrase of anonymous Christians' (used by Rahner to refer to those who lived by the grace of Christ without being aware of it). The slippery notion 'the spirit of the Council' has become 'an anti-spirit, an incubus'. Theologians have 'feminized God'. Since Sigmund Freud, paternity is viewed with suspicion – so out goes God the Father ('the death of God'). American moral theologians, in particular, are singled out for having fallen into 'consequentialism' (judging acts by their effects). Excessive optimism – about the world, about the chance of people being good, about the trends and movements of the age – has caused all these problems. So Ratzinger's 'pessimism' is not just a matter of temperament: in his own mind it is a lucid and conscious *reaction* to a situation of great gravity.

Now arguments between optimists and pessimists always tend to be frustrating and futile. They are looking at the same reality, but from opposite sides. The bottle is half full or it is half empty. But Nicholas Lash's contention is surely true: 'What has already been achieved in these last twenty years has in some respects already outstripped rather than cruelly contradicted preconciliar expectations.' ('Catholic Theology and the Crisis of Classicism', in *New Blackfriars*, June 1985.) And if there is a 'scandalous optimism' of which Ratzinger complains, there is also a 'scandalous pessimism' that he exemplifies. Lash claims that what is collapsing is not Catholicism, but only a certain version of it, 'the particular citadel that we once erected'.

Lash invokes the late Bernard Lonergan's distinction between the 'classicist' and the 'modern' world views. Ratzinger has the 'classicist' view which 'assumes that the unity of faith, hope and charity can only be secured by silencing dissent and eliminating genuine disagreement'. Modern culture demands that the truth be sought in obedience to the Lord while recognizing that cultural pluralism has come to stay. Ratzinger's basic illusion is to suppose that there is a single vantage point (for example the Vatican) that is somehow free from any cultural conditioning. 'A Church without tension,' says Lash, 'would be a Church gone dead, a mausoleum from which the Spirit had departed.' This does not mean that all tension is creative or all conflict compatible with charity. But it does mean that one should not dream of a Church that never was on land or sea. Conflict and tension are part of the Church's everyday life. One should argue hard, but fairly. It is the lack of fairness that, in the end, is the most striking feature of the C.D.F. today.

However, that is not the judgement of Pope John Paul, to whom Ratzinger is answerable. In his pre-Christmas address to the College of Cardinals in 1984, Pope John Paul alluded to the controversies that had swirled around Boff and Gutierrez and went out of his way to defend the work of the C.D.F.:

> Whoever considers the matter with dispassionate objectivity can-
> not fail to recognize, in certain recent events, that this dicastery
> (i.e. the C.D.F.) has always been inspired by the most rigorous
> respect for the persons with whom it was dealing. So one has the
> right to expect an equally respectful attitude on the part of those it
> deals with when they are called upon to speak, in private or in
> public, on the C.D.F.'s work. The same attitude of respect should
> be found in every member of the People of God, since the C.D.F.
> has no other purpose than to preserve from all danger the greatest
> good the Christian has – the authenticity and integrity of his faith.

That should console Ratzinger in his difficult watchdog mission. The trouble is that 'dispassionate' objectivity in such matters is in short supply.

8

Preferment and Patronage

The Congregation for the Doctrine of Faith, as we have just seen, is concerned with orthodoxy and soundness. Its predecessor, the Holy Office, used to carry the label '*Supreme* Congregation . . . ' and although the adjective has now been dropped, the C.D.F. still makes claims to universal competence since anything and everything is in some sense 'doctrinal'. That is why it remains the most powerful dicastery, or department, in the Vatican. The second most powerful is what is now known as the Congregation of Bishops. For it appoints bishops throughout the world (with the exception of mission territories, done by the Congregation for the Evangelization of Peoples, and Orientals, done by the Congregation of the Oriental Churches). But that still leaves an awful lot of episcopal appointments in the lap of the Congregation of Bishops (henceforward C.o.B.).

At this point the C.o.B. spokesman would intervene to say that it does not 'appoint' Bishops. Only the Holy Father can do that. What the C.o.B. does is to '*prepare* whatever is concerned with the nomination of Bishops, Apostolic Administrators etc.'. (*Annuario Pontificio*, 1984.) One grasps the nuance: the C.o.B. proposes, but the Pope disposes. It also deals with the division of dioceses and what is called the 'erection' of new ones. And it is the body to which Bishops report when they go on their quinquennial *ad limina* visits to Rome. Cardinal Sebastiano Baggio, for many years Prefect of the C.o.B., thought this was one of its most important roles and put it into Latin. The Bishops go to Rome 'to see Peter' (*videre Petrum*, allusion to Galatians where Paul goes to see Peter) and they travel 'to the heart of the Church' (*ad cor ecclesiae*). ('*A servizio della collegialità nello stile del dialogo*', *Osservatore Romano*, 20 October 1982.) This is very edifying and no doubt true.

But it glosses over a number of important facts. The first is that from its foundation by Sixtus V in 1588 until 15 August 1967 it was known as the Consistorial Congregation and it acted as the Ministry of the Interior of the Church. With its Prefect Cardinal Gaetano De Lai it was the principal agent of the anti-Modernist campaign in the early years of the century. Within Italy it imposed 'apostolic visitations' on dioceses (they were dubbed 'apostolic vexations' by the Cardinal Archbishop of Milan, Carlo Andrea Ferrari) which resulted in sackings of seminary professors.

Nor is it true to say that what we must now call the Congregation of Bishops was traditionally concerned with new episcopal appointments. One of the myths the Vatican can call upon is the idea that what is done now has been done 'from time immemorial'. That the appointment of bishops in the Catholic Church should be centralized is taken for granted by most Catholics. Apart from a few eccentric historians who bothered to look it up, who ever thought that bishops did anything other than drop down from the Vatican? The local Churches have to accept what they get with gratitude and sing '*Ecce sacerdos magnus*' ('Behold a great high priest') *molto allegro* and with welcoming vigour. It was ever thus.

But it was not ever thus. We are dealing with a very recent tradition. Two fourth-century episcopal appointments show the two methods that in one way or another prevailed for over a thousand years. Ambrose (339-97), for example, became the Roman civil governor of Liguria and Aemilia with headquarters in Milan in 370. Its heretical bishop, the Arian Auxentius, having died, Ambrose pleaded for peace and reconciliation in his province. That was in 374. Much to Ambrose's alarm, a voice (later said to be a child's – *ex ore infantium*) cried out, 'Ambrose for Bishop!' The cry was taken up by the whole assembly. What made it surprising was that he was not even baptized, but that was soon put right. Within a week he was both baptized and consecrated bishop, and later became one of the most influential bishops of all time. He was in effect elected by the people.

Meanwhile, at the other end of the Mediterranean in Asia Minor, John Chrysostom was living as a hermit in a damp cave. Ordained priest in Antioch in 386, he became the Bishop's secretary and had special responsibility for helping the poor. His eloquence became famous. Chrysostom means 'golden-mouthed', and he used his eloquence to lash the sins of the rich and to calm things down after the tax revolt of 387. This led the Emperior Arcadius to conclude in 397 that John was just the man to be Archbishop of Constantinople – but this was an imperial and not a popular choice. John Chrysostom's subsequent fate was heroic and tragic. He was banished and deposed, won the support of the Pope, and was finally killed by his many tribulations. Some thirty years after his death he was rehabilitated and reburied in the Church of the Apostles in Constantinople.

So we may say that at least in the first millennium bishops were either elected by the people or nominated by a lay patron (emperor or king, or eventually feudal lord). Elections by the people, where they were held, sometimes led to unseemly tumults, so election by the cathedral chapter, the clerical diocesan club, tended to replace them.

The most authoritative canonical statement on the question, the twenty-eighth canon of Lateran II, states very firmly that bishops shall be elected by cathedral chapters. It occurs to no one that episcopal appointments have anything to do with the Pope. The two systems – election by cathedral chapter and royal or imperial patronage – were still in vogue as late as 1829 when the Papal power to appoint bishops extended to a mere twenty-four dioceses outside the Papal States; since the Pope was sovereign within the Papal States, he was in the same position with regard to episcopal appointments there as Louis XVIII or Charles X was in France. It was as temporal ruler, not as Bishop of Rome, that he was appointing them.

But the situation was changing, and the United States accidentally played a key part in the story. The first bishop of the new republic, John Carroll (an ex-Jesuit only because the Society of Jesus had been suppressed), was elected in 1789 by the twenty-six priests who were active in the United States. They thought they were being as faithful as possible to the spirit of Lateran II. Pope Pius VI accepted Carroll as Bishop of Baltimore. His successor, Pius VII, varied in his methods. In five cases he accepted the candidates jointly nominated by the American bishops and clergy; four more were appointed *motu proprio* without any consultation in the United States; and in one case he rejected the proposed candidate and substituted his own.

At this point the U.S. bishops over-reached themselves and made an understandable tactical blunder. They wrote to Rome in 1810 requesting that the right of nomination be assigned to the Archbishop of Baltimore and his suffragans. Since the Pope was in captivity at that time, they may have thought they could get away with it. Hitherto, the American system had borne some resemblance to Lateran II. What was now being proposed was utterly different. Moreover, the Holy See had correctly perceived the danger: 'the development of a closed shop of inbred bishops, chosen by cronyism'. (Garrett Sweeney, in Adrian Hastings (ed.), *Bishops and Writers*.) The American Church at this period favoured French candidates; Rome imposed on it Irish bishops; the result was unhappiness.

But the Americans had delivered themselves, bound hand and

foot, into the power of the Holy See. They could not choose bishops by chapter elections, since they had no cathedral chapters. They could not hand over the *ius patronatus* (right of patronage) to the President, as happened in Latin America, because the constitution demanded the separation of Church and state. The pattern into which the Americans stumbled became a model for most of the rest of the Church: the American bishops could make recommendations to the Vatican, but the Pope would always freely decide – '*eos libere nominat Pontifex Romanus* (the Pope freely nominates bishops)' as the 1917 Code of Canon Law proclaimed. (Canon 320.) Few noticed, or anyhow complained of, how deeply untraditional this statement was.

So the present system of episcopal appointments by the Vatican is fundamentally a nineteenth-century invention. The Vatican's takeover of episcopal appointments was justified on the grounds that it was the only way to assert the 'freedom of the Church' from interfering governments. France with its 'Gallican' and separatist tradition, whatever the political regime, was a particular target: from Napoleon to de Gaulle, the French government was keenly interested in the appointment of bishops. The argument that papal patronage was a better system than state patronage carried all before it. And it was a good argument.

Yet despite this apparent triumph for the Holy See by 1917, when for the first time a universal Code of Canon Law was promulgated, the Pope appointed only 700 or about half of the world's bishops. Further threats from governments – now more likely to be Communist rather than 'Gallican' – strengthened still more the Vatican determination to retain or recover control over episcopal appointments. Modern methods of communication made it easier: the mule, the horse, the railway, the telegraph, the telephone, the telex, computers – these were the stages by which the Vatican became omniscient and omnipotent in episcopal appointments. By 1980, out of the 2,456 dioceses of the Catholic Church, only twenty-four still had chapter elections. They were mostly in Central Europe, and the Bishop of Basel in Switzerland is the best-known example. There were also 175 surviving examples of state patronage – but they were increasingly an anachronism and were fading tranquilly away. So to say that bishops are on the whole appointed by the Pope is perfectly true, but it should be clearly recognized as a very recent trend. In his *Utopia* Sir Thomas More, Chancellor of England, looked forward to the day when once again bishops would be elected (and, incidentally, married). That was no doubt one of the reasons *Utopia* was put on the Index of Forbidden Books, though More was more traditional

The *Portone di Bronzo* or Bronze Door is the ordinary pedestrian entrance to the Vatican. After Constantine's Portico, with a Bernini statue of the first Christian Emperor, the *scala regia* leads up into the Apostolic Palace, the papal apartments

The Vatican from the air, before the new audience hall was built just this side of St Peter's. The 109 acres are roughly divided into one-third buildings, one-third gardens and one-third pavements (the Square is part of the Vatican)

St Peter's Square in 1575
when 400,000 pilgrims
came for the Holy Year. A
print by de Cavaller is now
in the British Museum. The
new St Peter's arises behind
the façade and Portico of
Constantine's basilica

Pope Paul VI inspecting
the restorations at St
John Lateran, the
cathedral of the
Bishop of Rome, in
1963. When not in
exile, Popes lived here
until 1367. Pope John
XXIII wanted to revive
the Lateran Palace as
the centre of his diocese

The thirteenth-century bronze statue on the right in St Peter's Basilica. The left hand is raised in blessing while the right holds 'the keys of the kingdom of heaven' (Matthew 16,19)

Paul VI was the last Pope to wear the tiara. 'The real treasures of the Church,' said his successor, John Paul I, 'are the poor, the disinherited, the weak.' So he dispensed with the triple crown, of Asiatic origin, once held to symbolise the Pope's power over earth, heaven and hell

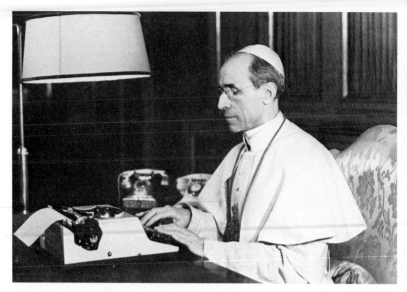

Pius XII at his famous white typewriter. On hearing the words '*Qui Pacelli*' (the Pope here) on the phone, cardinals and monsignori fell to their knees to receive the pontifical call

Pius XII with the man to whom he bequeathed his typewriter, Giovanni Battista Montini, then exiled to Milan and not made a cardinal. Montini is seen on 3 March 1955 congratulating the Pope on his eightieth birthday. It was their first meeting after Montini's removal from Rome

Pope John XXIII kissing the well-worn toe of St Peter – an ancient devotional practice – watched carefully by Cardinal Alfredo Ottaviani, then Prefect of the Holy Office, more usually known as the grand inquisitor

Apostolic succession: John Paul I, the 33-day Pope, greets Karol Wojtyla, in September 1978. Within a few weeks John Paul I died, in distressing circumstances, and Wojtyla, elected pope, inevitably took his name—John Paul II

John Paul II's Marian devotion is well known: he has a large unheraldic M on his coat of arms; his motto 'Totus tuus' (entirely yours) refers to the Virgin Mary. What is she saying to him?

Pier Luigi Nervi's new audience hall at its opening on 9 July 1971. The synod hall is built into its roof. It seats 6,300, not enough for today's audiences which move to St Peter's Square in the spring. The sculpture of the Risen Christ (inset) was added later. Hall and sculpture are the last major examples of papal patronage

Paul VI with Athenagoras, Ecumenical Patriarch of Constantinople, leader in some sense of the Orthodox Churches. They had three meetings in four years. The first was in Jerusalem in January 1963; at the Mount of Olives they recited the Lord's prayer together, embraced as brother patriarchs, and gave a joint blessing which meant: 'We are in agreement'

John Paul II at Canterbury on 29 May 1982. Prince Charles, heir to the throne, would meet him again with his bride, while Dr Robert Runcie, Archbishop of Canterbury, had already met the Pope in Accra, Ghana, and would meet him again in Bombay, India, on 9 February 1986

John XXIII's view of the
study-library where he
received important guests.
The chandelier was the
gift of the glass-blowers of
Venice, and the two statues
explain his choice of name:
John the Baptist and John
the Evangelist

The reading room in the
Vatican Library. It
contains precious
manuscripts such as a
fourth-century Greek
New Testament, a fifth-
century Virgil, the scores
of Palestrina, and many
other treasures. It also
houses 'the most important
archives in the world' –
protected by a seventy-five
year rule

Cardinal Joseph Ratzinger in the Vatican Press Office denouncing on 7 September 1984 the Marxism into which unnamed Latin American theologians were said to have fallen

Cardinal Agostino Casaroli toasting the revision of the Spanish Concordat on 28 July 1976. Franco's death enabled Spain to give up certain privileges. But the tall foreign minister, Laureano Lopez Rodo, was a member of Opus Dei. Cardinal Marcello Gonzalez, Archbishop of Toledo, the Spanish Primate, looks more enthusiastic than Casaroli

The cardinals' chorus line: with his last consistory on 27 June 1977, Paul VI made these men cardinals and completed the electoral college that would choose his successors. From left to right: Ratzinger, Benelli (a near miss in the second conclave of 1978, then died), Gantin (now head of the powerful Bishops' Congregation), František (still fighting the government in Prague), and Ciappi (an aged Dominican who was Karol Wojtyla's teacher in the 1940s)

Women's work in the Vatican: nuns restoring a tapestry in the Vatican Museum. Except in the Congregation for Religious and the Council for the Laity, women in the Vatican are strictly subordinate

The Cohors Helvetica or Swiss Guard, the last remnant of the papal armed forces. Middle-class volunteers from Swiss Catholic valleys evoke the sixteenth century. That Michelangelo or Raphael designed their uniforms is, alas, a legend

Men of the twentieth-century Central Security Office on the alert (mostly former Italian cops). Since the assassination attempt on John Paul II – 13 May 1981 – security has been tightened up

A pause for prayer – the Angelus at twelve noon – in the Secretariat of State.
Word processors have replaced the typewriters seen here

A pause for clerical conviviality in a Roman trattoria. Restaurants play an
important part in the 'informal Vatican'

One train a day brings EEC goods into the Vatican where they are sold, tax-free, to Vatican employees. Otherwise the massive steel door remains locked. The arms are those of Pius XI, Pope when this railway spur was opened in 1929. The size of bricks has remained little changed since Roman times. *Arrivederci*

than his detractors. It seems unlikely that the Congregation for the Causes of Saints (then called the Congregation of Rites) considered this aspect of his work when he was cleared for canonization in 1935.

The new Code of Canon Law (1983) echoes the old Code but leaves room for an elective system (of an unspecified nature): 'The Supreme Pontiff freely appoints Bishops or confirms those lawfully elected.' That could turn out to be important for the future. But in the present it is clear that in practice the Pope 'freely appoints bishops' or at any rate the vast majority of them.

This places a great burden of responsibility on the C.o.B. It has to keep tabs on likely candidates all the world over. It has immense power of patronage. It can directly influence a local church, since he who controls the leadership controls the church. What sort of qualities are sought for the Church's middle management? How does one become a bishop? An old chestnut has it that three qualities are required: to be baptized, to be male, and to have studied at the national college in Rome. The first two requirements may be dispensed from, but not the third.

The new Code of Canon Law takes a more serious view:

378 § To be a suitable candidate for the episcopate, a person must:

   1° be outstanding in strong faith, good morals, piety, zeal for souls, wisdom, prudence and human virtues, and possess those other gifts which equip him to fulfil the office in question;
   2° be held in good esteem;
   3° be at least 35 years old;
   4° be a priest ordained for at least five years;
   5° hold a doctorate or at least a licentiate in sacred Scripture, theology or canon law, from an institute of higher studies approved by the Apostolic See, or at least be well versed in these disciplines.

All of which seems rather obvious. A good priest ought to make a good bishop. Drunks and womanizers are best weeded out. But that still leaves an awful lot of candidates. Is there some other hidden principle of selection?

Since 'orthodoxy' in Catholic priests is to be presumed unless the contrary is canonically proven, that is not much help as a criterion. It tends to be replaced by the subtler test of 'soundness'. As Hans Küng, from Switzerland where elected bishops (and parish priests) were once the norm, put it with some irony:

In so far as Rome had a free hand, new bishops were selected preferably according to two tried and trusted principles of sound moral standards and the uncritical loyalty to Rome which is called 'obedience'. Fortunately mistakes were made in some instances, and some men were appointed who subsequently distinguished themselves by their independence of mind, courage and unexpected initiatives. (*Infallible?*)

The late Cardinal John Carmel Heenan, no great fan of Hans Küng, indirectly confirmed this analysis. Speaking of his own appointment to Leeds (immediately dubbed by clerical wags 'the cruel see'), he remarked: 'I knew that prudence was among the most highly prized virtues in episcopal candidates, and I did not count it among my attributes.' (*Not the Whole Truth.*) So Heenan slipped through the net.

The truth is that many men change when they become bishops, sometimes for the better. Fr Oscar Romero from El Salvador, for example, was an utterly docile and conservative priest who had an Opus Dei confessor and worried about laxity at the seminary: they actually wore shorts for football – shocking! Once Archbishop of San Salvador, he was transformed because gradually he learned that he had to embody and articulate the aspirations of his people, to become 'the voice of those who have no voice'. In this way, says Jon Sobrino S.J., who helped him write his great pastoral letters, he rediscovered the original ideal of the bishop in Latin America as the defender of the oppressed (the Indians) against their oppressors. That was why he had to be gunned down while saying Mass on 25 March 1981, an episcopal martyr to add to Stanislaw of Kraków and Thomas à Becket, two other 'turbulent priests'.

But I don't suppose that the C.o.B. is actually looking for such prophetic spirits. They are a bonus, one of Küng's 'mistakes'. More recently I have heard two other accounts of what the C.o.B. is looking for. In England Mgr X. would never be made a bishop because he had strenuously opposed Opus Dei in his university chaplaincy. In Holland Fr Y. could not be made a bishop, said Cardinal Adriaan Simonis, the Primate, 'because he did not say Mass every day'. It is certainly true that Cardinal Sebastiano Baggio, Prefect of the C.o.B. from 1973 to 1984, was an Opus Dei supporter. And little seems to have changed under Cardinal Bernadin Gantin, his successor.

But the appointment of Gantin does make one thing fairly clear. While Baggio had served as Nuncio in Chile and Brazil and Apostolic Delegate in Canada, Gantin's experience was confined to his native Dahomey (now the People's Republic of Benin) and Rome

Baggio also held the crucial post of President of the Pontifical Commission on Latin America. So while Baggio could be expected to know at least some of the candidates he was considering, Gantin is much less likely to. Moreover Baggio was a man with a 'career' in the Curia, whereas Gantin stumbled into it by accident when he was forced to leave Benin by its 'Marxist-Leninist' regime in 1971. Gantin has neither the knowledge nor the influence of Baggio. So one would expect episcopal appointments now to come 'from below' via the recommendations of local Vatican diplomats or 'from above' on the personal initiative of the Pope.

The system is this. Local bishops are invited to put names on a list of general candidates, and when a vacancy occurs the nuncio or his equivalent 'engages in wide-ranging consultations' until he comes up with three names: the *terna*. But since such consultations remain strictly confidential, there is no means of assessing how thorough they have been.

It does seem, however, that the views of the Vatican Nuncio or Apostolic Delegate carry especial weight, and that the role of the Congregation of Bishops is normally to process local information and then to inform the Pope of the options. It is simply not serious to imagine that the Pope can know enough to appoint every individual bishop in the Catholic world. If he even tried, he would have no time for anything else.

But in certain key dioceses, there has been evidence of direct papal intervention. This is particularly true where there are 'surprises'. In ecclesiastical terms, a 'surprise' means something that the media have not thought of (though others might have): it is simply a measure of previous ignorance and imperceptiveness. Thus the emergence of the Abbot of Ampleforth, Basil Hume, from his Yorkshire fastness to become Archbishop of Westminster, was a 'surprise'. It was also an example of Paul VI intervening directly, though Archbishop Bruno Heim claimed part of the credit for this original appointment. The proof of this is that he protested when I attributed it to the Duke of Norfolk and the London Catholic 'establishment'.

There have been some equally 'surprising' or 'personal' appointments in the pontificate of John Paul II. He was obviously keenly interested in the succession of Cardinal Stefan Wyszyński, who had astonishingly been Primate of Poland from 1948 to 1981, outlasting four or five First Secretaries of the Polish United Workers' Party. Obviously the succession was not something John Paul would want to leave in the hands of Baggio, who was deeply ignorant of Poland. So in the event the ambivalent and rather tragic figure Josef Glemp became Primate of Poland. There was direct papal intervention, too, in the case of Jean-Marie Lustiger, born of Polish Jewish parents, one of whom perished at Auschwitz, who was plucked from his Paris parish to become Bishop of Orléans on 10 November 1979, and promoted to Paris on 31 January 1981.

Other 'surprise' appointments involved two Jesuits who by their constitutions are not allowed to accept preferment, except in mission territories, unless the Pope gives them 'an order in holy obedience'. This evidently happened with French Jesuit Roger Heckel S.J., who became Archbishop of Strasbourg in 1981. He was already known to John Paul as Secretary of the International Justice and Peace Commission in Rome, in which post he confined himself to a careful analysis of the Pope's teaching as an expression of the ongoing 'social doctrine' of the Church. Unfortunately Strasbourg experienced only the shock of his appointment, for he died before he could do anything of note. As it turned out, John Paul merely annoyed the diocesan clergy of Strasbourg to no useful purpose.

The appointment of the brilliant Italian biblical scholar and Jesuit, fifty-three-year-old Carlo Maria Martini, till then Rector of the Gregorian University, to the see of Milan on 29 December 1979, was much more dramatic. It was not merely surprising. It was utterly astonishing. For Milan is by far the most prestigious, populous and wealthy diocese of Italy – the see of St Ambrose and St Charles Borromeo – and already two popes in this century have come from there: Ratti, Pius XI; and Montini, Paul VI. To have a Jesuit as bishop of an Italian diocese went against all tradition: the only previous example was St Robert Bellarmine in the seventeenth century – and he was only briefly Bishop of Capua, a small city that could not hold a candle to Milan. Another reason for astonishment was that the Pope was believed to be dissatisfied with the Jesuits. So Martini's appointment to Milan was puzzling, baffling even. Some said that the Pope was depriving the Jesuits of their next General – though why he should behave so quixotically was not explained. Baggio let it be known that he had come to favour Martini, having read his book on St Luke and on discovering that Martini was already spiritual director to a significant number of Italian Bishops. But that was merely Baggio climbing on to a rolling bandwagon. The merits of Martini are not in question: the entire Italian press is convinced that he will be next Pope. There is some evidence that an indefinable quality called 'spirituality', the capacity to talk about God credibly and to teach ordinary people how to pray, is what John Paul is looking for in his episcopal appointments.

But there are also cases where the Vatican asserts its authority through episcopal nominations. They can be used to restore order in a church that is believed to have fallen into error or 'secularism', or whatever the current bogey is. The obvious example is the Dutch church (which always calls itself the Roman Catholic Province of the Netherlands). At the special Synod held in Rome in 1980 the seven Dutch bishops were reminded that they should be 'true teachers of the faith' and not just interpreters of some vague '*sensus fidelium*' (the faith-instinct of ordinary Christians). This was designed to prevent bishops from appealing to their people to legitimate a particular approach. They are not 'delegates' of their churches. They are true 'leaders'.

One paradoxical way of making this clear was to appoint unpopular bishops. This is what happened in Holland after the Synod. First, four docile auxiliaries were named. Then in 1983, when Cardinal Jan Willebrands, the Primate, resigned to concentrate on his work as President of the Secretariat for Christian Unity in Rome, he was succeeded by Adriaan Simonis who swiftly became a Cardinal. Simonis had been Bishop of Rotterdam since 1970. He was not the most conservative of Dutch bishops; that title was easily held by pipe-smoking Jan Gijsen of Roermond in south-east Holland (Limburg). But he was conservative enough to cause protests on all sides. The co-provincial of the Dutch Dominican province, Andrew Lascaris, meeting Pope John Paul during the General Chapter in Rome, September 1983, told him that most people in Holland were unhappy with the appointment of Simonis. Somewhat taken aback by this bluntness, the Pope replied: 'You may become happy later.' ('A Disappointing Tale', *New Blackfriars*, March 1985.)

In fact Dutch unhappiness grew with a further series of barrel-scraping episcopal appointments. Henrik Bomers, the new Bishop of Haarlem, had been a missionary in a remote corner of Ethiopia since 1965. His auxiliary, Joseph F. Lescrauwaet, was a religious who had spent most of his working life at Louvain University in Belgium. This suggested a distinct lack of confidence in the local clergy. Was it conceivable that none of the 327 diocesan and 364 religious priests in Haarlem was thought fit for the episcopal ministry? It is more difficult to believe that than to imagine that a point was being made. Especially when exactly the same process was then repeated in the diocese of Den Bosch. Its bishop, fifty-seven-year-old Jan Bluyssen, the only surviving Dutch bishop who had lived through Vatican II, resigned on grounds of ill health (genuine). His replacement was Gijsen's auxiliary, sixty-two-year-old Jan Ter Schure, who had spent much of his life in the Curia of his order, the Salesians, in Rome.

This time the cathedral canons decided to reject the appointment and protest directly to the Pope. But in vain. The result was that when Pope John Paul drove through Den Bosch on 11 May 1985, ostensibly on a 'pilgrimage', the streets were deserted. An embarrassed Ter Schure was by his side in the popemobile. At one point they fell to prayer. Then, in the basilica of Saint John, the Pope did something quite unprecedented: with Ter Schure sitting sheepishly just ten feet away, John Paul defended his appointment. He said:

> I know you have been going through a difficult time in recent weeks. The recent appointments of bishops have deeply affected some of you who are asking the reasons for these tensions. I should like to say in all sincerity that the Pope attempts to understand the life of the Church in the appointment of every bishop. He gathers information and obtains advice in accordance with ecclesiastical law and custom. You will understand that opinions are sometimes divided. In the last analysis, the Pope has to take the decision.

The truth is, however, that opinion in Den Bosch had not been all that divided. On the contrary, it was solidly united against Ter Schure. Moreover, the picture of the Pope poring over the details of episcopal appointments everywhere was hard to accept. Holland is clearly regarded as in need of special treatment, a 'worst-case scenario' (as someone told *Time*). Once Pope John Paul had begun to defend his appointment in Den Bosch, it would have been useful to have explained it. The original draft of the address contained this: 'Must the Pope explain his choice? Discretion does not permit him to do so.' The fact that these words were cut only drew attention to them. The Dutch would have liked to have known by what criteria bishops are being chosen in Holland. If 'discretion' forbids an answer, they do not have much difficulty in guessing what it might be.

The Dutch Episcopal Conference was small enough to be reshaped and taken over within the space of five years. With larger episcopal conferences such methods cannot work. Brazil has over 300 bishops and has hitherto had the most influential episcopal conference in the world. The majority has been committed to some form of liberation theology. That will gradually change. Fr Bonaventura Kloppenburg D.F.M., who launched the first serious attack on his brother Franciscan, Leonardo Boff, was rewarded by becoming auxiliary of São Salvador de Bahia within the year. This set the trend for the future; all the more since Cardinal Eugenio De Araújo Sales,

Archbishop of Rio de Janeiro, and Cardinal Angelo Rossi, the only
Brazilian members of the C.o.B.'s council, are both sworn enemies of
liberation theology. Meanwhile other Brazilian cardinals such as
Aloisio Lorscheider and Paolo Evaristo Arns, who have supported
Leonardo Boff, are left conspicuously out in the cold.

The U.S. episcopal conference (officially called the United States
Catholic Conference, U.S.C.C.) is almost as big as the Brazilian one.
Moreover it is well organized and well led by Cardinal Joseph Bernadin, Archbishop of Chicago. It has put its collective mind to work
effectively and stimulatingly on the ethics of nuclear warfare and,
more recently, on the economy. It has evolved a good working
method, knows where to look for advice without surrendering to the
experts, and is as open to new questions (for example the place of
women in the Church) as it is possible to be. In short there was a new
generation of U.S. Catholic Bishops who were fully committed to
Vatican II. Belgian-born Archbishop Jean Jadot, Apostolic Delegate from May 1973 to 1980, was chiefly responsible for this transfor-
mation. Organization men like the late Cardinal John J. Cody ('I am
the corporation sole') were replaced by pastors sensitive to the problems of U.S. society.

Jadot was kicked upstairs to the Vatican and became Pro-Secret-
ary of the Secretariat for Non-Christian Religions. He did not long
survive, however, and in the reshuffle of 29 May 1984, he was
replaced by Archbishop Francis Arinze, an African. Jadot retired to
Switzerland, without the cardinal's hat he might have expected.

In Washington he was replaced by a more conventional type of
Vatican diplomat, Archbishop Pio Laghi, who arrived from Argentina with a bad or at least an obscure record on human rights. His
appointment was dated 10 December 1980. It was, of course, sheer
chance that his arrival at 3339 Massachusetts Avenue N.W. should
coincide with Ronald Reagan's election as President of the United
States. No doubt it was also a coincidence that full diplomatic relations between the Holy See and the U.S. were established in January
1984. Laghi became Pro-Nuncio and the first U.S. Ambassador to
the Holy See was William Wilson, a rich old Californian crony of
Reagan and a Knight of Malta. For years – 116 to be precise – it had
been said that diplomatic relations between the US and the Vatican
were out of the question because of the separation of Church and
state. Now Congress passed them on the nod, with hardly a whimper
of complaint from the Protestants who were supposed to be implaca-
bly opposed to papistry. Finally John J. O'Connor, well known as a
supporter of Reagan, became Archbishop of New York in time for

the 1984 election campaign. He was made a Cardinal in 1985. There were just too many coincidences for comfort.

President Reagan had been wooing Catholics for some time. He even has a special 'liaison officer to the Catholic community', Robert Reilly, who frankly admitted: 'We were pleased with O'Connor's appointment. We are pleased with his orthodoxy on abortion.' Did that mean that other U.S. bishops were unorthodox on abortion? Reilly plunged on: 'There is a natural alliance between the President and the Archbishop on a goodly number of issues.' (See Wayne Barret, 'Holier than Thou', *Greenwich Village Voice*, 25 December 1984.) He can say that again. Ex-naval chaplain O'Connor is a 'hawk' on nuclear weapons, believes in firm action against the Sandinistas, and has not observed the U.S. bishops' policy defined by Bernadin as 'a consistent ethic of life' or 'the seamless garment': that is, that respect for life covers the whole spectrum and applies equally to abortion and the use of nuclear weapons. Catholics should never, said Bernadin, become one-issue campaigners. (He developed these ideas first in a lecture at Fordham University, New York, and then in March 1984 at Saint Louis University.) O'Connor did not appear to have been listening. He also broke with the tradition that bishops do not comment on candidates during election campaigns. He contributed to Geraldine Ferraro's election defeat by digging up a two-year-old remark on abortion (which was, anyway, defensible).

Yet the silence of Bernadin on these matters has been positively deafening. He has been given a cuckoo in the nest. The irony is considerable. Earlier in this chapter we saw how the case for centralizing episcopal appointments was based on the need to be independent of the state; and I explained how the U.S. example contributed to this. But now it seems that President Ronald Reagan, the most powerful man in the world, has taken on the mantle of Louis XIV.

Probably it won't do him much good. Already there are signs that O'Connor, now that he is a member of the top team, grasps the importance of co-operating with Bernadin. He has also had his first taste of Roman arbitrariness. In May 1985 a fifty-two-year-old Chicago priest was 'offered' to O'Connor as an auxiliary bishop. The fact that Fr Edward Egan lacked pastoral experience and had spent the previous twelve years working on marriage cases in the Roman Rota looked ominous to some. It is notorious that the Vatican believes that American annulment procedure is lax and needs tightening up. O'Connor was somewhat put out at having this auxiliary parachuted down on him.

But he soon recovered. In August 1985 O'Connor attended a conference organised by *Comunione e Liberazione*, a right-wing youth movement, at Rimini on the Adriatic. It was somewhat bizarrely devoted to the theme of 'Parsifal, the Beast and Superman' (Parsifal was praised for seeking the Holy Grail, the Beast was to be unmasked and Superman denounced). O'Connor was bluntly asked whether it was true that to be made a cardinal under Pope John Paul you had to be a fervent supporter of all his policies. O'Connor prudently replied: 'The Pope's choices are always carefully thought through. Anyway, it is right that there should be harmony between the Vatican and the world's bishops. The choices of earlier popes were made on the same principle.' He was then asked whether he often talked with the Pope, and gave this astonishing reply: 'Sometimes his Holiness has to wait for me, because I am talking on the other line to President Reagan.' (*Corriere della Sera*, 26 August 1985.)

According to Catholic theology, bishops are the 'successors of the apostles'. So they are. But they get there in some pretty odd ways. There were, though, always two ways of looking at the bishop. He could be seen in relation to his people or in relation to the rest of the Church. If one stresses his relation to his people and their needs, then some sort of election, as envisaged by Lateran II, made sense. If one stresses his need to represent his local church to the universal Church, embodied in the Bishop of Rome, then a case can be made for acceptance by Rome or even for direct appointment.

Finally, and as a postscript to this chapter, one must point out the importance of the 'declaration' of the C.o.B. dated 27 November 1982. What it declared was that Opus Dei, the secretive and right-wing religious movement founded by Mgr Josemaría Escrivà de Balaguer y Albás, Marquis of Peralta, in Spain in 1928, had just been turned into a 'personal prelature' and was therefore shifted from the care of the Congregation for Religious and Secular Institutes to that of the C.o.B. itself. This was a great triumph for Opus Dei, because it vindicated its claim to originality: it was neither a religious congregation nor even a secular institute. Was it then a pantomime horse? No, it was a personal prelature. And what was that? It was a quasi-diocese: not exactly a diocese because it covered (in principle) the entire world and was not defined by territory; but resembling a diocese in that it was made up of both priests and laity, men and women. At the time of the application, Opus Dei claimed a membership of '72,375 faithful from 87 countries, of whom 2 per cent are priests'. It was a bit like a military chaplaincy which has a bishop for the pastoral care of the troops overseas.

But that parallel doesn't hold water. The military bishop exists to cope with a particular problem that ceases when the men and their families return home. There is no other instance of a quasi-diocese that people can choose to join. If Opus Dei is a quasi-diocese, it is a curious anomaly, a canonical monstrosity, and no matter how vehemently it seeks to deny the fact, its new status means that it slips out of the control of the local bishops.

We thus reach the paradoxical conclusion that a movement of which a great number of local bishops are exceedingly suspicious is now championed by the very congregation which is supposed to represent their interests. As Cardinal Sebastiano Baggio himself conceded in making the announcement: though the majority of those consulted were in favour of this change (he gave no precise statistics), 'not a few had made observations or requests for clarification'. Indeed they had. We will meet Opus Dei again. Meanwhile, we need to move from bishop-making to saint-making. The two processes have something in common.

9

The Meanings of Canonization

Whoever appoints leaders in the Church has control of it. But there is another more intangible but no less important form of control: 'models' of Christian life can be set before the faithful as examples to follow. Such models of holiness are called saints. Just who is raised to the altars (to use the hallowed phrase) in any given pontificate is indicative of the outlook of the Pope and the direction he wishes the Church to take.

In dealing with beatification and canonization we notice once again that what happens today is the result of quite recent decisions (mostly from the last four hundred years). Yet it is founded in the most ancient tradition of the Church: the doctrine of the communion of saints is fundamental to Christian faith. We are not saved as isolated individuals, but by incorporation into the Body of Christ, which is the Church. In New Testament usage the 'saints' are simply Christians, the baptized, in whom God's grace is already at work. So the number of saints far exceeds the tally of officially declared saints. Jean-Baptiste Bossuet preached a sermon in the seventeenth century in which he warned that, on judgement day, the birettas of eminent clerics would fly off their heads in astonishment at the unlikely rabble who preceded them into the Kingdom of Heaven.

So the communion of saints, made up of the living and the dead, is a democratic doctrine in so far as it asserts that all Christians have a radical equality in grace that is not altered by subsequent distinctions between those who do or do not hold office in the Church. Probably we have all met some saints who were unaware of their holiness. There is even a contradiction between being aware of sanctity and actually being saintly: like all good Christians, the saint starts out from the conviction of his or her own sinfulness. The good in himself he attributes to God. With Mary he says: 'He that is mighty has done great things in me.' (Luke 1:49.) So there is in principle nothing extraordinary about sanctity. It is the ordinary path for all Christians.

But as things have turned out, that is not what most Catholics believe. They tend to suppose that their parents or their children are unlikely to be saints because saints are a tiny, privileged group who have 'St'. in front of their name and a halo round their head. Saints are those who have gone through the mill of the Sacred Congregation for the Causes of Saints. The first stage is to be accepted by the local bishop as a 'servant of God' (*servus Dei*); the second and most difficult stage is to be granted the title of Blessed (*Beatus*), which means that the person in question enjoys the beatific vision – they have moved from grace to glory. And the third is that of 'canonization', being entered into the 'canon' or official list of recognized saints, characterized by heroic holiness and cheerfulness. 'The whole process,' said one observer, 'is a cross between a complex court case and promoting a particularly contentious Act of Parliament.' (Philip Mould, *The Times*, 9 May 1984.) It is entrusted to the Sacred Congregation for the Causes of Saints (henceforward C.C.S.). Its work will be the subject of this chapter.

The C.C.S. is a relatively modern development. For example, the distinction between 'blessed' and 'saint' dates back to Pope Urban VIII in 1634. (Pierre Delooz in *Saints and their Cults*.) The most important systematization of the procedure came in the eighteenth century under Benedict XIV, the 'humanist Pope', who corresponded with Voltaire and the most learned men of the age. After many years as Devil's Advocate, he had a keen nose for the fraud and the hoax, and brought to his work the most rigorous standards of historical accuracy. (See Renée Haynes, *Philosopher King*.) Though many popes were tempted to tinker with the rules, the biggest changes after Benedict XIV have come in this pontificate.

But all these changes in the last four centuries built upon a tradition that was much more ancient and very different. We may distinguish six stages in the history of the recognition of holiness:

1. Those designated in the first thousand years by a local church. What happened was simply that a 'cult' developed around the tomb of a local martyr or holy bishop. When persecution ceased, religious life was sometimes regarded as an alternative to literal martyrdom ('white martyrdom') and earned the same crown and palm.

2. Those designated by popes between 993 and 1234. The popes tried to impose some control over the proliferation of local cults, and, incidentally, to boost the claims of their own office. But they did not succeed completely, and many saints were still spontaneously canonized.

3. Those canonized between 1234 and 1634 with papal approval, though there were still some tenacious local cults that won through.

4. Urban VIII's 1634 legislation, which introduced for the first time the distinction between beatification and canonization, and insisted on Roman approval.

5. Benedict XIV's thorough revision of this legislation.

6. John Paul II's modifications, *Divinus Perfectionis Magister*, 1983.

As in most questions of Church history, the story is one of spontaneity being replaced by bureaucratic order, of charism giving way to juridical precision, of legend being subjected to scientific winnowing. And as usual there is a contrast between the Orthodox tradition, which is less organized and closer to the original tradition, and Rome's insistence on the correct juridical procedure. There is gain as well as loss in this development. Whether the gain outweighs the loss is a moot point.

In this respect, Anglicans are more like the Orthodox: Bishop Edward King, who died in 1914, and Nicholas Ferrar of Little Gidding, appeared in the Alternative Service Book calendar thanks to local pressures. Canon Donald Allchin of Canterbury Cathedral complained that Rome's procedure is 'elaborate and expensive' and wanted to see it decentralized.

But that was precisely the effect of the apostolic constitution, *Divinus Perfectionis Magister*, of 26 February 1983. It 'simplified' the procedure. Someone could be canonized as early as ten years after death. The responsibility for investigating potential saints and presenting their causes now rests with the diocesan bishops and their episcopal conferences. The 'promoter' of the cause will be a local man (or woman), and the role of the C.C.S. will be to see that canon law has been duly observed. In other words it will take over the role of the old 'devil's advocate', probing and testing the heroic virtue of the candidate, and, in the end, committing the 'conscience of the Church' to the judgement that he or she is now 'in Heaven', at one with Christ who now is for them 'all in all'.

The new system has not been in operation long enough for us to judge how well it will work. It looks at first blush like a welcome measure of decentralization. But the explanation given by the under-secretary of the C.C.S., Mgr Fabijan Veraja, did not stress that the move had been made to highlight the importance of the local Church. Instead he attributed it to the increasing workload of the

C.C.S. He refused to be drawn on the details, but vouchsafed one statistic of great importance: whereas the 1950s saw the introduction of forty-seven causes, the single year of 1982 comfortably surpassed that with fifty-three. Maybe they will not all come through successfully. But the number of canonization processes has escalated dramatically. There are at present over 2,000 candidates for sainthood on the books.

That is the first novelty of this pontificate. The second is that Pope John Paul is the first Pope to have presided at canonization ceremonies outside Rome. Of course the question did not arise with non-travelling popes who considered themselves to be prisoners of the Vatican. John Paul II seems to regard canonization as a special treat or bonus to be granted when he visits a local church. Thus in the Philippines he canonized Lorenzo Ruiz, the first Filipino saint – a Chinese servant of the Dominicans who boarded by mistake the vessel taking them to Japan and shared in their excruciatingly slow death suspended upside down over pits of excrement. In Korea it was the turn of the 100 Korean martyrs. On his second visit to Poland in 1983, at Poznan on 20 June he beatified Mother Ursula Ledochowska, who in 1907 had organized the first school for Polish girls living under Russian occupation; and then in Kraków two days later he beatified the Carmelite Father Rafal Kalinowski and the founder of the Albertines, Brother Albert Chmielowskie. Kalinowski came from his home town in Wadowice where he died, 'the martyr of the confessional', in 1907; and Chmielowski was the painter about whom the young Karol Wojtyla had written in 1950 a thinly veiled autobiographical play, *The Brothers of God*.

And so it went on. In September 1984 there was the first-ever beatification on North American soil, in Jarry Park, Montreal. Blessed Marie-Léonie was an estimable woman who founded a religious order largely devoted to the domestic service of the clergy. This did not seem altogether to meet the demands of Canadian feminists.

But if beatifications and canonizations outside Rome are designed to encourage the local church, they also make a theological point. The most striking example was the beatification in Kinshasha, Zaïre, of Anuarite Nengapate on 15 August 1985. The Blessed Anuarite was a twenty-three-year-old Zaïrean nun. During the Simba rebellion of 1964 she refused to submit to the sexual advances of Openge Olumbe, who hacked her to pieces while her sisters sang the *Magnificat*. Olumbe is now a pious if simple-minded Catholic and was present at the beatification of his victim. The Pope forgave him in the name of the Church. His homily was one long hymn to 'the

primordial value of virginity' and he placed the African Anuarite in
the long roll of Roman martyrs, Agatha, Lucy, Agnes, Cecilia. . . . So
by this beatification Africa enters the universal Church; and those
who have argued for married priests on the grounds that 'celibacy' is
not an African value are implicitly rebuked.

The escalation of beatification processes raised a number of questions. Why were there so many priests and nuns? Where were the
models of lay holiness? Cardinal Pietro Palazzini, Prefect of the
C.C.S. from 29 June 1980, attempted to answer this at the 1980
Synod by saying that priests and nuns inevitably came from families,
and that their parents were honoured even as they were. It seemed a
far-fetched argument. Why not beatify or canonize the parents?

Next there was the danger of devaluing the currency of holiness.
So many candidates have been sped through with what seems like
immoderate haste. Contemporary judgements are notoriously falli-
ble. Does ten years leave enough time to place someone's holiness in
historical perspective? At Vatican II the idea was put to Pope Paul
VI that John XXIII, his predecessor, should be canonized by accla-
mation. Paul VI took fright and cunningly ordered that the process
of investigation should begin of both John XXIII and Pius XII,
according to the ordinary rules. Pope John was entrusted to the
Franciscans, in fact to Fr Antonio Cairoli, while the Jesuits in the
person of Fr Paolo Molinari were landed with Pius XII. That held
things up, as no doubt it was intended to.

Quite clearly the canonization policy of any pontificate reflects a
very conscious selection of models of holiness to be put before the
whole Church. In 1979 Pierre Delooz pointed out that of those
declared 'blessed' in this century, only 33 per cent were women and
only 20 per cent lay. (*Concilium*, 1979.) Despite the endless talk about
lay holiness, it remains true that the surest path to beatification,
unless you happen to be martyred, is to be a religious or the founder
of a female religious order. It helps to be Italian, French or Spanish
or, in this pontificate, Polish. It is not really surprising that mother
foundresses should be so frequently canonized. Their congregations
have the money needed to push the canonization through with the
requisite doggedness. And they have every interest in doing so: the
canonization of one's holy mother foundress is a proof that one's particular *charisma* is recognized by the Church. It has produced fruits of
holiness; it is a Good Thing. Therefore it may recruit with added
zest. It has upon it the seal, if not of the Spirit, at least of the C.C.S.

On 14 April 1985 Pope John Paul II beatified two more
nineteenth-century nuns: Caterina Troiani, foundress of the Fran-

ciscan Sisters of the Heart of Mary; and Pauline von Mallinchrodt, foundress of the Sisters of Christian Charity (who specialize in looking after blind children). The next day the Pope characteristically replied to the murmurings that have been heard about his beatification policy. First he declared that saints were ordinary people like ourselves:

> Blesseds and saints are not an exotic breed of human beings to be marvelled at as strange. They are human beings like us who show us the way, who give us the courage to strive unerringly for the goal that is set before us. (*Osservatore Romano*, English, 13 May 1985)

The fact that Blessed Pauline began her work for blind children as a laywoman leads the Pope to conclude that she has a lesson for all:

> Thus we see that love for the poor and the urge to help them concretely are possible also outside the religious life. Now as then we adults should give young people as much recognition and encouragement as we can when out of their youthful idealism they strive for social commitment, even if such involvement at first seems to us to be reckless and unplanned.

This looks like a concession: it is *possible* to be a lay social worker. It is difficult to think of anyone who would deny that proposition. However, Pauline is not a very good role model for the lay social workers since she was soon to enter religious life. And the Pope evidently believes that it is preferable that social work should be in the hands of religious. So he concluded his address with an exhortation to parents to foster religious vocations among their children and not to be deterred by those who wonder whether happiness 'can be found in the life of vows and whether they can fulfil themselves in this way'. So quite clearly these particular beatifications serve the general policies of the pontificate. The waves of secularization are to be driven back by an army of new saints, and religious life is to be commended by showing that it is the ordinary path to holiness.

But not all religious orders wish to be commended in this way. The Franciscan Friars of the Atonement and Opus Dei (which is not, of course, a religious order, nor even any more a secular institute) have a very different approach to the beatification of their founders.

The Friars of the Atonement (F.A.) were founded at Graymoor, a hill in the Hudson Highlands in New York State, by Lewis T.

Wattson (1863-1940), an Anglican priest, in 1898. In religion he took the name Father Paul James Francis. In 1909 his small community, together with the Sisters of the Atonement, founded by Sister Lurana White (1870-1935), 'went over to Rome' amid a storm of abuse and misunderstanding. These origins explain their ecumenical vocation. At a chapter meeting in the 1970s, the Friars of the Atonement decided that they would not press for the beatification of their founder, not because they thought him insufficiently holy, but because they thought it would be a misuse of money with no important spiritual recompense. (See Joseph P. Eagan, *Pilgrim from Canterbury*.)

Opus Dei has displayed no such inhibitions, even though their founder, Mgr Escrivà de Balaguer, died as recently as 1975 (so the change in the rules makes him admissible from 1985). On the contrary, they have done everything possible to see that their man get rushed through, aided by the Prefect of the C.C.S., Cardinal Pietro Palazzini. One clue was that on 19 March 1982, at a solemn ceremony to mark the new status of Opus Dei, Archbishop Romolo Carboni, Vatican Nuncio to the Republic of Italy, no less, 'looked forward to the day when Mgr Escrivà would be raised to the altars'. He said this in the presence of Palazzini; the whole event was televised and a commentary was provided by the well-known newscaster and Opus Dei member Alberto Michelini. Unlike the Graymoor Friars, it is evident that Opus Dei regard the money devoted to this cause as well spent.

Their campaign has been thorough. On the seventh anniversary of his death in 1982, his successor, Alvaro del Portillo, preached a homily in which he declared that there was 'widespread popular devotion to the Founder' and that 'without anticipating the judgement of the Church, he is a figure that cannot be ignored'. Just to drive the point home, the same day, the Secretary (shortly to be President) of C.E.L.A.M. (the Latin American Bishops' Conference), Argentinian Archbishop Antonio Quarracino, wrote an article in *L'Avvenire*, the Italian Catholic daily, in which he said: 'I don't know whether Mgr Escrivà will be canonized, but when I see that prudent and serious people who know the meaning of words judge him to be a saint, I say to myself that this must happen.' He attributed opposition to the beatification to the work of the Devil. Meanwhile the 'postulator' of Escrivà's cause, Father Flavio Capucci, revealed that an Opus Dei sister in Madrid had been cured of a tumour, and that this was 'occasioned by a prayer to the Founder of Opus Dei'. Given that Pope John Paul is an enthusiastic admirer of Opus Dei, the chances of Escrivà being beatified soon must be considered very strong.

This is all the more likely in that Palazzini is another keen supporter of Opus Dei. He has had a curious career. Paul VI made him a Cardinal in 1973 but did not trust him with any significant post. He seemed to be heading for the safe haven of retirement, his only task being acting president of a society dedicated to the beatification of Pius IX, the Pope of the Syllabus of Errors and Vatican I. Pope John Paul made this atavistic throwback Prefect of the C.C.S. on 27 June 1980. Palazzini was then sixty-eight. Almost exactly five years later it was announced that *Pio Nono* had overcome the first hurdle; he could now be called by the title 'Venerable'. Giancarlo Zizola, one of the best Vaticanologists, has described Palazzini in these terms:

> He is the real strong man of the pontificate, the one who determines decisions of fundamental importance. During the years of Popes John XXIII and Paul VI he was in opposition. Paul VI denied him until the last moment the office of cardinal because he knew how far Palazzini had hated John XXIII. Palazzini is the central pillar of Opus Dei's influence in the Vatican, and he is the one who secures for the Pope the constant financial flow from this enormous Catholic multi-national for all his needs, but especially for the development of Wojtylian movements and the transfer of Polish priests to other countries. ('The Counter-Reformation of John Paul II', *Magill*, Dublin, 7 March 1985)

Palazzini's job, then, is to see that no disturbing saints get through. One would not, for example, rate Pope John XXIII's chances of beatification very highly. Yet in his case the preliminary historical spadework is complete, miracles have been plausibly reported, and there can be no doubt about the cult that has grown up around him. It is Pope John's tomb in the crypt of St Peter's which always has the most flowers. So why the delay? Because his beatification would not serve the overall purposes of this pontificate.

The same reasoning also excludes the beatification of Oscar Romero, Archbishop of El Salvador, murdered at the altar of a hospital chapel on 29 March 1980. It would seem to be a clear case of martyrdom, and immediately a cult sprang up. He was, as the saying is, already 'canonized in the hearts and minds' of Latin Americans. Gustavo Gutierrez, the 'father' of liberation theology, declared that Romero's death divided Latin American history into 'before' and 'after'. He was the first episcopal martyr of liberation theology (though about 800 priests, religious and laypeople had already been killed). Romero was murdered because he defended the poor and the oppressed against the government. He was killed because he became 'the voice of those who have no voice', and it was an inconvenient, prophetic voice. One of the things he told Pope John Paul may have been held against him: 'In my country it is very difficult to speak of anti-communism because anti-communism is what the right preaches, not out of love for Christian sentiments, but out of a selfish concern to promote its own interests.'

That was not music to John Paul's ears. In any event, he has never called Romero a martyr. And though he prayed privately at Romero's tomb when he went to San Salvador – he could hardly have omitted that gesture of respect – he did not betray any great enthusiasm for the late Archbishop's causes and indeed warned against 'manipulating' his memory. With his voice rising in a dramatic crescendo (I still have the cassette) he cried: 'Let no ideological interest exploit the sacrifice of this great pastor!' Since El Salvador was in a state of civil war and since there was no way in which the government could exploit a man they regarded as their opponent, this cry must have referred to the left-wing guerrillas in the hills who were listening on their crackling transistors. So Pope John Paul was trying to deprive the left of their hero. Perhaps he half gives credence to the theory put about by Cardinal Alfonso Lopez Trujillo: Romero was not murdered by a government death-squad (as everyone else believes) but by left-wingers wishing to provoke a revolt.

But if Oscar Romero will have to bide his time, the cause of Francesco Forgione, better known as Padre Pio, is being hastened along. We know this because Pope John Paul II himself has taken the unusual step of giving evidence to the tribunal investigating Padre Pio. To understand what is happening one needs to go back in history, Padre Pio, a Capuchin Franciscan, had been a great cult figure in the pontificate of Pope Pius XII: he had the marks of Christ's wounds on his hands and feet, and was said to emit 'the odour of roses' and reputed to use 'second sight' in the confessional. (There is a story that Graham Greene once queued up to go to confession to Padre Pio, but fled in panic just as his turn came round.)

But there was always controversy around Padre Pio, and in 1962 Pope John ordered an investigation and forbade him to see pilgrims while it was under way. Karol Wojtyla, however, in Rome for the first session of the Council, continued to have faith in Padre Pio and asked him to pray for Wanda Poltawska, a Kraków psychiatrist, mother of four and survivor of a concentration camp, who was now dying of cancer at the age of forty. 'One cannot say no to such a request,' Padre Pio is reported to have said. Ten days later Cardinal

Wojtyla wrote a second letter to Padre Pio to say that Wanda was already cured. (See Bruno Bartoloni, *Corriere della Sera*, 4 October 1984.) This correspondence, which was in Latin, was presented to the C.C.S. by the Pope. No doubt Cardinal Palazzini will know what to do with it. But one can point to no other comparable example of direct papal intervention in a beatification process.

However, I am not suggesting that the contemporary C.C.S. is lacking in integrity or that its history is unreliable. It is simply being invited to look harder in some directions than in others. Canonizations have nearly always had an additional motive besides the obvious one of declaring someone to be in Heaven. They always express a choice of certain values. The beatification of the Curé d'Ars in 1905 was a tribute to his holiness, but it also suggested that 'simplicity' was of more importance in a priest than 'learning' (which was deemed to be leading the 'Modernists' astray).

The canonization of Joan of Arc in 1920 was not only the putting right of an historical mistake – she had been burned at the stake as a relapsed heretic – it also had a political dimension. It sealed the reconciliation of the Vatican with the French government after the '*union sacrée*' in the First World War: Catholics had shown that they were as patriotic and ready to die for France as anyone. So diplomatic relations could be resumed. The canonization of Thomas More, former Chancellor of England, and John Fisher, Bishop of Rochester, in 1935 was intended to flatter the 'English' while making an apologetic point about the necessity of union with Rome. They 'died for the Pope'.

Canonization, in other words, is not a univocal act with a single meaning. Its meaning can be pushed this way and that. One of the most striking examples was that of the canonization of the forty English and Welsh Martyrs in 1970. Their 'cause' had been hanging fire for generations. It seemed to many Anglicans and to the British Council of Churches that to proceed with the canonization was inopportune: it would revive enmities and passions just as they were dying down thanks to the ecumenical movement. The English and Welsh Bishops wanted canonization as a confirmation of Roman Catholic identity put in jeopardy, some of them believed privately, by all this ecumenical nonsense. Though the forty seemed to have displayed a very English lack of enthusiasm for miracles, that requirement was waived and the great day came on 25 October 1970.

It was then that Paul VI changed the meaning of the event and gave it a new dimension. For he chose to make his most welcoming statement about the Anglican Communion in this very homily:

May the blood of these martyrs be able to heal the great wound inflicted on God's Church by reason of the separation of the Anglican Church from the Catholic Church. . . . Their devotion to their country gives us the assurance that on the day when – God willing – the unity of faith and life is restored, no offence will be inflicted on the honour and sovereignty of a great country such as England. There will be no seeking to lessen the legitimate prestige and usage proper to the Anglican Church when the Roman Catholic Church – this humble servant of God – is able to embrace firmly her ever-beloved sister in the one authentic communion of the family of Christ: a communion of origin and faith, a communion of priesthood and rule, a communion of the saints in the freedom and love of the spirit of Jesus.

This is a very clear example of what is meant by the 'plasticity' of canonization. It does not have an absolute meaning in itself: it acquires its significance from the words that accompany and explain it.

The consensus of theologians is that the Church's infallibility is engaged in a canonization. That means that the wrong people cannot be canonized. But it has recently been claimed that such a mistake was made in the case of Maria Goretti, a twelve-year-old from Ancona on the Adriatic who resisted sexual advances and was murdered in 1902. Her killer lived to see her canonized in 1950, a 'martyr of chastity'. The problem was that her last words, '*Si, si*', could be read as a confirmation of her previous remark, '*Dio non vuole*' (God doesn't want this); or they could be ready as meaning that she was now prepared to give way. This was argued about for many a long hour, and seven volumes of evidence were gathered. Maria was cleared, which was the gentlemanly thing to do, and how anyone could expect total clarity about such a passionate and fleeting moment is beyond me.

The source for this story is the late Cardinal William Theodore Heard, Scotsman and Oxford rowing blue (Balliol, 1911). He got a third in law, which no doubt helped him become a celebrated Roman canonist. He told the young Anthony Kenny that he 'preferred to deal with annulments in the mornings and canonizations in the afternoon; the canonizations were less depressing, because even the failed candidates had at least tried to be good'. (Anthony Kenny, *A Path from Rome*.)

This chapter may conclude with some reflections based on the work of the Belgian Jesuit, Pierre Delooz. He has made a sociological study of canonizations. ('Towards a Sociological Study of Canonized Sainthood' in *Saints and Their Cults*.) He shows that saints can be made to perform any number of roles. So in iconography St Anthony of Padua – usually depicted today with the Christ Child in his arms – has been presented as a sage, a healer, or a Spanish admiral driving the Moors out of Oran. That reinforces the theory of the 'plasticity' of canonization.

St Anthony of Padua was at least a verifiable historical personage. Some saints have been even more 'constructed', either because practically nothing was known about them, as is the case of St Anne, Jesus' grandmother, or because they did not exist, like the unfortunate Philomena or Catherine of Alexandria. Delooz concludes that saints are 'for other people' and are made by 'other people'. One can complicate the problem still further by noting that the requirement of 'heroic virtue' for canonization does not mean very much unless we know which particular virtues are to be prized.

Consider this example: St Thomas Aquinas says that the virtue of fortitude is shown in 'constancy of purpose'. Many canonized saints have signally failed to display constancy, and have been in and out of religious orders like yo-yos. St Anthony Mary Claret (1807-70), for example, entered a seminary but left it to become a Carthusian. Before reaching the monastery, however, he changed his mind and returned to the seminary, where he was ordained a diocesan priest. After an unsatisfactory spell in the Jesuit noviceship, he went to Latin America, became an archbishop, survived several assassination attempts, returned to Spain as the Queen's confessor, accompanied her into exile in Paris after the 1868 revolution, and finally retired to a Cistercian Abbey to escape the French police. Constancy! He was canonized in 1950 at the request of the religious congregation he had almost absent-mindedly founded, the Claretians. In a footnote, Delooz gives even more remarkable instances of instability.

In short, no matter how hard one tries, there is a certain hit-or-miss quality about those who are selected for the accolade of canonization. That brings us back to our starting point in this chapter. The 'saint' is an everyday Christian who tries to take seriously the demands of the Gospel in his or her life. That some should be singled out for 'raising to the altars' is no doubt a good thing, for it publishes the fact that the Holy Spirit is still at work among the people of God and that in Christ a new era, salvation history, began.

That is the theological justification for the existence of the Congregation for the Causes of Saints.

10

They also Serve

The general outlook of the Roman Curia has already been conveyed in the previous chapters. It remains to complete the survey of the 'old Curia' (that is the Curia as it was up to 31 December 1967). In this chapter the work of three more congregations will be described, and a 'typical' problem will illustrate their work and attitudes. Do not expect any new ideas.

The Congregation for the Clergy dates back to 1564. Until 1967 it was known as the Congregation of the Council: both its date and its title are a reminder that its task was to implement the Council of Trent. Since Trent reformed the priesthood, the clergy belonged to its competence, but it was something of a rag-bag department that picked up a lot of other loose ends. Even Paul Poupard, a most respectful writer on the Vatican, and now a cardinal, admits it has 'less historical continuity' than any other dicastery and describes it somewhat ambivalently as 'an anachronism into which Paul VI breathed new life'. (*Il Vaticano Oggi*.) But it still has the three sections or 'offices' it traditionally had.

The first is concerned with the intellectual and spiritual life of priests; the second with preaching the Word of God which embraces catechesis in all its forms, and the approval of local catechetical directories; and the third and most yawn-inducing busies itself with the temporal administration of the Church – legacies, oratories, shrines, chapels, paintings, tapestries and works of art generally, taxes, clergy pensions, health care, and sacerdotal alcoholics.

Presiding over this multifarious activity – most of which could be dealt with on the local level – is Cardinal Silvio Oddi. Born in 1910, the twelfth of fourteen children and a member of what is known in the Curia as the 'Piacenza Mafia', he spent most of his working life as a Vatican diplomat in the Middle East, though he ended up as Nuncio to Belgium where Cardinal Léon-Joseph Suenens caused him sleepless nights with his spectacular interviews. In 1969 he returned to Rome, when Paul VI gave him a cardinal's hat but no serious job. Like his friend Palazzini he was in effect put out to grass.

It was assumed that he was quietly preparing for death. His theological views were hardly distinguishable from those of dissident Archbishop Marcel Lefebvre. He regarded Vatican II as the cause of the crisis in the Church. It was therefore a great surprise – to the uninformed – when in 1979 John Paul II made him Prefect of the Congregation of the Clergy. To call Oddi 'conservative' would be an understatement. He is linked with the most right-wing Catholic groups, including 'Catholics United for the Faith' (C.U.F.) in the U.S.A. In interviews in *The Wanderer*, he urges them to write to Rome denouncing unorthodoxy wherever they encounter it.

So one usually hears about the Congregation for the Clergy only when it has banned something. Oddi's own explanation of how the Office of Catechetics came into being suggests that it is another of those temporary expedients that were made permanent. He says:

The Office for Catechetics came into existence originally when countries which had concordats with the Church insisted on approving religious texts used for teaching the faith in public schools. Since the negotiations often involved relations with national governments, local bishops were often at a disadvantage and welcomed the help of the Holy See. In those days, many countries had a single national catechism which was acceptable both to the civil government and to the Church. In recent years, however, many countries lack a single national catechism. Instead each diocese supervises the books that may be used as religious texts. From your American experience, you can easily imagine how the work of our catechetical office has expanded. The reason the Office of Catechetics is located in the office for the Clergy is that the parish priest or pastor is the first teacher of faith in his parish, immediately responsible, of course, to the Bishop. (Interview with Richard Cowden-Guido, in *The Wanderer*, 28 July 1983)

So a system devised for dealing with the Empress Maria Theresa of Austria is now employed against episcopal conferences. Poupard was right to talk about anachronism. Armed with this comprehensive principle, Oddi has acted against catechisms in France and Italy. The French played for time. The Italians, knowing their man better, said in effect they had a catechetical commission of their own with which they were perfectly happy, and that Oddi should mind his own business. The Americans caved in when in April 1984 the *imprimatur* (official permission to print) was withdrawn from *Christ among Us*, an adult catechism. It was not explained how a book which had sold over 1,600,000 copies and been used in the instruction of countless converts had so suddenly forfeited its *imprimatur*. It was like closing the stable door after the horse had bolted – as swiftly as possible, as it turned out, in the direction of a secular publisher, who did not need to bother about an *imprimatur* and welcomed for sales purposes this Vatican equivalent of an X certificate.

The C.f.C. has also produced a declaration 'On Certain Movements and Associations Forbidden to the Clergy' (8 May 1982). This said that priests should not belong to organized political movements of any kind. It could be used against any priest who 'engaged in party politics' such as those who were ministers in the Sandinista regime in Nicaragua. But the real target was the *Pacem in Terris* movement in Czechoslovakia. It was alluded to cryptically in the condemnation of associations of priests which 'directly or indirectly, openly or undercover, pursue goals that are related to politics, even when they present themselves as seeking to promote humanitarian ideals, peace and social development'. In an interview with Domenico Del Rio in *La Repubblica* (11 March 1982), Oddi admitted that his document had *Pacem in Terris* in its sights. The result in Czechoslovakia has been total impasse. Priests are not allowed to come together except as members of *Pacem in Terris*. The Vatican refuses to appoint bishops from among them. Loyal priests cannot meet at all. The individual priest has no support. The outlook is bleak.

Pope John Paul addressed the plenary assembly of the C.f.C. – its annual get-together – on 20 October 1984. He showed himself to be much less conservative than Oddi. On one hand he made the anti-Brazilian point that the parish (and not the basic community) is 'the first school of faith, prayer and of Christian conduct . . . the first field of ecclesial charity . . . the primary seat of catechesis'. (*Osservatore Romano*, 21 October 1984.) One might be permitted to observe that in the developed world it is not 'basic communities' so much as the fact that people have cars that makes the territorial parish less important. They are free to choose where they will worship. But on the other hand the Pope spoke of lay ministries in terms unfamiliar to Cardinal Oddi: 'The laity are not only the object of pastoral ministry, but they must become active workers in it, because of their innate vocation as laity and because of the intrinsic need of the Church.' These questions will surface at the Synod of 1987 which is devoted to the 'Mission of the Laity in the Church and the World'. Since laity and priesthood are defined by contrast with each other, the two topics are very closely connected. In a later chapter, we will look at this from the side of the laity.

Oddi's predecessor at the C.f.C. was the American Cardinal John J. Wright, formerly Archbishop of Philadelphia, known in the 1960s as 'the egg-head bishop', largely on the grounds that a bishop who read books at that date was an odd man out. He was also extremely fat, and the splash as he dived into the swimming pool had to be experienced to be believed. Following the unstated post-conciliar principle that there has to be an American in a top curial post, Cardinal William Wakefield Baum, Archbishop of Washington, became Prefect of the Congregation of Catholic Education on 25 January 1980. He is also *ex officio* Grand Chancellor of the Gregorian University. There can be few who have never heard of Baum's birthplace: Dallas, Texas. The date, 21 November 1926, is less well known. But the family soon moved to Kansas City, Missouri, where the young Baum studied, was ordained, and became parish priest and eventually chancellor of the diocese.

He keeps as low a profile as his congregation. Catholic Education is the Cinderella among Vatican dicasteries. It began life under Sixtus V in 1588. Its task was to supervise the Roman universities and the other great universities of the Catholic world – Bologna, Paris and Salamanca for example – as well as those of the New World such as León in Nicaragua. Hitherto, universities had been independent fiefdoms and were represented at councils in their own right. They were, after all, the original *magisterium*, that is, the teaching authority. The new congregation did not have much success. The proof is that in 1824 Pope Leo XII needed to make a fresh start with a *Congregatio Studiorum* (Congregation of Studies) whose brief, however, extended only to the Papal States. From 1870 it began to claim a wider and more universal authority. Gradually, seminaries were brought in as providing more tractable subjects than universities.

Finally, the congregation reached its present form in 1967. There are three sections which include seminaries (except those which fall under the Oriental Churches Congregation or Propaganda), most universities, faculties and institutes of higher studies in clerical hands (*dipendenti da persone fisiche o morale ecclesiastiche, Annuario Pontificio*, 1984), and Catholic schools generally.

There is not much that Cardinal Baum can do about Catholic schools generally, except to encourage them to stay in business. But teachers in seminaries and other institutes of tertiary education are required to have a 'canonical mission', which means in effect permission to teach from the bishop. This is what Hans Küng lost in Tübingen (though it could not affect his teaching in the Ecumenical Institute). The professors in the seminary of São Paulo are threatened with a similar sanction after a special visitation by Cardinal Joseph Höffner of Cologne early in 1985. It is true that he went as an emissary of the Congregation for the Doctrine of Faith rather than for Catholic Education. But that may merely indicate Baum's weakness. Cinderella does not go to the curial ball.

Since the Congregation for Divine Worship (C.D.W.) is concerned with the liturgy, it touches the lives of more Catholics than any other dicastery. Few are aware of this, however, except when edicts appear forbidding the use of girls as altar servers, insisting on the retention of 'sexist' language or 'restoring the Tridentine Mass' (Indult of 3 October 1984). On these occasions Fr Cuthbert Johnson O.S.B., responsible for the English-speaking desk in the C.D.W., emerges to explain what has happened. In 1980, for example, the U.S. bishops had recommended that the eucharistic prayers should be revised to 'eliminate the exclusively male tone of the original language'. The C.D.W. rejected this because 'the problem is not universal': the whole English-speaking world must move together or no one can move at all. 'Personally,' Dom Cuthbert added, 'I object to individual groups or movements claiming the right to change the meaning of words, such as man and mankind.' (*National Catholic Reporter*, November 16, 1984.) This example sums up the problem of the C.D.W.: it tries to represent 'the universal' in a world of particular churches.

The C.D.W. was given its present shape on 5 April 1984, when the Congregation for the Sacraments, which deals with certain dispensations and unconsummated marriages, was hived off again. But despite various changes of name, one can say that the C.D.W. is in continuity with the bodies responsible for implementing the liturgical changes demanded by Vatican II. That won't commend it in the eyes of everyone. Liturgical change was based on the following principle: 'That sound tradition may be retained, and yet the way be open for legitimate progress, a careful investigation is to be made into each part of the liturgy which is to be revised. This investigation should always be theological, historical and pastoral.' (*Sacrosanctum Concilium.*)

Those three dimensions, theological, historical and pastoral, define the work of the C.D.W. I will say a word about how each of them applies to the Eucharist, the central act of worship.

Every liturgical act implies and expresses a theology. *Lex orandi, lex credendi*: as we pray, so we believe. The Council of Trent was more concerned with who had the power validly to celebrate the Eucharist than with its effective celebration. The result was that the worshipper was often reduced to being a passive and silent spectator. St Pius X began to break with this tradition in the first years of the century when he stressed the 'active participation' of all the faithful in the Mass. Vatican II developed the logical consequence: if all the faithful were to participate in the Mass, then it ought to be in a language they understood. Vatican II also brought out the communitarian aspect of worship. Trent's rite stranded the worshippers in prayerful isolation as separate monads, merely accidentally alongside each other. Vatican II hoped that Christians would become aware of the social nature of their redemption by praying and singing together. Why sing? *Qui cantat, bis orat*, said St Augustine: he who sings prays twice over.

The second aspect of the C.D.W.'s work is historical. People tended to forget the obvious truth that the Mass had a history. Various items were put in for accidental reasons. Some customs – such as communion in the hand – dropped out. The meaning of other parts of the Mass was obscured. The offertory prayers, for example, were said inaudibly by the priest. True, one could 'follow it all in spirit' in a book. But we are not disembodied spirits, and there is every reason why all five senses (those that will be anointed on our death-bed) should be brought into worship. The opponents of liturgical change in the 1960s, though they appealed to tradition, were for the most part a-historical in their thinking. They did not realize that the 'Mass of Pius V' (or Tridentine Mass) was itself the product of centuries of development and was, in its own time, a reform. It could not provide a fixed, timeless and immutable standard. The lesson of history was that the Church had a perfect right to regulate its own worship.

The third criterion of liturgical reform used by Vatican II was that it should be 'pastoral', that is, directed to the real needs of people in their own settings. It stressed liturgy as pedagogy. It led, for example, to greater variety in scriptural readings to make more of the Bible familiar to Catholics. It led to greater flexibility in liturgy for special groups such as children and the handicapped. It also led to greater adaptation to local cultures. This can, however, cause problems.

One of the unresolved issues facing the C.D.W. is that of liturgical dance. David danced before the Ark and the canons of Seville still dance (or at least gently sway) on Corpus Christi. Some scholars claim that dancing played a greater part in early Christian worship than has been acknowledged. (J.G. Davies, *Liturgical Dance: An Historical and Practical Handbook*.) But it has to be admitted that it had dropped out of use and sight. One cannot imagine Cardinal Augustin Meyer and Archbishop Virgilio Noè, Prefect and Secretary of the C.D.W., engaging in a liturgical *pas de deux*. Even 'The Lord of the Dance' is probably not in their repertoire.

But where dancing is part of the local culture, as in many parts of Africa and India, some argue that it has its rightful place in the liturgy just as local music does. It is as natural for an African to dance as to sing. It is certainly not natural to sit on benches in neat rows singing Frederick Faber's 'Faith of Our Fathers'. In developed countries experiments in liturgical dance have mainly been confined to children ('music and movement') or to stately and dignified gestures, or to miming scripture stories. Some prefer to call it choreography on the grounds that the word raises fewer hackles; others think the charismatic movement has usefully helped to break down inhibitions. These matters were raised at the meeting organized by the C.D.W. held in Rome from 23 to 28 October 1984 (full account in '*Vent'Anni di riforma liturgica*', *Il Regno*, 1 February 1985).

This international congress illustrates one way in which the C.D.W. differs from other Congregations. Once the liturgy went into the vernacular, the C.D.W. was plainly incompetent to act as the centre of all initiatives, experiments and translations. It was obliged to work with and through local liturgical commissions at a national or diocesan level. Making a virtue out of necessity, it adopted a more 'collegial' and consultative style: in the last twenty years liturgical texts have been approved in an astonishing 345 languages – and that's not the end. So the C.D.W.'s task is to ensure that in all these texts there is 'substantial unity with the Roman rite'. Obviously, one can argue about the presence or absence of 'substantial unity' for a very long time.

However, the local churches do not seem to feel that the S.C.W. is on their backs; and when it is, they advise it to get off. The 228 bishops and experts who met in October 1984 for what was in effect a mini-synod on the liturgy did not mince their words. Some of them were incensed by the Indult which gave permission for the 1962 (i.e. Tridentine) missal to be used. They were angry because they had been consulted on this question in 1981 and given a firm no to it. (*Notitiae*, December 1981.) The verdict of the bishops and the C.D.W. in 1981 was that the Tridentine Mass was definitively and irrevocably superseded, and that its restoration would do nothing to bring back dissidents like Archbishop Marcel Lefebvre, since the traditionalists' basic objection was to what they called 'the hybrid and democratic Mass of Paul VI'. They rejected liturgical change just as they rejected Vatican II. As Paul VI, who loved the Tridentine Mass, said, 'This rite has become a symbol, like the white flag of the monarchists after the French Revolution – a symbol of opposition to the Council.'

The Indult granting permission was signed by Meyer and Noè. It was dated 3 October 1984. It looked like a pre-emptive strike just two weeks before the Congress. The English-language discussion group reported, to applause, that the Indult marked 'a step away from the ecclesiology of Vatican II which insists on the involvement of all the people of God in the Eucharist according to their different functions and ministries'. Again, 'the Indult seems to bring comfort to those who have resisted the liturgical movement and shows a lack of consideration towards those who have accepted liturgical renewal and loyally followed the directives of the Council.' But the final charge was the most grievous. This was a manifest flouting of collegiality. They had been consulted. They had given their views. Their advice had been peremptorily overturned.

Unfortunately, these objections were sent to the wrong address. The decision came from the Pope, and Noè had been overruled. We know this from a remark of Lefebvre, who welcomed the Indult as slightly better than nothing and added: 'This document has been in preparation for more than four years. Publishing it has always been problematic; there has been fierce opposition. The Pope must have taken a personal decision against the advice of a certain number of cardinals and Mgr Noè.' So here is an instance of a dicastery caught between loyalty to its 'constituency' and loyalty to the Pope. It must happen not infrequently, but it rarely comes to light.

11

Propaganda and the East

Africa and Asia have already been mentioned in the previous chapter in connection with liturgical dance. But strictly speaking they fall under the Congregation for the Evangelization of Peoples (C.E.P.). This unwieldy mouthful was invented by Paul VI in 1967 as a new name for the Congregation *de Propaganda Fide* (which meant propagating or spreading the faith).

Propaganda began life, somewhat chancily, as covering a geographically definable 'sector' of Catholic life rather than a particular category (priests, bishops or religious). Since the same applies to the much more modern Congregation for the Oriental Churches (C.O.C.), they slot easily together into one chapter.

Propaganda started in the sixteenth century under St Pius V and Gregory XIII to handle two rather distinct problems: the evangelization of what were known as the East and West Indies, and the survival of the Church in the parts of Europe that had succumbed to some form of Protestantism. So its ambitious task was to conquer the new world and recover the old.

But it faded out of existence altogether at the start of the seventeenth century and had to be resuscitated by Gregory XV in June 1622. Thereafter it rarely looked back. The Prefect of Propaganda was known as 'the red pope' because his power was thought to rival that of the Jesuit General, dubbed 'the black pope'. It is still in the sumptuous buildings handily placed near the Spanish Embassy (and the Spanish Steps). This proximity is not accidental. Spain was the leader in Catholic missionary work until the nineteenth century, when France began to play a leading role and Holland, Belgium and Ireland had an importance far exceeding their numbers. Today, as the *Annuario Pontificio* puts it with infuriating vagueness, 'the territories dependent on the Sacred Congregation comprise some regions of south-east Europe and the Americas, almost all Africa, the Far East, New Zealand and Oceania with the exception of Australia and almost the whole of the Philippines.'

So the C.E.P. is responsible in practice for the 'young Churches' in

what were once called 'mission territories'. The semantic change
came about with the realization that the whole Church was missionary and because the Church has a mission to the whole world. Paris
was equally a mission territory. Ghana could send missionaries to
England. The difference between local churches is that some have
been implanted for a very long time, and grown a little weary, while
others are relatively fresh and full of life: most African churches go
back not much more than a hundred years. They are all sister
churches, as Pope John Paul told me on the way to Africa in 1980.

But if the sister churches are equal, it does seem that some are
more equal than others. Those who are the object of the C.E.P.'s
benevolence tend to grumble a lot about their state of humiliating
dependence. They may be young, but they are not immature. For
example, the Church in Zaïre has fifty-six bishops, and half its population of 20 million are baptized as Catholics. When Pope John Paul
visited it for the first time in May 1980, it was celebrating the hun-
dredth anniversary of the first missionaries. It would seem that the
Church in Zaïre is by now firmly established. It would like to take its
place in the ranks of its sister churches. But it is still firmly under the
tutelage of the C.E.P., tied to its apron strings.

Does this matter? Yes, because the C.E.P. has almost complete
jurisdiction over the young churches – not quite complete, for the
rights of the Congregations for the Doctrine of Faith, the Causes of
Saints, Divine Worship, Catholic Education (as far as universities
go) and the Eastern Churches (where they exist) continue to prevail
in these sometime missionary churches. But that still leaves in the
hands of the C.E.P. the appointment of bishops, which is clearly
decisive. There is also the bond of finance: C.E.P. churches are
dependent on disbursements from the Congregation which, it is
widely believed, go where most 'fidelity' and 'orthodoxy' are displayed. This makes them feel immature, second-rank, dependent.

When Pope John Paul went to Zaïre in 1980, he was greeted by
Cardinal Joseph Malula who regretted, however, that he would not
see a truly African liturgy during his visit: the Vatican organizers of
the journey had forbidden it. Difficult questions of symbolism are
involved in the administration of the sacraments. Bread and wine,
for example, make sense within a Mediterranean culture, but are not
in common use in equatorial Africa. So these symbols are imported
and have to be learned. The question this raises is how much diversity is compatible with unity. At Kampala, Uganda, on 31 July 1969,
the feast of St Ignatius Loyola, Pope Paul VI declared: 'Your Church
must be above all Catholic. But given this first response, we must

pass to the second. . . . You can and must have an African Christianity.'

But when it comes down to the practical expression of 'African
Christianity' there has been considerable hesitation on the brink.
Great declarations of principle do not seem to lead anywhere. Pope
John Paul's attitude to Africanization is, to put it mildly, quizzical.
In the capital of Zaïre, Kinshasa, he expressed himself dialectically
in 1980:

> You seek to be both fully Christian and fully African. The Holy
> Spirit asks us to believe that the leaven of the authentic Gospel has
> the power to raise up Christians in various cultures, with all the
> riches of their heritage, in a purified and transfigured form.
> Africanization involves broad and deep areas which have yet to be
> fully explored, whether this is the question of the language needed
> to present the Christian message in a way which attracts the spirit
> and heart of the people of Zaïre, or the catechism, or theological
> reflection, or the most suitable expression of the common forms of
> Christian life in the liturgy or sacred heart.

What one really needs to know about 'dialectical' expressions is
where exactly the accent falls. Unless we know that, we cannot know
what such sentiments mean.

On his third visit to Africa in August 1985 – the Catholic population of the continent had gone from 56 million to 67 million in the
meantime – Pope John Paul defined the problem of Africanization as
'how to be fully Christian and at the same time fully African'. What
was needed, he said, was a process of 'inculturization'. He recognized that the early missionaries had tended to reject African traditional religion as barbarism and superstition. Yet it contained some
religious values: the omnipresent sense of the divine, the attachment
to the extended family, the appreciation of fecundity. So in the
Cameroons John Paul said there must be no question of rooting out
traditional religion. On the contrary it should be 'purified, elevated
and regenerated'. This formula goes back to Pius XI. But it is
perhaps less helpful than it sounds. For everything depends on how
much 'purification, elevation and regeneration' is required and to
what it must be applied. The twenty-three episcopal conferences of
Africa, meeting in Madagascar in July 1984, formally requested to
be allowed to hold a 'Council' for Africa to discuss, among other matters, Africanization. On the plane on the way out John Paul said he
would prefer to think in terms of a 'Synod'.

One incident which suggested that Pope John Paul was unenthusiastic about certain aspects of Africanization was the abrupt dismissal of Archbishop Emmanuel Milingo from the see of Lusaka, Zambia in August 1982. Born in 1930, ordained priest in 1958 and bishop in 1969, Milingo did not like the way expatriate missionaries in Zambia spurned African culture and religion. They could be charged with cultural imperialism. Their Latin-style worship was too cerebral and dull for Africans. They disapproved of crying babies and women's bare breasts. They thought Mass should start punctually rather than when everyone felt in the right mood.

The result was that many frustrated African Catholics privately returned to *nyanga* (witch-doctors) and the cult of ancestral spirits. A spell at Ann Arbor in Michigan convinced Milingo that Christianity itself had a tradition of healing that could bridge the gap between Christian faith and African culture. The charismatic movement had merely drawn attention to what was in scripture. Moreover, he found that he had a special charism for healing. It became the most notable feature of his ministry. But healing often involved exorcism, the casting out of evil spirits, and the weeping, screaming, shouting, rolling on the floor that accompanied the exorcising disconcerted those unfamiliar with such matters.

Milingo was inevitably denounced by expatriate missionaries, some of them Polish, to the Pro-Nuncio in Lusaka, Archbishop Giorgio Zur. It was said that his healing services were a form of witchcraft. There were other nasty innuendoes. The fact that most of those he healed were women put him in a bad light. But anthropologists said this was only to be expected: in rural areas, African women have a clear place in society; in the cities they have no role, and suffer crises of identity and psychosomatic ailments. In 1978 Milingo was ordered to stop holding healing services. He did his best to obey, sometimes going into hiding to escape his more importunate fans.

The first sign that the C.E.P. had decided to sack Milingo came in a letter he received from Archbishop Zur in April 1980. Milingo was ordered to Rome 'for a period of theological studies and quiet reflection, as well as to seek medical aid from the doctors'. Since there was nothing wrong with his physical health, Milingo assumed that doubts were being cast on his sanity. This was confirmed by Zur's next remark: 'If at the end of such a period the doctors find you in good health, and if the Holy See receives from your Grace all the necessary guarantees that could make it possible for you to lead the diocese in a positive and fruitful manner, you will be allowed to resume office. If not, the diocese will have to be entrusted to a new ordinary.' It is fair to describe this as a threatening letter, even an ultimatum: conform or face deposition and exile. It is full of cant, and represents the *stylus curiae*, the curial style, at its embarrassing worst.

By now the press had got hold of the story. The Secretary of the C.E.P., Indian Archbishop Simon Lourdasamy, impotently protested, 'This is a family matter, internal to the Church – it does not concern the international press.' That only made the story more irresistible. Lourdasamy had a more valid point when he complained that *Time* and *Newsweek* had not hitherto shown great enthusiasm for the cause of 'Africanization'. Their interest was aroused by the heady brew of witchcraft, sex and authoritarianism.

Milingo never returned to Zambia and was given the newly invented post of 'special delegate' in the Pontifical Commission for Migration and Tourism, an insignificant office under the control of the Congregation of Bishops. No one seems to have thought that the C.E.P. would be the most appropriate perch for an African ex-archbishop. The irony of the whole affair is that Milingo has become internationally known thanks to his sacking. He has acquired a reputation that he would never have had in Lusaka. He has become a symbol, and a rather cheerful one. 'If God made a mistake in creating me an African,' he says, 'it is not yet evident to me.' He has published books, and holds a monthly healing service in Rome.

The reason he appears in this chapter is that he illustrates a point about the Curia in general and the C.E.P. in particular. Perhaps there were good grounds for removing Milingo from Lusaka. An anthropologist on the whole favourable to Milingo pointed out that in African culture 'the functions of healing and leading cannot be combined: the healer is not the chief, and the chief is not the healer.' This may be so, though the Vatican is not usually so sophisticated in its judgements. What matters is that the case against Milingo has never been properly explained or expounded. At the very least there was a miscarriage of justice. Secretiveness and lack of due process are inevitable when administrative and judicial powers are concentrated in the same body. The Milingo story also illustrates that authority of the C.E.P. over its bishops is more thoroughgoing than that of the Congregation of Bishops over those it has helped to appoint.

It would be virtually impossible to dismiss a European or American Archbishop. They would start beating their big drums and saying they were successors of the apostles. Cardinal John J. Cody, for example, survived various attempts to unseat him, ignored all hints to resign and died, Archbishop of Chicago to the last, with these immortal words on his lips: 'I may forgive my enemies – but God won't.' Africans note the contrast: Cody stayed on despite financial scandals that earned a Federal investigation, while Africans can be pushed around at will like children.

The fact that the two most recent Prefects of the C.E.P. have been Europeans with no first-hand experience of work in the third world confirms this gloomy analysis. It suggests that in Pope John Paul's mind the principal function of the C.E.P. is one of control. In the summer of 1984 Dr Dermot Ryan, Archbishop of Dublin, was named as Prefect. This caused as much surprise in Dublin as in Rome. Though not without ability, he was tall, shy and awkward in company, had been Professor of Semitic languages at University College, Dublin, and knew little about the missions. One theory was that he was appointed because there are still a large number of Irish missionaries in the world, some of whom have been infected with the blight of 'liberation theology'. But Ryan had hardly time to unpack his bags, let alone show his hand, for he died on 21 February 1985. At his Requiem Mass the Pope described Ryan as 'practical and courageous, pastorally interested in all, and convinced – as he used to say – that the Church must do what it can to save its members where they are to be found'. That did not help much. It entered the anthology of Pope John Paul's riddles.

Ryan was succeeded by the sixty-one-year-old Slovak, Archbishop Jozef Tomko. Tomko has been in Rome since the late 1940s. He has a doctorate in social sciences from the Gregorian University (1951–4) but has spent most of his life working as a canonist in the Congregation for the Doctrine of Faith. Pope John Paul II made him Archbishop and General Secretary of the Synod in 1979. So he organized the Synod of 1980 on marriage, and that of 1983 on penance and reconciliation. Under his guidance the Synod as an institution lost whatever independence it might have had, and became an echo of the pontifical voice. It is difficult to find anything in Tomko's background that would make him the right man to head the mission department. He is an organization man, sound on Africanization and liberation theology. The idea of a special council for the sister churches of Africa has been mooted; but if it is to be conducted under Tomko and if previous form is anything to go by, it will be a ruthlessly organized and utterly predictable event.

What makes this all rather sad is that between the 1920s and the 1950s Propaganda had a great tradition and was easily the most innovatory congregation in the Curia. It anticipated the process of decolonization that many missionaries, if no one else, already knew was inevitable. One of the great unsung heroes of the Church at this time was Mgr Celso Constantini. (See Agostino Giovanogli, '*Pio XII e la decolonizzazione*', in Riccardi, *Pio XII*.) Constantini was Secretary of Propaganda from 1933 to 1952. He came from a small village near Udine in the Veneto, was in the Pope John mould and, like him, had been a chaplain in the First World War. He was sent to China as Apostolic Delegate in 1922, where his brief was to set up a Chinese hierarchy. In 1924 he held the first Council of Chinese Catholics, and in 1926 led his first Chinese bishops on pilgrimage to Rome. This roused the ire of the French, who claimed the right to oversee the nomination of bishops.

China was the testing ground of the most advanced missionary theologies. On his return to Propaganda as Secretary Constantini began to apply them more widely. By raising missionary awareness – and also by collecting money through the local Associations for the Propagation of the Faith – Propaganda gave practical expression to what later was called 'collegiality'. The sister churches were seen to be interdependent and in solidarity with each other.

By its emphasis on the importance of a 'native' clergy and bishops, it anticipated what the Council taught on 'the local church'; it implicitly contains the 'whole Church' and has all its tasks. The need for a vernacular liturgy became increasingly clear the more the Church moved into remoter and non-European cultural realms: the Mass in Latin might make sense in Perugia or Paris, but in Peking it did not. Constantini was made a Cardinal in December 1952; he was in effect kicked upstairs. It broke his heart. He complained to Montini and was disappointed, but he did not give in. Almost his last act was to write a 200-page memo on the urgent need for better ecumenical relations in mission territories. Constantini's argument was simple: quarrels originating in Europe in the sixteenth or seventeenth century made no sense whatsoever when transported to China or India. Christian divisions were a scandal. (Text in *Irénikon*, 1959.) Constantini died on 16 October 1958, just a few days before Angelo Roncalli was elected Pope John XXIII. He would not have voted for Roncalli (at least in the first ballot), but he set the agenda for his Council. (See Hebblethwaite, *John XXIII, Pope of the Council*.) With his breadth of vision, Constantini puts to shame his successors.

The Congregation for the Oriental Churches (C.O.C.) started in 1862 as a specialist commission within Propaganda. It became an independent congregation in 1917 and its range was extended in 1938 when its prefect, the former French cavalry officer, Eugène Tisserant, took charge and ran it for the next twenty years. It has always been small, its waters have rarely run smoothly, the churches it deals with have known tragedy and dissolution; and yet its theological importance remains great. The C.O.C. deals partly with a geographical area and partly with specific churches. Its patch is mostly the Middle East (Egypt, Ethiopia, Bulgaria, Cyprus, Greece, Iran, the Lebanon, Palestine, Syria, Jordan, Turkey and Iraq). The systematic use of 'Palestine' instead of 'Israel' makes both a semantic and a diplomatic point: Israel has not yet been recognized by the Vatican; certainly the 'Uniate' Churches have a good deal to do with this judgement, which is seen as offensive by Jews. These Oriental churches in communion with the Bishop of Rome are sometimes known as Uniate Churches, a term they do not much like. They have their own rites, their own forms of worship, their own traditions and customs – including, usually, a married clergy. They are therefore a witness to the diversity that is possible within Catholicism. And diversity is an enrichment.

So 'Roman' Catholicism is not the norm for everyone: there are also perfectly legitimate and valid Coptic, Ethiopian, Maronite, Malabar, Melchite, Syrian, Armenian, Chaldean, Greek, Georgian, Hungarian and Slovakian versions of Catholicism. I have left out of the list the two churches which up to the end of the Second World War were the largest: the Ukrainian Catholic Church, which numbered 4,340,000, was forcibly and shamefully 'converted' to Orthodoxy, and the Romanian Catholic Church of a million and a half was also suppressed. If they survive at all on their home ground, it is as 'underground Churches'.

But while it might be consoling to have such great theological importance – so much so that the 'Uniate solution' has been proposed as the key to the reconciliation of the Anglican Communion with Rome – in practice the Oriental Churches are overwhelmed by their much more numerous Roman Catholic brothers. They are only 11 million out of 810,484,000. (*Osservatore Romano*, English, 29 October 1984.) They feel they do not count for much. They are a mere tootle on the fife in the great Catholic symphony. They dread 'Latinization' and the loss of their venerable traditions, and fear they may be sacrificed on the altar of ecumenism. The Russian Orthodox Church, for example, plainly detests the Ukrainian Catholic Church and does not wish to see it revived in the Soviet Union. Since the Catholic Church is in dialogue with the Russian Orthodox, the Ukrainians and other Oriental Churches feel squeezed out. Exile augments neurosis, and they also think that the C.O.C. is merely the instrument of these repressive policies.

True, they joined in the general rejoicing over the election of the

Slav Pope in 1978. For the first time in history they had a Pope who could speak their language. Moreover, Pope John Paul shares in the messianic nationalism which holds that the appalling sufferings of the Slav peoples – the Golgotha of the Ukraine, for example, and the martyrdom of Poland – mysteriously prepare a resurrection.

On the other hand he is Polish; and the Poles, Slavs by race but Latin by Church tradition, have been notorious as 'Latinizers'. No one was more aware of this than Cardinal Josef Slipyi, the Major Archbishop of the Ukrainians, who ruled over the remaining 823,000 Ukrainian Catholics in exile, mostly living in Canada and the U.S.A. Slipyi had been released from a Soviet labour camp in 1963, thanks to Pope John. Though gratified at being named a Cardinal, he considered this a 'Western' label of little relevance and claimed instead the traditional Oriental title of 'Patriarch'. Pope Paul VI said no: the Ukrainians had no historic tradition of a patriarch and, anyway, no longer had a territory. But a patriarch must have a territory. The Ukrainian Church was split into pro- and anti-patriarchate factions. The Ukrainian Bishop in London was stoned by hotheads, and Slipyi showed his mettle by calling a Synod (illicitly, according to the C.O.C.).

Pope John Paul tackled these problems with despatch and panache. He was able to lecture the Ukrainians in their own language. To show who was really in charge, he himself – not the would-be patriarch – called a Synod of the Ukrainian Church in the spring of 1980. He summoned the Ukrainian bishops to Rome. He set them the task of electing a 'co-adjutor with right of succession' to the now eighty-eight-year-old Slipyi. Not surprisingly they elected Miroslav Lubachivsky, whom the Pope had personally ordained Ukrainian Metropolitan of Philadelphia, and who was thought to be opposed to the patriarchate. He succeeded Slipyi when this astonishing old man eventually died in September 1984.

Meanwhile, Polish Cardinal Ladislaw Rubin was made Prefect of the C.O.C. in June 1980. File closed: end of the Ukrainian affair. Pope John Paul's words to the Ukrainian Synod in 1980 seemed to have come to pass: 'With all my heart I wish to ensure the internal unity of your Church and its unity with the see of Peter.'

But of course that did not stop the complaints. The C.O.C. had always been worried about married priests. They would be fine in the Ukraine to which, however, they were no longer admitted; but elsewhere they made Roman priests look enviously in their direction, and so ordinations were banned outside the Ukraine. Slipyi got round this by ordaining the married men in Rome and slipping them into North America as 'missionaries'. No sooner had Slipyi died than Rubin wrote a reproachful letter to Ukrainian bishops everywhere. I quote this as another example of the 'curial style' which still prevails in the Vatican:

> It is not without true regret that I fulfil my duty of calling your Excellency's attention to the shortcomings and the abuses that have been occurring in the Ukrainian eparchy for quite some time and greatly worry the Holy See.
> 1. A certain number of priests, ordained *illicite et in fraudem legis* (illicitly and in defiance of the law), for which they were suspended *a divinis*, continue to celebrate Mass and carry out the pastoral ministry to the great scandal of the faithful. . . . I ask your excellency to present to this Sacred Congregation a list of all these priests. . . .
> 2. As regards the question of the Ukrainian patriarchate, I am sure that your Excellency will not fail to comply with the decisions and instructions from the Holy See. . . . A difficult attitude, at such a delicate moment, would gravely upset many faithful and do serious damage to the Ukrainian Church, especially the one in the motherland.
> 3. Among the Ukrainian clergy of the eparchy, a certain dissatisfaction is spreading because of a lack of discipline and spiritual life, giving rise to a pseudo-patriotism, dangerous for ecclesiastical life. The duty of your Excellency as a good shepherd is to re-establish peace and harmony with the aid of Our Lord Jesus Christ. (*National Catholic Reporter*, 30 November 1984)

So the C.O.C., like most Roman departments, knows exactly what is going on, and brandishes concepts such as 'scandal of the faithful' and 'grave damage in the motherland' (i.e. the Ukraine) without any need to produce evidence for its peremptory judgements. A tone of unctuous piety combined with bureaucratic smugness is maintained throughout the missive. The language is that of service; the implication is one of power. In autumn 1985 Rubin retired on grounds of ill-health, and was replaced by . . . Lourdasamy.

There remains one dicastery of the 'old Curia': the Congregation of Religious and Secular Institutes. Does it have the same concern with power?

12

The Professionals

The Vatican Council's decree *On Religious Life* (Latin title: *De Accommodata renovatione*) was one of its most radical documents. It not only exhorted religious – those under the three vows of poverty, chastity and obedience – to renewal; it offered them five criteria of renewal which, taken seriously, could lead a long way.

The five criteria were:
1. 'Since the fundamental norm of the religious life is a following of Christ as proposed by the Gospel, such is to be regarded by all communities as *their supreme law.*'
2. Communities should have their 'own spirit and character' based on their founder's special grace or charism.
3. But they should share in the life of the Church generally and catch up where need be on the biblical, liturgical, ecumenical, social and missionary movements.
4. They must be aware of the needs of the Church and the world *today*. This will enable them to serve the people of today more effectively.
5. But even the most desirable changes will fail unless sustained by a spiritual renewal which brings out the point of religious life: it is a sign to the world that God matters overridingly. (Paraphrased for clarity)

General Chapters were to be summoned to bring about this renewal. An attempt was made – more or less energetically – to involve all the members of a given community in the process of renewal. Historical studies had to be done to define more precisely what this elusive 'spirit of the founder' was. For the older religious orders – Benedictines, Dominicans, Franciscans, Carmelites and Jesuits, for example – the task was relatively easy: at least there was something to work on and a substantial body of spiritual literature. Many nineteenth-century orders, especially of women, had founders who could be distinguished only with difficulty from other founders. They were mostly pious women who had gathered a local group to help the bishop in schools, hospitals or social work. Or they were missionaries. Many resolved the difficulty by saying they shared in Jesuit or Franciscan spirituality. But there was an immense amountof fairly agonizing reappraisal. The ten years from 1965 to 1975 were spent in a quest for identity. The roots were taken up and shaken vigorously. In certain cases this killed the plant.

Overseeing and monitoring, though not exactly controlling all this many-sided activity was the Congregation for Religious and Secular Institutes (C.R.S.I.). Its history was not particularly glorious. Most of its time was spent in ordering women back into the enclosure whenever they wanted to venture out among the poorest. Founded in 1586 by Sixtus V, it was incorporated into the Congregation of Bishops in 1601, where it plodded along, forbidding and dispensing, until St Pius X made it autonomous in 1908. In addition to every aspect of religious life, the 'third orders' also fall under its competence. 'Secular institutes' were thrown in in February 1947. The New Code of Canon Law defines a secular institute as 'an institute of consecrated life in which Christ's faithful, living in the world, strive for the perfection of charity and endeavour to contribute to the sanctification of the world, especially from within'. For some time Opus Dei was happy with this description: in fact they sang the *Te Deum* when it was granted to them. But later Opus Dei changed its mind and then its status: from being a 'secular institute' it became a 'personal prelature', a quasi-non-territorial diocese, and so moved out of C.R.S.I. and into the charge of the Congregation of Bishops.

C.R.S.I. has two distinct sections, each with an under-secretary: Fr Jesus Torres C.M.F. for religious and Fr Mario Albertini for secular institutes. One feature of C.R.S.I. is that it employs a fair number of religious and – surprise, surprise! – some of them are women. American Sr Mary Linscott, of the Sisters of Notre Dame of Namur, ranks just below the under-secretaries. Her task, and it is a hot seat, is to 'deal with the chapters and constitutions for religious communities of women'. In October 1985 she was promoted and given the same responsibility for men. Of the twenty-seven religious assigned to C.R.S.I. ten are women – which scarcely seems a fair proportion when we consider that at the last count there were 941,031 sisters in the world compared with 154,148 religious priests and 68,994 brothers. But at least the sisters have secured a modest bridgehead in the Curia from which they could fan out in other directions. In C.R.S.I. they are not merely typists and telephone operators.

The Prefect of C.R.S.I., Belgian Cardinal Jérôme Hamer, is a Dominican; his predecessor from 1976 to 1984 was Argentinian Cardinal Eduardo Pironio, who was not a religious. Before that, from 1963 to 1976, there was the wholly catastrophic figure of Cardinal Ildebrando Antoniutti. He was not a religious either. So there is no rule about it, or even custom.

Pironio was shunted sideways in 1984 to the Pontifical Council for the Laity, which in a secular administration would have been seen as 'downward mobility'. That he should be replaced by Hamer, who earned a hard-line reputation in ten years at the C.D.F., confirmed the view that Pironio had shown insufficient resolution in dealing with C.L.A.R. (the Federation of Religious of Latin America). Pironio's sympathies with liberation theology, together with his informality – he has actually been seen in his office in his shirtsleeves – counted against him. Cardinal Alfonso Lopez Trujillo, Archbishop of Medellín, convinced Pope John Paul that the renewal of the Latin American Church would have to begin with the religious. But there had to be a firmer hand than the relaxed Pironio could provide. He was too much a man of the 1970s and post-conciliar optimism.

This was not a mood ever shared by Cardinal Karol Wojtyla. As early as October 1972 he suggested to the Synod Council that Religious Life (*De Vita Religiosa*) would make a good theme for the forthcoming Synod. This suggestion was not adopted, because no one thought it was such an urgent matter. But Karol Wojtyla wrote a brief paper which showed how deeply concerned he already was.

He began with the blunt statement that religious life is in a state of *crisis*. The evidence was crisply summarized: 'Defections; lack of vocations; infidelity in the keeping of the vows'. The second paragraph proposed remedies for this sad state of affairs based on the principle of 'a better insertion in the present-day mission of the Church'. He proposed that this 'better insertion' should be achieved on the universal level by closer links with the Pope, and on the local level by closer links with the bishops. That 'better insertion in the life of the Church' was really a euphemism for greater control by the bishops was apparent from the remark that there should be another look at 'exemption', the juridical device which makes some orders less dependent on the local bishops. (Giovanni Caprile. S.J., *Karol Wojtyla e il Sinodo dei Vescovi*.) The Jesuits thought this was aimed at them. They were not mistaken.

At the 1974 Synod on Evangelization Cardinal Wojtyla, whose role was merely that of *rapporteur*, nevertheless launched an attack on liberation theology, which had been defended by Cardinal Evaristo

Arns and Dom Helder Câmara, both of Brazil. Wojtyla replied:

> As for the link between liberation and the Gospel, some think that
> the effort to liberate man is connected with the very nature of the
> Gospel; others regard it as the proof of the credibility of the Gospel
> and quote 'the poor have the Gospel preached to them'; others,
> finally, consider the effort towards human promotion to be the
> fruit of the virtue of charity. This last approach is the most accept-
> able since there is a danger that social justice, deprived of the
> impulse of love, may fail to be directed to the service of man. (*Ibid*)

Wojtyla held and holds the last approach: in his third encyclical,
Dives in Misericordia (30 November 1980), he explains that the exclusive pursuit of justice can lead to profound injustice. He cannot be
charged with inconsistency: a straight line can be drawn from 1972
to the actions of the 1980s.

The crisis in religious life was exemplified in the Jesuits, still with
25,990 the largest religious order – but they had had 9,000 'defections' in the previous ten years. Yet the Jesuit General, the Basque Fr
Pedro Arrupe, seemed unruffled. He did not lose hope or speak of
'defections'. He expected people to go on serving the Church. 'You
will make a good layman but never a good Jesuit,' he said to the
Dutch poet Huub Oosterhuis as he charismatically dismissed him.
Arrupe also believed that there were two ways to leave the Society of
Jesus: some left to resolve a psychological problem and all one could
say was 'God bless you'; but there were others whose departure sig-
nalled that the Society of Jesus was in some respects failing. These
attitudes were anathema to Karol Wojtyla. Moreover, Arrupe's position as President of the Conference of Major Superiors (a Union of
Fathers and Mothers General in Rome) meant that his influence had
extended to other orders of men and women – even to the Dominicans, their traditional rivals. So the Society of Jesus would have to be
made an example of, *pour décourager les autres*.

The Jesuits provided the rope by which they would be hanged
when they opposed known or suspected papal policies on Central
America. The position of the Pontifical Commission for Latin
America (C.A.L.), a dependency of the Congregation of Bishops,
presided over by Cardinal Sebastiano Baggio, was that an all-encom-
passing or 'global' solution could be found to the problems of Central
America. The religious, who provide 70 per cent of the priests of the
region and were in touch with what was happening on the ground,
thought that the Church's approach could not be identical where a

civil war was raging as in El Salvador, a military dictatorship was in power as in Guatemala, or a left-wing regime had replaced a hated dictatorship as in Nicaragua. These matters were debated in a highly secret meeting of C.A.L. from 8 to 12 June 1981.

The religious were allowed to win the theoretical debate, but when the conclusions of the meeting were eventually published it was clear that they had lost the practical argument. It was resolved, for example, that 'in view of unity and ecclesial communion, the conferences of religious should refrain from taking positions or making statements without the previous agreements of the Bishops.' Major religious superiors such as Arrupe or Vincent de Couénongle, Master General of the Dominicans, would be allowed to visit the countries concerned, provided that 'the visits were announced in good time and had sufficient preparation'. Religious, in short, were perceived as a source of trouble. They would have to be curbed.

Arrupe's letter to the Provincials of Latin America (8 December 1980) was particularly resented. In it he had asked, 'Can a Christian, a Jesuit, adopt Marxist analysis, so long as he distinguishes it from Marxist philosophy or ideology, and also from Marxist praxis, at least considered in its totality?' Arrupe's answer, lengthy and carefully stated, was 'no': 'To adopt therefore not just some elements or some methodological insights, but Marxist analysis as a whole, is something that we cannot accept.' This qualified rejection of Marxism, however, was regarded as inadequate by Baggio, Lopez Trujillo and the Pope. Arrupe's removal now became inevitable.

Arrupe inadvertently helped matters by suffering a stroke on 7 August 1981. He was left paralysed down one side and largely dumb. A New Yorker, Fr Vincent O'Keefe, became his Vicar according to the Constitutions. But on 5 October 1981, Cardinal Agostino Casaroli appeared unexpectedly at the Jesuit Curia and read out to Arrupe a letter which informed him that the eighty-year-old and almost blind Jesuit, Fr Paolo Dezza, had been named the 'personal delegate of the Supreme Pontiff to the Society of Jesus'. This was known, not entirely humorously, as 'the *putsch* of Borgo Santo Spirito'. Rumour had it that some unemployed Roman Cardinal, possibly Paolo Bertoli, had originally been envisaged as the man most likely to 'normalize' the Jesuits, but that Cardinal Carlo Maria Martini had persuaded the Pope that this would be a catastrophic mistake: to fire a warning shot across the Jesuit bows was one thing; to deprive them of sails, rigging and compass would be quite another and equivalent to a second suppression.

The Jesuits took the body blow very well. There were neither resignations nor very public protests. John Paul later admitted in his speech to Jesuit Superiors on 27 February 1982 that they had passed 'the test' (*la prova*) with flying colours. So was it all much ado about nothing? The 'personal delegate of the Supreme Pontiff', Fr Paolo Dezza, Paul VI's confessor, had in fact quietly outmanoeuvred Pope John Paul. He left everything as it was, and gave unimpeachable assurances of loyalty while kicking boldly for touch and playing for time – that is, the return of properly constitutional government. The Pope could not allow the anomalous situation to continue indefinitely, and the Jesuits had not risen in rebellion, so normal service was resumed in September-October 1983 when the thirty-third General Congregation elected the Dutchman Peter-Hans Kolvenbach, at the first ballot, as successor to Pedro Arrupe. The Italian press had predicted that Sardinian Fr Giuseppe Pittau, Dezza's number two and the Pope's candidate, would be elected. Wrong again.

The first thing Kolvenbach did was to embrace Arrupe and thank him for his exemplary obedience. There was not a dry eye in the Curia. The election of Kolvenbach and the documents of the General Congregation proved that the Jesuits were not repudiating Arrupe or the policies associated with him. Sovereignty was restored to the General Congregation.

At the same time there was drama at the Dominican General Chapter to elect de Couénongle's successor. The first man chosen, on 2 September 1983, was Fr Albert Nolan, who lives in a Johannesburg slum among the blacks he serves. He warned the delegates that he would not accept. They ignored this and he was elected despite his protests. He resigned immediately saying that he 'questioned the idea that the order needed someone to symbolize the aspirations to justice found among today's Dominicans. All Dominicans should be committed to this work – not just the Master-General.' So instead they elected the Irishman Fr Damian Byrne, who said how much he admired Fr Albert and also Fr Edward Schillebeeckx, the Flemish theologian working in the Netherlands, who was an object of C.D.F. curiosity first for his work on christology and then for that on ministry.

What all this indicated was that the Jesuits and Dominicans were now shoulder to shoulder, and were not going to be intimidated. The weakness of C.R.S.I. became apparent: unlike Propaganda it has no funds to disburse, unlike the Congregation of Bishops it has no patronage to offer and, unable to dictate to the Conference of Major Superiors, it has to negotiate from a position of weakness.

The Jesuits and Dominicans were strong enough to resist papal pressures and remain faithful to their vision of Vatican II. They bide their time, knowing that the pontificate will not last for ever. It might seem that the 13,000 Carmelite nuns, enclosed, contemplative and voiceless in the counsels of the Church, would prove easier game. One of the first 'decisions' under the new regime of Hamer was to impose on the Carmelite sisters the 1581 Constitution of St Teresa of Avila rather than the revised Constitution drawn up after Vatican II, which had been used experimentally for five years. Eighty per cent of the sisters, the wave of the future, voted for the new Constitution, whereupon the 20 per cent minority, mostly nostalgic Spanish sisters, cried foul and appealed to Rome.

To everyone's surprise, Cardinal Agostino Casaroli, in a letter dated 15 October 1984 and addressed to the Carmelite General, Fr Felipe Sáinz de Baranda, took the side of the minority. Once again the unfortunate Casaroli was cast as the hatchet-man, as he had been in the case of Arrupe. Yet he was merely carrying out papal orders.

It was an odd letter in any terms. The criteria laid down at the start of this chapter were reduced to one, and Casaroli's letter said that 'unity must be indissolubly tied to fidelity to the charism of the founder.' That begged the question. The letter also made the insulting suggestion that those who could not accept the 1581 Constitution should 'seek other forms of consecrated life'. Sáinz de Baranda dutifully wrote to the Carmelites asking them to accept the decision 'despite the judgement which we think the dispositions of the Pope and the letter of the Secretary of State may deserve'. He meant that they didn't think much of either.

But at the same time Sáinz de Baranda courageously wrote to Pope John Paul objecting to the 'harsh and polemical tone' of Casaroli's letter. He pointed out that the new Constitution had been approved by Pope Paul VI, and that the vast majority of sisters wanted legislation 'loyal both to the Teresan charism and to the documents of Vatican II'. Six months later C.R.S.I. climbed down just a little. There was no apology. It announced that it would 'act in the light of the second Vatican Council and consider the experiments and events of recent years'. That ought in principle to rule out a simple return to 1581, though 'in the light of Vatican II' can prove a fairly elastic concept.

All the negotiations in this affair were conducted according to custom by the General of the male Carmelites. However, there are some Carmelite prioresses, among them Ruth Burrows of Quidenham, near Norwich, England, a well-known spiritual writer, who are more capable of redefining St Teresa's charism than the staff of C.R.S.I.

Carmelites like others knew that they had a choice: to adapt and renew themselves – or go under.

Of all religious families, the Franciscans are the least likely to founder. Francis' love for Lady Poverty is capable of endless applications in the modern world: the 'option for the poorest' made by Leonardo Boff and Cardinals Evaristo Arns and Aloisio Lorscheider is not unconnected with the fact that they are Franciscans. Franciscans have been prominent in the peace movement. Besides, if the three branches of the Order are taken together, they are the largest order in the world. There are 20,262 Friars Minor (O.F.M.), 4,013 Conventuals (O.F.M. Conv.), and 12,206 Capuchins (O.F.M. Cap.). That makes a total of 36,881 assorted Franciscans. Here is a rule of thumb to tell them apart: Friars Minor (like Boff) shave, while Conventuals (like St Maximilian Kolbe) and Capuchins (like Padre Pio) wear beards; but the Conventuals have a black habit and the Capuchins a brown one. They work together increasingly, but keep their organizational independence.

The Franciscans had so far kept a low profile and, it seemed, led a charmed life. True, the Brazilians were in trouble because of liberation theology. There were also strange goings-on in mountainous Bosnia-Hercegovina, Yugoslavia, where for many centuries the Friars Minor had run the Church in a Turkish Islamic setting. They had the privilege of growing moustaches as a display of symbolic *machismo*. In 1981 C.R.S.I. summoned the entire leadership of the Franciscans in Bosnia-Hercegovina to Rome and dismissed them for insubordiantion to the local bishops. Our Lady then appeared (it was said) at Medjugorje and supported the ousted Franciscans.

But apart from such limited and exceptional cases, the Franciscans did not appear to have incurred the wrath of the Holy See in a general way until in May 1985 the Friars Minor, the largest group, met in chapter at Assisi. Where else should they meet than in the place where the spirit of St Francis is almost palpable? They assembled on 13 May 1985, feast of Our Lady of Fátima and fourth anniversary of the assassination attempt on the Pope. On that very day the *Osservatore Romano* published an astonishing letter from Pope John Paul virtually ordering the Chapter to reject the work of the last fifteen years and return to the true spirit of St Francis. This time he did not shelter behind Casaroli. The tone was as tough as anything the Jesuits had to bear, and even in some respects harsher. The Pope insisted that 'the Rule of St Francis must be observed just as it was approved by the Church.' The Franciscans were not a 'a mere "movement" open to new options continually replaced by others in an incessant search for identity as if this had not been found'. The Pope criticized endless 'new readings' which 'threaten to replace the text of the Rule with interpretations of it or at least to obscure the simplicity and purity with which it was written by St Francis'.

This was, to put it mildly, a rather jaundiced and one-sided account of what the Franciscans had been up to. But the real reason for this vehement attack was only revealed in the second part of the letter. The allusion to liberation theology was implicit but clear. 'Fraternity', for example, to which St Francis attached so much importance, must not – John Paul went on – 'assume ambiguous meanings which, while favouring independence, fail to protect justice'. What precisely is the danger lurking in 'fraternity'? The Pope said it could lead to 'a ruinous crisis of authority' (which sounds more like 'fraternity' as conceived by the French Revolution than by St Francis). Finally the cat was let out of the bag when the Pope reminded the Franciscans that the poverty preached by St Francis 'does not confine itself to proclamations in defence of the poor'. It should, on the contrary, be lived out in daily life and should be largely invisible so that the life of the Franciscan 'is more one of silence than [of] propaganda'. In the Italian magazine *Panorama*, Giancarlo Zizola claimed that the papal letter was the work of Bishop Bonaventura Kloppenburg O.F.M. working in cahoots with Fr Umberto Betti O.F.M., a consultor of the C.D.F. That could well be so. But the Pope signed it. Apart from question of authorship, it might have been relevant to ask how many of the 20,262 Friars Minor were thought actually to have fallen into these traps. Was this not another *procès de tendance*, a 'worst-case scenario'?

Before these questions could be asked, let alone answered, it was revealed that Archbishop Vicenzo Fagiolo, Secretary of C.R.S.I., would personally preside over the Franciscan chapter to ensure that the considerations mentioned above would be taken into account and the right people would be appointed to implement them. The Pope said he had assigned Fagiolo 'a delicate task'. That was an understatement. Fagiolo did not improve matters by declaring early on that there was 'no substantial difference between the Word of God and the word of the Pope'. (Mark Day, *The National Catholic Reporter*, 5 July 1985.)

Nothing is more calculated to rouse a religious order from lethargy so much as an attack on its autonomy. No matter how pacific St Francis was, his followers have always proved resolute in the defence of their own interests. That is what happened on this occasion. Forelocks were vaguely tugged in the papal direction, but the view

was that the Pope's letter was about some imaginary body, an
invented bugaboo, and not about the Friars Minor. On the day it
was published, Californian Fr John Vaughn, the outgoing Minister
General, spoke about the new challenges the Order had to face, especially in third world countries. He reproached his brothers with com-
placently accepting traditional patterns of ministry and being too
much influenced by consumerism. This, said Fr Vaughn, stopped
them grasping the chance to serve the refugees and the victims of
world hunger.

These blameless remarks were greeted with a five-minute stand-
ing ovation. Not surprisingly, on 25 May 1985 Vaughn was re-
elected as Minister General by 117 out of the 135 delegates. This was
an endorsement of his policies and a polite rejection of the caricature
of the Friars presented in the papal letter. It was also a rebuff to
Fagiolo of C.R.S.I., whose attempt to discredit Vaughn in the wings
totally failed and caused some delegates to leak chapter news to the
press (though they had been forbidden to talk to anyone).

Moreover, the Friars released a statement which any ordinary
person would have construed as an outright rejection of the papal letter. The key passage read:

> It is too late for us to turn back. As Franciscans, we cannot start all
> over again. We are not going in search of our identity. Our move-
> ment in the world is not generated by a search for our identity. It
> *is* our identity. It is the fruit of centuries of history, doctrine, trad-
> itions and of commitment to the world. (*National Catholic Reporter*,
> 21 June 1985)

The re-elected Vaughn, however, took the advice of a commission of
the chapter which recommended the restoration of the post of 'cardinal protector'. St Francis had certainly found Cardinal Hugolino
helpful in his day. But Pope Paul VI abolished this office (for Franciscans and others) on the grounds that he should communicate
directly with the General of an order without the need of an intermediary. John Paul II wants it restored. Why? The theory is that the
'cardinal protector', far from being a curial watchdog over the Franciscans, would enable them to have 'better communications' with
the Pope. But that assumes that the only problem is 'inadequate
communications'. It might be that there is a different conception of
what Franciscan life is all about, in which case adding the buffer of a
'cardinal protector' will make little difference.

With Jesuits, Dominicans, Carmelites and Franciscans all holding out for renewal, where can Pope John Paul turn for support and consolation? He might have turned to Opus Dei, but they have migrated into another place. Or, to judge by his address to the twenty-second Salesian General Chapter, held in Rome in April 1984, he can turn in hope to the sons of St John Bosco, the Salesians (named after St Francis de Sales, the seventeenth-century bishop of Annecy in Savoy, whom Leigh Hunt called 'the gentleman saint'). Their special task was the education of the children of the poor. There are plenty of them: 16,869 at the end of 1982.

Founded in the pontificate of Pius IX, they were even more ultramontane than the nineteenth-century Jesuits. The Jesuits at least sometimes remembered they had another tradition, as Fr Polanco, Ignatius' secretary, wrote to the Jesuits at the Council of Trent: 'If the members of the Society are papists, they are so in so far as they should be and not otherwise, and even then only out of a desire for the glory of God and the common good.' (*Monumenta Nadal*.) This liberating distinction was recalled by the Jesuit General Kolvenbach in his first major letter to the whole Society dated 3 March 1985. The Salesians had no such alternative tradition to fall back on.

They commended themselves to Pope John Paul for their general docility and because Cardinal August Hlond, Primate of Poland at the outbreak of the Second World War and throughout its course, was a Salesian. John Paul quoted fragments of his spiritual teaching: 'In the Salesian Congregation I have learned that work is neither a burden nor a cross but a joy...' and 'Every cross is a stone, every suffering a brick, and tears provide the cement. This is the way the saints build, this is how Don Bosco built.' (*Bolletino* of the Vatican Press Office, 3 April 1984.) It is possible without spiritual snobbery to find such maxims less than wholly convincing. It remains to add that two of the most 'delicate' episcopal appointments in Central America have gone to Salesians: Arturo Rivera y Damas in San Salvador, who succeeded the murdered Oscar Romero after a suspicious three-year hesitation, and Miguel Obando Bravo, Archbishop of Managua, Nicaragua, whose sterling opposition to the Sandinistas was rewarded with a cardinal's hat early in 1985.

But this survival of Victorian values is rare. The Salesians are unthreatening so far. One cannot guarantee the future: Don Bosco's desire to work among the poor could turn into a form of liberation theology. One is forced to conclude that C.R.S.I. is more often than not its own worst enemy. It alienates the very people whose support it needs to enlist: the Church's professionals (both in the sense that they are employed full-time and that they are professed of the three vows). Its role has become entirely negative as though it were saying: whatever you are doing, stop it immediately. It resembles Sydney Smith's Mrs Partington who during a storm was observed 'with mop and pattens . . . vigorously pushing away the Atlantic Ocean. . . . The Atlantic Ocean beat Mrs Partington.' It is time to turn to the 'New Curia'.

13

Dialogue with the Lord's Brothers

It has been rightly said that a problem does not exist in the Vatican until there is an office to deal with it.

As Pope John was preparing for the Council in 1960, he realized that the 'old Curia' had little sympathy with the ecumenical cause. Most Italian priests had never met a Protestant, and shunned the occasional Waldensian they might come across. Paul Johnson – the other one – then in charge of the Quaker Conferences for Diplomats, once invited a member of the Roman Curia to lunch. The prelate hesitated and said, 'Well, I think I probably could speak to a Quaker: but *lunch* – no, I think not.' (Stella Alexander, *The Friend*, 11 January 1985.) Cardinal Alfredo Ottaviani, then at the Holy Office, imaged he was showing an ecumenical spirit by encouraging the friars of Taizé to 'come over' to Rome. In true Counter-Reformation spirit 'Protestants' were material for conversion – or for burning.

Matters were little different in England. Bishop Andrew Beck, in a letter to *The Times* in 1949, solemnly explained that he could not say the Lord's Prayer with an Anglican because when Catholics say 'Thy Kingdom come' they are praying for the conversion of all to Catholicism, an intention in which Anglicans obviously could not join. He also refused to give a joint blessing with the Bishop of Winchester on the grounds that the Bishop did not have valid orders and was 'only a layman'. (Christina Scott, *A Historian and his World, A Life of Christopher Dawson*.) These examples illustrate the magnitude of the ecumenical task, and the distance we have travelled.

Pope John's experience in Bulgaria, Turkey and France convinced him that such Counter-Reformation attitudes were outdated. What united Christians was far more important than what kept them apart. John's goodness and spiritual intuition transformed those who hitherto had been regarded as 'heretics', 'schismatics' or, at best, 'dissidents', into 'separated brothers'. And he deplored the separation. His reading of the New Testament told him that Christian divisions were literally a scandal, that is, a stumbling block. His constant prayer was that of St John's Gospel: '*Ut unum sint!* That all may

be one!' (John 17:21). But all this would have petered out unless his
aspirations had been given institutional, even bureaucratic, shape in
the Secretariat for Promoting Christian Unity (known as S.P.U.C.
from its Italian initials). Here was something totally new: a Roman
office whose mission was to learn from others.

The choice of the German Jesuit, Augustin Bea, as the first President of the new body, was inspired. Bea, son of a Bavarian woodcut-
ter, was born in 1881, the same year as John himself. So the two
immensely old patriarchs surprised everyone by embarking on a
great adventure. They demonstrated the youthful vitality of old age.

Bea's orthodoxy was difficult to impugn (which didn't stop Ottaviani trying to impugn it): after all, he had been confessor to Pope
Pius XII, the most nervously orthodox of popes. Yet at same time
Bea had contributed through his teaching and articles to the revival
of Catholic biblical studies, and he felt at ease and on equal terms
with scholarly Protestants and Orthodox.

Bea's long years as Rector of the Biblicum in Rome meant that he
already knew most of the Catholic exegetes who mattered. He
became an indefatigable traveller, and used his travels not only for
ecumenical contacts but to spot likely talent. Bea knew just who had
written on antisemitism in the New Testament (the Canadian Gregory Baum) and who had been following very closely the work of the
World Council of Churches (the Dutchman Jan Willebrands). Bea
brought such men into his Secretariat whether as consultors or as
full-time staff members. Willebrands came and never left, becoming
Secretary and then President on Bea's death in 1969. The present
Secretary and Under-Secretary, White Father Pierre Duprey and
Mgr Jean-François Arrighi, have also been there from these early
years. Some cannot stay away: the American expert on Orthodoxy,
Fr John Long S.J., returned in January 1986 after a few years in
Washington.

One could simply conclude that the members of S.P.U.C. have all
grown old together and are now like hardened veterans for ever
rehearsing the nostalgic tales of the conciliar yesteryear. It is more
relevant to observe that no other department in the Curia can claim
such continuity of personnel and consistency of purpose. S.P.U.C.,
therefore, embodies in a special way the 'spirit of Vatican II'. When
this is attacked, it is the Council that is being attacked. It continues
to keep alive the basic principles, now somewhat threadbare from
repetition, on which ecumenism rests. Christians share, on a deep
level, 'one Lord, one faith, one baptism'. They are therefore properly
called brothers. Those living today are not responsible and not to be

blamed for the divisions that they have inherited. There is an 'ecclesial reality' of other Christian Churches which cannot be denied. The Holy Spirit is at work in the ecumenical movement.

Two conciliar passages in particular constitute the charter of S.P.U.C. The first says that the 'one, true, holy, catholic and apostolic Church . . . subsists in the Catholic church'. (*Lumen Gentium*.) The phrase 'subsists in' replaced the original 'is', and means that there is no simple identification of the two terms and that valid though incomplete 'ecclesial elements' may be found elsewhere.

S.P.U.C. also had to develop the implications of the Council's statement: 'When comparing doctrines, they (i.e. Catholic theologians) should remember that in Catholic teaching there exists an order or "hierarchy" of truths, since they vary in their relationship to the foundation of Christian faith.' (*Unitatis Redintegratio*, 11.) This crucial text was inserted in the final document in response to a speech by Archbishop Andrea Pangrazio, then Archbishop of Gorizia and Gradisca, the diocese next door to Yugoslavia. But it was S.P.U.C. who put him up to it, and the speech was actually drafted by Lukas Vischer of the W.C.C. Without this text, serious theological dialogue could not start: for some doctrines bring us closer to Christ than do others. It further requires that Catholic theologians should be able to demonstrate, so far as they can, the *Christian* content of disputed doctrines, especially those the Roman Catholic Church had introduced after the break-up of Christian unity. Infallibility and the Assumption are the two trickiest examples.

S.P.U.C., then, differed from the rest of the Curia in that its function was to listen to others: it would learn as much as it would teach. It also used a different language, that of the separated brethren. Italian lost its stranglehold and French, English and German – in that order – took over. It had from the start a different style. It was welcoming and hospitable, acting as guide and chaperon to baffled ecumenical visitors to Rome. It also had a different method of work. Instead of toiling away in separate compartments, S.P.U.C. members know what their colleagues are doing, since their work almost invariably overlaps at some point. The late Mgr Richard Stewart, former Professor at Wonersh Seminary, explained how this was achieved. Each member of S.P.U.C. has a threefold responsibility: (1) for a given church (e.g. the Anglican Communion); (2) for a geographical area (his was the United Kingdom and Africa); (3) for a particular problem or theme (such as mixed marriages or intercommunion). The themes are as vast as the geographical areas. But this system makes for greater sharing and communication.

August Hasler, a Swiss priest from the diocese of Chur, had been spotted by Cardinal Bea at an early age. His church was the Lutheran Federation, his geographical area the German-speaking lands, his topic infallibility. He had a row with the *sostituto* at the Secretariat of State, Mgr Giovanni Benelli, whom he accused of confusing the Lutheran doctrine of the Eucharist with that of the Calvinists. This was more than likely. But Hasler was harried out of the S.P.U.C. and slammed the door as he departed – taking with him files, some of them classified, on infallibility at Vatican I. This was widely regarded as ungentlemanly conduct. He then went to work at the *Goethe-Institut* in Rome and, on the basis of the material he had gathered, produced his controversial book, *How the Pope became Infallible*. An introduction by Hans Küng pointed out that according to Hasler, Vatican I was not a truly free Council, and that therefore the doctrine of infallibility ought to be re-received, did not make the book any more welcome in the Vatican. Hasler died in 1981, just winning the race against involuntary laicization. He remains in S.P.U.C.'s folk-memory as the *enfant terrible*.

Apart from a different language, a novel method of work, and some distinguished old boys, S.P.U.C. has another originality that marks it off from the old Curia. It is not alone in the ecumenical field, but is in close contact with some seventy national ecumenical commissions that engage in local ecumenical work. This is where Christians actually meet each other as the people next door. Top ecclesiastical people cannot make Church unity; that was the lesson of the Council of Florence in 1439.

So S.P.U.C. expects from the local churches not just a faithful echo of its own voice, as the C.D.F. does, but authentic feedback. 'They can prod us,' said Mgr Stewart, 'and sometimes we can get them to prod us.' Does S.P.U.C. do any prodding itself? It hasn't usually been necessary. The national delegates like to come to Rome for their annual plenary meeting to 'meet the faces behind the signatures'.

At the 1985 meeting Pope John Paul dropped a broad hint that some local commissions had been proceding too far too fast. 'When you return to your own countries,' he said, 'I hope you will resolve to work in close contact with the Secretariat, since its irreplaceable work is at the service not only of the universal Church but of the local Churches. With its help you can go ahead with imagination and prudence. . .' and so on. (*Osservatore Romano*, English, 13 May 1985.) Was that a warning shot, a touch on the brakes? Were some local commissions, in the celebrated phrase, 'trying to run before they could walk'? As Robert Murray S.J. once said to a Westminster

canon who warned against this danger: 'Canon, no one is asking you
to run, not even to walk; what is expected is that you should be seen
to put one foot in front of the other.' Twenty years after Vatican II,
that seems a modest enough ambition.

In fact S.P.U.C. has achieved much more than that. Its activity
has been prodigious for a body that has never had more than twenty
full-time members. At present there are no fewer than eight important bilateral dialogues under way. In a progress report towards the
end of 1984 New Zealander Mgr Basil Meeking summed up the state
of play. Here it is in his own words which, incidentally, provide a useful introduction to 'ecu-speak', the special jargon in which such discussions are conducted:

1. *The Joint International Commission for the Theological Dialogue between the Catholic Church and the Orthodox Church* came into being only
in 1980 but a major part of the Secretariat's efforts from before the
Council had been devoted 'to the work of restoring the full communion that is desired between the Eastern Churches and the
Catholic Church' (*Unitatis Redintegratio*, 14), giving due consideration in the special aspects of the origin and growth of the Churches
of the East, and developing the attitudes and behaviour which are
suitable between sister Churches. The 'dialogue of charity' which
owes so much to Popes John XXIII and Paul VI and to Patriarch
Athenagoras developed with growing intensity not only through
visits and acts expressing both courtesy and communion but especially through the statements and speeches of Pope Paul VI and
Pope John Paul II and those of the Ecumenical Patriarch and his
assistants. This material, collected in the volume *Tomos Agapis*,
gives ever more explicit theological statement of the relationship
and now forms a rich point of depature for the formal dialogue
which is in progress. This dialogue which involves all 14
Orthodox Churches has produced a joint document on 'The mystery of the Church and the Eucharist in the light of the Mystery of
the Holy Trinity'. Now with a further theme 'Faith, Sacraments
and the Unity of the Church' the discussion is fully launched in a
promising direction which is looking at problems and at common
faith. As well as this pan-Orthodox dialogue there are bilateral
discussions with some individual Orthodox Churches to look at
questions specific to that Church. An important recent event was
the visit of the Holy Father to the Orthodox Centre of Chambésy,
one more in the series of continuing signs of communion which are
forwarding this relationship.

As well the Secretariat is fully concerned with the relations with the ancient Oriental Churches where there is a similar pattern of fraternal contacts and gestures of communion. Here, while there is no formal theological dialogue it has been possible to make two highly significant joint statements: the Joint Statement of Christ-ological Faith between Pope Paul VI and Pope Shenouda III of the Coptic Church in 1973; and the recent joint declaration bet-ween the present Holy Father and the Syrian Orthodox Patriarch of Antioch and the East, Zaaka II Iwas which is a profession of faith including the doctrine of the Incarnation expressed in terms of the Council of Nicea. Also noteworthy are the 'Principles for guiding the search for unity between the Catholic Church and the Coptic Orthodox Church', drawn up by the Catholic-Coptic Commission, signed by Pope Shenouda III and now officially accepted by both Churches.

2. *The Anglican-Roman Catholic International Commission* completed the first phase of its work in 1982 with the major theological report on Eucharist, Ministry and Authority. As a theological statement referred by a dialogue commission to its authorities this rep-resented an unprecedented step in the dialogue process. The report is before the Secretariat for promoting Christian Unity and the Sacred Congregation for the Doctrine of the Faith and is being studied by Catholic episcopal conferences, and by the provinces of the Anglican Communion. Replies are due by Easter 1985 but it will take time to process them and undertake the further processes of consultation which will have to precede any final judgement of the significance of the report. That on the Anglican side is expected only at the time of the Lambeth Conference in 1988.

3. *The International Evangelical-Lutheran/Roman Catholic Joint Commis-sion* was the first of the dialogue commissions to come into being and was set up and had its first meeting already during the Coun-cil. With its meeting earlier this year in Rome, it concluded the present phase of its work. The Commission has published the fol-lowing major documents which give an idea of the scope of its task:
– the Eucharist (1978)
– Ways to Community (1980)
– All under One Christ (1980), a statement on the Augsburg Con-fession
– The Ministry (1981)
– Martin Luther: Witness to Jesus Christ (1983)
– Facing Unity: Models, Forms and Phases of Lutheran/Roman Catholic Unity (to be published soon).

4. *The Reformed/Catholic Dialogue* held its first meeting in 1970 after preliminary discussions. The theme was the Presence of Christ in Church and World. In 1977 a report was published and the following years were spent in trying to get reactions to it and an eventual evaluation of the dialogue took place. Meanwhile, plans were made for a second round of talks. The first meeting in the new series will take place in 1985 with the theme: 'The Church as People of God, Body of Christ and Temple of the Spirit'. Attention will be given also to the Reformation and to remaining causes of friction between Catholics and Reformed in some places.

5. *Catholic/Methodist International Commission.* A joint commission began meeting in 1967. The first two series of discussions dealt with problems of Christian life and spirituality. The following period was devoted to discussion on the Holy Spirit in relation to Christian experience and authority, and a report was published. The present series is looking at questions of the Church, its sacraments, life and ministry.

6. *The Disciples of Christ/Catholic Dialogue* began in 1977 and has focused on the question of unity. A second round of talks has begun to discuss the Church as agent and realization of communion (*koinonia*). This dialogue has been able to make good use of developments in other dialogues and in the work of the Faith and Order Commission of the World Council of Churches.

7. *The Catholic/Pentecostal Dialogue* began in 1972 and has published two reports. In the beginning it dealt with questions of spirituality and pentecostal phenomena but has moved to more central theological and even ecclesiological questions. Its scope is chiefly to improve mutual understanding.

8. *The Baptist World Alliance/Catholic Dialogue* began this year and looks to mutual understanding, overcoming prejudices and difficulties and examining possibilities of common witness. The discussions will develop under the general theme of Evangelization: the Mission of the Church. Its next meeting will take up the aspect of witness in reference to the person and work of Jesus Christ and to conversion and discipleship. (*Osservatore Romano*, English, 3 December 1984)

As well as these bilateral dialogues, the Secretariat has also been involved in multilateral dialogues, particularly in the Faith and Order discussions which led to the Lima Report, *Baptism, Eucharist and Ministry*, of 1983. There should be no conflict between bilateral and multilateral dialogues: an improvement in understanding bet-

ween any two churches has a ripple effect on other dialogues. The
same questions crop up again and again because they are the fundamental. And the fundamental questions are the right ones. These
dialogues are not like diplomatic negotiations in which to draw
closer to one party is to pull away from another. They are all heading
towards 'convergence in Christ' – Paul VI's favourite ecumenical
phrase.

Moreover, some churches, notably the Lutherans and the Anglicans, have found that it is only in ecumenical dialogue that the true
originality and nature of their self-understanding as churches comes
to light. The Lutherans, for example, came into existence as a protest
against the excesses and abuses of the late mediaeval Church; how
do they define themselves if those excesses and abuses have been
removed? Again, the Anglican Communion, comprehensive though
its theological umbrella may be, has always understood itself not as
the exclusive embodiment of the 'one, true Church' but as a reformed
branch of the Catholic Church with which it is, so to speak, an
unacknowledged fellow-traveller or, better, fellow-pilgrim.

But the Roman Catholic Church itself is also engaged in this process of discovering its true identity through dialogue. No one expects
it to abandon its doctrine that the Bishop of Rome, as successor of St
Peter, provides a focus for the visible unity of the Church. The
Lutherans, for example, considered whether they could recognize
'the possibility and desirability of the papal ministry, renewed under
the Gospel and committed to Christian freedom, in a larger communion that would include the Luthern Churches'. (See Paul C.
Empie and T. Austin Murphy, (eds.), *Papal Primacy and the Universal
Church.*) They did not rule it out. The Anglican-Roman Catholic
International Commission (A.R.C.I.C.) went much further and and
said in 1977:

> The only see which makes any claim to universal primacy and
> which has exercised and still exercises such *episcope* is the see of
> Rome, the city where Peter and Paul died. It seems appropriate
> that in any future union a universal primacy such as has been
> described should be held by that see. (*Authority*, No. 23)

But both these statements belong to the optimistic 1970s, when there
was a reasonable hope that the Petrine ministry would adopt a more
'collegial', more 'evangelical' and less aggressively Counter-Reformation style. Pope John Paul II, despite his many gifts, has dashed
such expectations.

The dilemma of S.P.U.C. is that it cannot publicly admit this fact. It has to act on the assumption that Pope John Paul is on its side and is an enthusiastic supporter of its work. There is enough truth in this idea for it to be plausible. On the great ecumenical occasions – notably the visits to Constantinople, Canterbury and the World Council of Churches – Pope John Paul has said all the right things. In Constantinople he talked of his own office in acceptable 'Greek' terms. He defined Peter, brother of Andrew, patron of Constantinople, as 'the chorus-leader of the apostles' (a phrase used in the Orthodox liturgical texts, where Peter is always linked with Paul). Again, he described Peter 'as a brother among brothers, who was entrusted with the task of confirming them in their faith'. Most important of all, on 30 November 1979 he quoted the principle of the Council of Jerusalem on 'not imposing anything other than what was necessary'. (Acts 15:28.) This was a far cry from Vatican I with its all-embracing claims to universal primacy and jurisdiction.

At Canterbury, once again Pope John Paul did not put an ecumenical foot wrong. He seemed to have assimilated the contents of the A.R.C.I.C. report when he described his own role in terms of 'presiding over the assembly of charity'. And as in Constantinople, the symbolic gestures spoke even more eloquently than the words. The Pope made no attempt to upstage the Archbishop of Canterbury. Together they venerated the Canterbury Gospel, reputedly brought from Rome by St Augustine in 598. Together they renewed their baptismal promises: baptism sets up a dynamic drive towards full communion. And together they lit candles for the modern martyrs whose blood is the seed of the Church. John Paul lit a candle for St Maximilian Kolbe, the Polish Conventual Franciscan who gave his life at Auschwitz so that a married man might live; and Dr Runcie lit a candle for Archbishop Oscar Romero, slaughtered at the altar in San Salvador two years before. Just as important as the great set-piece in Canterbury was the visit to Liverpool's Anglican Cathedral, where John Paul was applauded in and out in most un-Anglican fashion. The unexpected lesson of the visit to England, Scotland and Wales was that ecumenism is a popular cause.

The snag is that S.P.U.C. has drafted the Pope's speeches on these big ecumenical occasions. Acknowledging his own inexperience in the ecumenical field, he turns to S.P.U.C. as a specialist body which is competent in these matters. He adds his own emphases, usually to make the point that ecumenism is essentially a spiritual matter; but on the whole he reads out what is prepared for him. Thus it becomes rather difficult to answer the key questions: what does Pope John

Paul really think on ecumenical matters? What priority does he give them? Has he subordinated them to the restoration of Catholic identity that seems to be the main plank of his pontificate? How far is his interest in Orthodoxy a function of his desire to strengthen believers in Eastern Europe and the Soviet Union?

S.P.U.C. may well feel that it has quite enough to work on positively without attempting to answer such big questions. But the problem of contradictory utterances will not just go away. For example, the C.D.F. commented on the A.R.C.I.C. Final Report in rather discouraging terms. Its 'Observations', dated 29 March 1982, were particularly severe on the method used by A.R.C.I.C., saying that it ought to have compared the foundational documents – the Thirty-nine Articles and the Council of Trent, for example – to pave the way forward. But this revival of sixteenth-century controversies would merely have led to sixteenth-century conclusions. As Professor Henry Chadwick said, the originality of A.R.C.I.C. was precisely that it strove to get behind the sterile Maginot Line of past controversies in order to state what is the faith of the two churches today.

On this question, S.P.U.C. had a fine card to play: Pope John Paul had commended A.R.C.I.C.'s method when he met its members at Castelgandolfo on 4 September 1980:

> Your method has been to go behind the habit of thought and expression born and nourished in enmity and controversy to scrutinize together the great common treasure, to clothe it in a language at once traditional and expressive of the insights of an age which no longer glorifies in strife but seeks to come together in listening to the quiet voice of the Spirit.

That was a splendid and even eloquent statement of A.R.C.I.C.'s method. 'Listening to the voice of the Spirit' is diametrically opposed to comparing the polemical texts of the sixteenth century. However, Pope John Paul did not write this speech. It was written by someone in S.P.U.C., quite possibly Mgr William Purdy. The important thing, S.P.U.C. will say, is not who wrote it but that the Pope was prepared to read it out: that is the commitment.

It is nice to be so sanguine. The truth is that S.P.U.C. has to argue its corner to survive at all. It has to exploit every favourable pontifical remark and ignore the unfavourable ones in order to stay in business. This is not a discreditable position: it is inevitable in a system in which even everyday papal statements are regarded as an expression of 'the ordinary *magisterium*'. This does not imply any nonsense about them being 'infallible', but that they have a special weight and authority of a somewhat indefinable kind. Pope John Paul takes this doctrine seriously: in one audience he urged the members of the Cagliari football team to subscribe to the *Osservatore Romano* so that they could regularly follow 'the ordinary *magisterium*'.

What the Cagliari footballers, supposing that they obeyed the papal injunction, would have made of Pope John Paul's address in the Paushuis in Utrecht on 13 May 1985 is a moot point. They are even less likely to have followed the correspondence in *The Times* on the subject. Fr Bruno Brinkman S.J. and others said that the speech was a setback to the ecumenical cause. In particular they noted a contrast on mixed marriages. At the Knavesmire Racecourse, York, on 31 May 1982, Pope John Paul had said of mixed couples, 'You live in your marriages the hopes and difficulties of the path to Christian unity.' But now in Utrecht, in what was allegedly the house of Pope Adrian VI, the last non-Italian Pope, John Paul said that mixed marriages did more harm than good and that they tended to lead to 'indifferentism' – that is, both parties lost interest in their faith.

What no one seemed to notice was that Pope John Paul had not made the supposedly offensive remarks at all. They were indeed in his published text, but in delivery he cut those sections devoted explicitly to 'certain delicate problems', in order to save time. The result was that his Dutch Reformed listeners, not having a text, did not even know what he had to say about the counter-productive effect of mixed marriages; nor did they hear him denounce 'wildcat' intercommunion or that there could be no question ever of admitting women to the priestly ministry. The Dutch Calvinists, blissfully unaware of such sentiments, imagined they had been addressed in the most friendly fashion. Dr Henk Huting, President of the Synod, said so on television immediately afterwards. This raised a novel theological conundrum: what is the status of non-pronounced papal speeches?

The answer appears to be that they have to be taken seriously if the non-delivered speech has nevertheless been published. I conclude this from a remarkably revealing letter written by Mgr Richard L. Stewart to *The Tablet*. He was writing in his own name, but his letter reveals the alarm of S.P.U.C.

Mgr Stewart begins by setting the scene. Huting had said that 70 per cent of marriages in the Netherlands are ecumenically mixed. Stewart says that the correct figure is nearer 37 per cent in the country as a whole, rising to 70 per cent only in the big cities. He then points out that the Pope had mentioned the York address, remarked that 'such delicate issues cannot be resolved by an exchange of speeches', and stressed that it is an obligation of the Catholic partner to 'do everything possible' to transmit the Catholic faith to the children but that this is qualified by the phrase 'within the unity of the marriage'. Cash that if you can.

Here is the conclusion to Mgr Stewart's letter. Call it casuistry, but observe S.P.U.C. striving to keep open its little area of freedom:

> He (Pope John Paul) urged couples to face the 'difficulties and *possibilities*' of their marriage (nowhere in the speech does the word 'errors' appear). Pastoral care is necessary here; having quoted Pope Paul VI's teaching on the need for good contacts between pastors to enable them to ensure such care, the Pope went further and spoke of the part local communities can play here, 'also in the first years of married life, in which the spouses discover one another more fully and grow together in a life of faith which is capable of expressing not only a minimal concord' ('an agreed minimum' might be a better translation) 'but even an authentic appreciation of all that can be esteemed valid in the traditions and spiritual practices of the other. I pray for those couples who make a valid contribution to the work of reconciliation. I pray also for pastors, communities and associations that seek to offer the pastoral care and support to which such couples have a right' (I do not recall any previous papal references to 'associations' of this kind).
>
> All in all, then, I would suggest that the Popes's speech at Utrecht gives at least as much emphasis to possibilities as to difficulties. (*The Tablet*, 22 June 1985)

This is rather like watching a man struggling to open an umbrella in a high wind. Mgr Stewart draws what consolation he can from the fact that the speech *could be* interpreted positively and that it contained a wholly new idea: a commendation of associations of the mixedly married. He died on 30 July 1985 at his sister's home in Surrey at the age of fifty-eight. I suspect he drafted the sentence about 'associations' himself. Thus does ecumenism advance from nuance to nuance.

Part of the problem lies in the nature of 'ecu-speak' itself. There are only a finite number of things to be said, and they have all been said many times over. On every particular issue one can look at the distance already travelled together and rejoice in the progress made; or one can look ahead at the road to actual unity and find it long, rocky, beset by dragons and full of perils. S.P.U.C. professionally takes the optimistic view; the Congregation for the Doctrine of Faith (C.D.F.) is professionally pessimistic.

S.P.U.C. members know that they are being 'shadowed' by members of the C.D.F. The rivalry between the two bodies has sometimes led to tense scenes. In a meeting with journalists on 22 March 1985 Fr Pierre Duprey, Secretary of S.P.U.C., tried to state as delicately as he could the complementary relationship between them: 'The Doctrinal Commission is concerned with the purity of faith. We are concerned with the purity of faith and rising above the traditional ways of expressing it to find common ground with other Christians.' Though this is not luminously clear, one gathers that the C.D.F. and S.P.U.C. have one common goal, sound doctrine; while S.P.U.C. has an additional goal, finding common ground with other Christians, in which the C.D.F. does not share. Of necessity, then, the C.D.F. will be critical of S.P.U.C.'s efforts at dialogue. So some degree of conflict is built into the situation. One can even high-mindedly claim that this is a good thing: as the moment of unity comes closer, any agreements will have to be sieved through an even finer mesh to guarantee the conscience of the Church. That is presumably what Fr Duprey meant when he added: 'The relationship is not always smooth, but this is healthy.' (*N.C. News Service*, 25 March 1985.) One senses a wealth of experience behind that simple remark. If Duprey is prepared to say that much on the record, what might he not say off the record?

The C.D.F. case was put the following day by its Secretary, Archbishop Alberto Bovone. 'We are not opposed or unsympathetic to ecumenism,' he confidently began, and went on:

> The Congregation does not replace other Vatican bodies, but offers contributions so that faith is expressed accurately. The fundamental concern of the Congregation is to defend and promote the idea of a unified, redeeming faith which is expressible in a unified and exact way. The Congregation's role also involves promoting doctrine and giving new energy to people who announce the Gospel so that faith moves in all aspects of Church life. (*Ibid*)

It is a little difficult to know what to make of these circumlocutions, but a rereading of Chapter 7 in this book should clear the mind. The crucial question is: what happens in case of conflict?

The Pope could intervene, but in practice does not (or not

directly). Articles in the *Osservatore Romano*, such as Fr Daniel Ols
O.P.'s intemperate attack on the late Karl Rahner in March 1985 act
as straws in the wind. Reunion cannot come about, the Angelicum
professor maintained, unless other churches submit to 'each and
every one of the dogmas professed by the Roman Catholic Church'.
Though this was said without authority, and despite the French
Dominican being so notoriously right-wing that his own province
refused to profess him (he sneaked back via Bologna), such incidents
cause concern in S.P.U.C. The decisive question is who will be
appointed to succeed Cardinal Willebrands when he finally steps
down. Born on 4 September 1909, he is already over the normal age
limit of seventy-five for top curial posts. The appointment of his successor will be a declaration of intent: either the spirit of dialogue will
be kept alive in the Curia or it will be quietly, bureaucratically snuf-
fed out.

What is unlikely to change is the sub-section of S.P.U.C. which
goes under the name of the Commission for Religious Relations with
Israel. It consists of the same people wearing different hats. Willebrands is its President and Pierre Duprey its Vice-President, and the
Argentinian Mgr Jorge Mejia here rises to the dignity of Secretary. It
was set up in its present form in 1974, but the 'Jewish question' as a
religious problem had always been dealt with by the Secretariat.
There were two reasons for this. No one at the council, other than
Bea and his team, had the toughness and the desire to ward off those
Christian Arabs who did not take kindly to benevolent or forgiving
statements about the Jews: and since Christianity began as a schism
within Judaism, there remained a common bond with it which has
no parallel in the other great non-Christian religions. So politically
and theologically, this was the right home for it.

The Commission has built steadily on the decree of Vatican II,
Nostra Aetate, which said not only that 'what happened in Christ's
passion cannot be blamed upon all the Jews then living without distinction nor upon the Jews of today', but also stressed the 'spiritual
patrimony common to Christians and Jews'. If today the first statement seems somewhat grudging and the second rather trite, they
represented a big step forward in 1965. But the problem was always
how to move from sophisticated theology to unsophisticated
attitudes. How were these principles to be brought to bear on the
Church's everyday catechesis and preaching? For antisemitism was
a cultural fact that was partly nourished by some New Testament
usages: 'the Jews' in St John's Gospel, for example, are invariably
presented as the enemies of Christ. Much scholarly ink has been

expended in showing that 'the Jews' does not mean the Jewish people or Judaism itself. Willebrands himself dealt with this and related questions in a remarkable lecture at the Oxford Union in March 1985. ('Is Christianity Anti-Semitic?' in *Briefing*, 22 March 1985.)

Two months later the Commission published *The Common Bond*, a workmanlike text which was modestly described as 'notes for teaching and preaching'. It suffered a predictable fate: as each fresh document on Jewish-Christian relations comes out of the Vatican, it is eagerly scrutinized on the Jewish side to discover whether it represents an advance or a retreat from the previous statement. *The Common Bond* was harshly judged by the Chief Rabbi of Great Britain, Sir Immanuel Jakobovits, on two counts. First its reference to the holocaust was 'painfully casual'. Here it is: 'Catechesis should on the other hand help in understanding the meaning to the Jews of the extermination during the years 1939-1945, and its consequences.' This is certainly bland, but who, anyway, can comprehend the mystery of iniquity? The Jewish demand for expressions of Christian guilt and remorse has an insatiable quality that makes it difficult to fulfil.

The Chief Rabbi's other objection was, of course, to the one sentence devoted to the state of Israel: 'The existence of the state of Israel and its political options should be envisaged not in a perspective which is itself religious, but in their reference to the common principles of international law.' The Chief Rabbi found it 'difficult to fathom the meaning of this enigmatic statement . . . when in fact throughout the ages the vision of the Jewish return to Zion has been essentially religious'. (*The Times*, 29 June 1985.) One sympathizes with the Chief Rabbi's bewilderment. Christians make a distinction that he does not. The Commission's brief is to deal only with 'religious relations' with Jews. The existence of Israel is undoubtedly a political fact. Therefore in Vatican terms any political comment would have to come from the Secretariat of State. So far it has propounded the unlikely utopia of the 'internationalization of Jerusalem' and withheld diplomat recognition on the grounds that Israel's frontiers have not yet been guaranteed by international treaty. True, but consciously or not, this makes Israel's status dependent on the political interests of her declared enemies. The Vatican could clear the air by recognizing that Israel has come to stay. But that is not a decision that could ever be taken by the Commission for Religious Relations with the Jews.

Sharing the premises, a creaking lift and an elderly porter at Via dell'Erba 1, just off the Via della Conciliazione, is the Secretariat for

Non-Christian Religions (S.N.C.R.). Paul VI announced its creation on Whit Sunday, 19 May 1964. This was a hint to the Council Fathers that they should get on with their document on non-Christian religions, which they eventually approved on 28 October 1965.

The declaration, *Nostra Aetate*, became the charter of the S.N.C.R. But it proved rather difficult to determine exactly what the great world religions had in common. The declaration suggests that they share 'a quest for answers to those profound mysteries of the human condition which today even as old deeply stir the human heart'. This echoes, though oddly it does not quote, the second-century theologian Justin Martyr who attributed all the truths found in non-Christian religions to the Holy Spirit who 'enlightens everyone who comes into the world'. (John 1:9.) The declaration simply says: 'The Catholic Church rejects nothing which is true and holy in these religions.'

That may sound distressingly tautological – the problem is to know precisely what is true and holy in these religions; but it represented a new respect for non-Christian religions, and a willingness to sit down and talk with their spokesmen.

The first President of the S.N.C.R. was Cardinal Paolo Marella, whose reign lasted from 1964 to 1973. He very properly resigned at seventy-eight. He was roughly qualified for the post by being a Constantini-trained man (see Chapter 10) who had been Apostolic Delegate to Japan during the difficult war years. That explained his interest in Shintoism and Zen. But unlike S.P.U.C., which never lacked eager partners in dialogue, the S.N.C.R. had to work hard to find interlocutors. A large painting in the S.N.C.R. meeting room depicts Pope Paul VI with arms extended welcoming various saffron-robed Buddhist monks, gorgeously arrayed bonzes, sundry mullahs and other obscurer religious leaders. The painting has a certain symbolic truth. But there are so many internal divisions among Buddhists and Muslims themselves that no dialogue ever led to any very durable or ascertainable result.

The painting belongs to the time when Cardinal Serio Pignedoli was President of the S.N.C.R. (1973-1980). Pignedoli had been one of Pope Paul's closest friends, and was his auxiliary in Milan. So his appointment enhanced the importance of the office: it was not just a piece of window-dressing. Pignedoli made friends wherever he went. As Apostolic Delegate in Canada he drove a battered Volkswagen from coast to coast and up into the Yukon to say farewell to his many friends. Everyone he met was entered on his voluminous card index. They were all invited to visit him in Rome, and sometimes one stumbled across prone students in sleeping bags in his dining room. These human qualities, rather than any remarkable learning, endeared him to the representatives of non-Christian religions. Not that he was a duffer in this field. He had served his time in Vietnam and some of the Buddhists who came to see him in Rome were old friends.

There is a legend that Pignedoli made a terrible gaffe in 1976 in Tripoli, Libya, when Colonel Muammar al-Qaddafi held a celebrated Christian-Moslem dialogue in the opera house. While Moslems prayed towards Mecca, Christians enjoyed imaginative non-alcoholic beverages. Needless to say, from Qadaffi's point of view the purpose of the meeting was to make propaganda for T.I.T. (the Third International Theory) which was the foundation on which his People's Republic is allegedly based. Everyone present knew that.

Pignedoli's so-called gaffe was his failure to notice that a resolution predictably condemning 'Zionism as racism' had been slipped past the translators at the last moment. His mistake was in not knowing enough Arabic. I was present on that occasion, and thought the mistake forgivable. But this incident was exploited by Pignedoli's enemies in the Curia who resented his approachableness and popularity. It was whispered that he was too inclined to be 'all things to all men'. The S.N.C.R.'s reputation went down with Pignedoli's. It was considered to be fundamentally non-serious. It did not carry much weight in curial politics. He got a few votes in the 1978 conclaves, but was never in with a serious chance.

Pignedoli died in December 1980. His successor was Archbishop Jean Jadot, a Vatican diplomat from Belgium who, like Pignedoli, had served in Vietnam. His more immediate claim to fame was that he had renewed the American episcopacy during his seven-year stint as Apostolic Delegate in Washington. But he only lasted three years as Pro-President of S.N.C.R., was not made a cardinal, and in April 1984 was abruptly replaced by Francis Arinze, who was born in 1932 and from 1967 had been Archbishop of Onitsha, Nigeria. So Arinze became one of the leading Africans in the Roman Curia, balancing the French-speaking Mgr Emery Kabongo from Zaïre, the first black papal private secretary who helped, but did not displace, the Polish Stanislaw Dziwisz. Since Nigeria, with over 100 million inhabitants, is the largest country, in terms of population, in Africa and not the poorest (it is a member of O.P.E.C.), and since it is in the front line of the encounter of Moslems (47 per cent) and Christians (34 per cent), the appointment of Arinze made a good deal of sense. The mark of confidence that was withheld from Jadot was conferred on Arinze within the year: he was made a cardinal in spring 1985.

Yet Pope John Paul's remarks on Islam reveal an ambivalence that is confusing. On special occasions he is friendly, but he can be sharp when recalling the past. When he went to Turkey in November 1979 he was very ecumenical. Though Turkey is officially a secular state, it had an Islamic tradition and shared a common frontier with Iraq and Iran where the Ayatollah Ruhollah Khomeni had given a new and sinister content to the 'Islamic revival'. John Paul, however, with a vision of monotheists pressing in upon the Soviet Union from Lithuania to Iran, claimed at the Italian Embassy Chapel in Ankara on 29 November 1979: 'Now that Christians and Moslems have entered into a new phase of history, it is urgent to recognize and develop the spiritual bonds that unite us so that we may "protect and encourage for all men social justice, moral values, peace and liberty"'. The quotation came from *Nostra Aetate*.

This speech was over-optimistic. One result of the 1979 papal visit to Turkey was that a young Turk, Mehmet Ali Agca, told the press that he intended to murder this 'Christian crusader'. No one paid much attention to him until, on 13 May 1981, he shot and wounded the Pope in St Peter's Square. Where bullets fly, there is not much room for dialogue.

John Paul showed himself keen to recall the more heroic Christian exploits against the Turks. The defeats were as heroic as the victories. In October 1980 he went to Otranto, where a castle juts out into the Adriatic; it is the easternmost part of Italy and Shelley wrote a violent play about it. Five hundred years earlier, 800 Christians had been frog-marched up the Hill of Minerva in Otranto and beheaded by the Turks. John Paul spoke from the very spot where they were butchered. But he did not dwell on the past. Instead he glanced across the Adriatic towards Albania, only seventy kilometres away, where suffer 'the martyrs of our own age who are often unknown and yet not so far away from us'. That the Albanian Communists were to be thought of as the successors of the Turks was not exactly a compliment to either party.

In September 1983 Pope John Paul went to Austria to commemorate the victory of the Austro-Polish Alliance which 300 years before had routed the Turks at the gates of Vienna. Hungary was rescued and Europe saved. It was a great victory. But Austrian and Polish schoolbooks do not record the fact that on 12 September 1683, three thousand wounded Turks were burned alive 'to purify the air'. Turkish sources say they were ten thousand. Throughout the baroque period and well into the nineteenth century the 'Turkish head', made of wood or papier-mâché, stood outside imperial post offices. Gentlemen would cut it down with their swords or shoot it down with their pistols and then spit on it.

None of which encouraged dialogue with the Turks, who historically represented the avant-garde of Islam in Europe. True, in Vienna Pope John Paul called for 'a spiritual crusade of prayer and action', directed against some unnamed enemy; it should be engaged upon 'with the same commitment and heroism that our forefathers displayed in saving Vienna'. The Viennese, who from bitter experience have become prudent compromisers, listened to these bold words with some puzzlement. They were spoken in the *Heldenplatz* (Heroes' Square) where fifty years before Austrian Catholics had applauded the Nazis.

In all this the original purpose of the Secretariat for Non-Christian Religions was somewhat lost sight of. It was becoming not a means of dialogue so much as an apologetic instrument. The proof was that in 1984 under its new President it embarked on a study of the 'sects', and in particular the Moonies. No one seriously thought there was anything positive to be learned from the Moonies (though a comparison with Opus Dei would have proved instructive, if embarked upon). Cardinal Arinze was reduced to sending out messages of goodwill to Moslems at Ramadan. In Pakistan the Catholics join in the month-long fast.

On 19 August 1985 Pope John Paul addressed 60,000 enthusiastic young Moslems in a stadium in Casablanca, Morocco. 'Today,' he said, 'God is inviting us all to change our old habits, to respect each other and stimulate each other on the pathway to God.' This was rapturously received. John Paul was the guest of King Hassan II of Morocco, spiritual and religious leader of his nearly 20 million people. The King claims direct descent from the prophet Muhammad through thirty- five generations – the Islamic version of 'apostolic succession'. But King Hassan is regarded as unrepresentative by the rest of the Islamic world, and his gaols are full of political prisoners. Even as the Pope was declaring an end to the Crusades, the idea of the *jihad* or holy war was being revived in Islam, not least in the Lebanon, once a place where Christians and Moslems lived in peace.

So most dealings with Moslems so far have been rather speculative, a bit like throwing a message into the ocean in a bottle.

14

The New Curialists

The success of the Secretariat for Christian unity prompted Pope
Paul VI to set up another one for Non-Believers in April 1965. From
the outset this title caused trouble because few people were ready to
accept that they were total non-believers, i.e. that they believed in
nothing at all. The agnostic or atheist might well protest that
although they did not believe in God, that did not prevent them
believing in truth, justice, fraternity – the whole realm of values.
These look better (more like 'transcendental' truths) with capital letters. There is not much evidence that actual non-believers were
really worried by this nomenclature, but Catholics worried deeply
on their behalf. However, it was too late. The label stuck, and no one
could think of a better title. A one-eyed Lebanese Jesuit, Gabriel
Malik, went round Europe advocating a 'Secretariat for the Study of
Contemporary Ideologies'. But his remedy seemed considerably
worse than the disease.

In any case, everyone knew perfectly well whom Paul VI had in
mind. In his first programmatic encyclical, *Ecclesiam Suam*, he
sketched out his vision of the Church of Rome and the 'concentric
circles' by which it was surrounded. In Chapter 13 we saw how he
dealt with the first two circles: the separated brethren, those who
share a common baptism and faith, and the Jews, of the same trunk.
Then came the historic non-Christian religions. But the 'outer circle'
consists of everyone else, the residue of humanity, those otherwise
left out. They might be adherents of certain political ideologies, such
as Marxism; or they might not. But Paul VI was persuaded that
'wherever men are striving to understand themselves and the world,
we are able to communicate with them.' (*Ecclesiam Suam*, 97.) It was
to reach out towards this widest area of common human discourse
that Paul VI set up his Secretariat for Non-Believers.

He was also giving a hint to the Council, whose fourth and final
session was due to begin in September 1965. 'All things human are
our concern,' wrote Paul VI, 'and we share with the whole of the
human race a common nature, a common life with all its gifts and

problems.' (*Ecclesiam Suam*, 97.) This corresponds with the magnificent opening chord of the conciliar pastoral constitution, *Gaudium et Spes*: 'The joys and hopes, the griefs and anxieties of the men of this age, especially those who are poor or in any way afflicted, these too are the joys and hopes, the griefs and anxieties of the followers of Christ.' (Note by the way, the phrase, 'especially those who are poor', which is at the origin of liberation theology's 'option for the poor'.) Normally it is superfluous to congratulate a group of people on admitting that they belong to the human race. But from the nineteenth century onwards the Church had so often belittled the world and defined itself in contrast with it, that this simple recognition of belonging struck home with the full force of novelty. So the Secretariat for Non-Believers symbolized the passage from the disapproving Church of Pius IX to the Church in dialogue of Paul VI.

More precisely, its purpose was to 'probe the mind of the contemporary atheist in order to understand the reasons for his mental turmoil'. (*Ecclesiam Suam*, 104.) That suggested a picture of the atheist as an invalid, a desperately sick man. Theologians were invited to gather round his bedside like doctors anxious to discover an antidote for this dreadful condition. One puts it rather satirically, but probably the Christian has to believe that to be an atheist is unnatural. He banks on the 'restless heart' of St Augustine and George Herbert ('If goodness may lead him not, yet weariness/May toss him to my breast'). But if complacent atheists could never engage in dialogue with complacent believers, critical atheists could talk with critical believers. They sometimes did. The adventures and misadventures of the Secretariat for Non-Believers in its first decade were chronicles in Chapter 9 of my book *The Runaway Church*, 'Dialogue with Humanism in a Secular World'. Here we pick up the story late in 1984 when I had an interview with Archbishop (now Cardinal) Paul Poupard, President of the Secretariat for Non-Believers, in his apartment in the Palazzo San Calisto.

This enormous barracks-like building – Pius XI's answer to Fascist architecture – was built in the heart of Trastevere, a working-class quarter of Rome known for its restaurants, its crime rate and the Regina Coeli prison. Most of the 'new Curia' to be examined in this chapter is housed there. One enters the courtyard and there, behind a tiny fountain, is an immense statue of Pius XI in his tiara. His right hand is raised, but whether this is in blessing or warning remains somewhat uncertain.

Everywhere in the offices of the Secretariat, as elsewhere in the Vatican, are photographs of the reigning Pope. They serve the same function that portraits of the King performed in seventeenth-century France: they make the 'prince' visible, present everywhere. The Pope is indeed ubiquitous here: even the light switches are surmounted by the papal coat of arms. I was shown into a parlour with a vast ceiling and four brocaded chairs drawn up as though for a conversation piece in act four of a play that will never happen. It is a place of some gloom and austerity. I remembered the Californian priest who used to work here: they decided he was mad and sent him home when he pulled a revolver on his superior.

But on this occasion Mgr Poupard had a broken leg and was unable to descend from his apartment on the top floor. So I was led up to a kind of cloister or open gallery four storeys up. From here there is a magnificent view of the Janiculum and the dome of St Peter's. Sundry cardinals live up here safe from terrorism and in modest but enviable comfort. There is no collegiate life. Each has his own establishment: at least a secretary, two reliable sisters of a certain age, a study, a reception room, a dining room, and an oratory. With his right leg in plaster and propped up on the desk, Mgr Poupard explained that while the other Secretariats that do not lack partners in dialogue, 'non-believers' are hard to talk to, as they are a rather disorganized lot. 'Non-believers,' he remarked, 'are usually freethinkers, and they resent anyone presuming to speak in their name.' But he made the important claim that even if dialogue was impossible, to speak with the problems of outsiders in mind was already a form of dialogue, though of an internal kind.

This conversation was in French. Poupard, who has a magnificent library (*'J'ai toutes les collections'*) confessed his ignorance of 'the Anglo-Saxon world'. He did not seem unduly concerned to remedy it. I put it to him that the Anglo-Saxon unbeliever was less likely to be the heir of Karl Marx and Friedrich Nietzsche so much as an ordinary bloke (*type*) who didn't want to outrun the available evidence. He was more likely to be a man pushing a bicycle up a hill than Sisyphus vainly pushing his boulder, as recalled by Albert Camus. He was neither Prometheus stealing fire from the gods nor Nietzsche's Superman. He was the man next door who just didn't know. Poupard said I was making a very Anglo-Saxon statement. He asked me to send him an article on the subject. I never did. Let these remarks be a substitute for the unwritten article.

The Secretariat for Non-Believers makes one very aware of how our thinking (and consequently our perceiving) is shaped by different intellectual traditions. Pope John Paul has always advocated a *'pastorale de l'intelligence'* and defined this as the purpose of the Sec-

retariat. How are we translate this very Gallic phrase? 'The pastoral
care of the mind'? 'The apostolate of the intellectuals'? 'A pastoral
approach to the university and scientific community'? Perhaps the
rest of the Pope's statement in his address to the Secretariat on 3
April 1981 will provide some clue to its meaning:

> The Secretariat for Non-believers has an important role to play in
> this *pastorale de l'intelligence* by stimulating interest, deepening
> questions, making suggestions and proposals within the Roman
> Curia while being at the service of the local Churches who have to
> face the challenge of atheism and the drama of unbelief – always in
> conjunction with university people. In this way it could help many
> believers to bear witness to the values that provide their *raisons de
> vivre*, to find words to share them with others, and to be fearless in
> declaring themselves witnesses to God in the name of the obsti-
> nate quest for the Truth which, through centuries of scientific
> research, has constituted the greatness of humanity. (Published in
> *Atheism and Dialogue*, 1, 1985)

The very vastness and windiness of this project make it difficult to
grasp. For it embraces all the questions which used to belong to fundamental theology, the so-called 'frontier questions': faith and science, the rationality of faith, the status of the human sciences. When
a local branch of the Secretariat meets – many have only a phantom
existence – the first thing they discuss is what to do. Given the broad
description of aims, what is the next step? What should they actually
do first? Some never got beyond this preliminary question, and took
the easy way out by answering the numerous questionnaires sent out
by the Secretariat.

But then they found themselves trapped, because in 1984 there
came a questionnaire designed to 'evaluate' the work of the Secretariat over the previous twenty years. It would hardly do to admit
that their time had been spent in answering questionnaires like this
one. But that is what some episcopal commissions had to confess.
The Philippines said that their commission existed largely on paper
and that apart from a few seminars on contemporary ideologies they
had done nothing. Concerning the Secretariat's quarterly, *Atheism
and Dialogue*, they frankly admitted that 'the publication has not
helped for the quite simple reason that it has not been read'. The
Japanese found this talk about atheism (*munish-ron*) and the habit of
dividing people into 'believers' and 'non-believers' foreign to their
cultural tradition. Fr Francis J. Buckley S.J. reported that the Uni-

versity of San Francisco California 'hired an atheist philosopher to
team-teach with eminent Catholic philosophers and theologians
courses in philosophy and theology'. This was a success, with both
sides learning respect for each other. But the atheist 'was not given
tenure and left the university', no doubt a sadder and a wiser man.

It is always useful to study Polish responses to such questions,
especially when they come from Fr Marian Jaworski of Kraków, a
friend of the Pope. He says bluntly that 'because of the limitations
imposed by the system, there is not and has never been a dialogue
with Marxist atheism in Poland.' The conditions for dialogue are
simply not given; any meeting would be manipulated for political
purposes. Jaworski then goes on to give an account of the formidable
'religious revival' in Poland which found expression in the two papal
visits of 1979 and 1983. The first Polish Pope in history was not the
cause of this movement, but he was its catalyst. Solidarity and then
martial law brought Poles together in the defence of human values.
There were many conversions, particularly in prison. Jaworski sums
up: 'In general the Church has emerged from its confrontation with
Marxist atheism strengthened and purified. It has even deprived its
enemies of the ethical initiative by becoming the champion of human
rights, of liberty and justice and so its credibility has been reinforced
in the eyes of unbelievers.' As evidence of the religious revival he cites
the interest of young people in pilgrimages and the underground 'flying universities'. (*Atheism and Dialogue*, 1, 1985.)

No doubt this is all perfectly true. But it cannot be extended to
other countries, except perhaps for neighbouring Czechoslovakia.
We can hardly be expected to pray for the advent of Communist
regimes so that we can all experience a similar bracing atmosphere.
So the relation between what we presume to call 'believers' and 'unbelievers' in Poland cannot be a paradigm for the rest of the world.

Moreover, if the lessons of Poland are extrapolated elsewhere,
they would subvert the very principles on which the Secretariat for
Non-Believers is based. Poland shows that 'dialogue' is impossible
because of the intransigence of the other side. Any notion of 'learning' from them is out of the question. They are described as 'our
enemies' (*adversaires*). The goal is to defeat or convert them. The idea,
found in *Gaudium et Spes*, 19, that Christians can contribute to
atheism by their inadequacies, is dismissed as weakness, a self-
inflicted wound. In short there is a crusade going on, a battle to the
finish, and the Christians have seized the initiative.

Yet Cardinal Poupard strenuously denies that his Secretariat has
changed its nature in this pontificate. Local commissions continue to

make 'study and dialogue' their watchword. But one cannot help noticing that *Atheism and Dialogue* has become an apologetic review, revealing what can only be called an obsession with Galileo Galilei. And to Pope John Paul's apocalyptic vision of the world described in Chapter 4 corresponds a deeply pessimistic judgement on European intellectual history. Everything started to go irrecoverably wrong at the Renaissance:

> Modern man, since the Renaissance, in a tremendous challenge (*un gigantesque défi*), rose up against the mystery of salvation and began to refuse God in the name of dignity of man. At first limited to a small group, the intelligentsia that considered itself an élite, atheism today has become a mass phenomenon which assails the Churches. What is more atheism infiltrates the hearts of the believers, including those who call on the name of Jesus Christ, and brings about a secret and ruinous complicity in the undermining of faith in God – and does so in the name of the autonomy and dignity of man. (Address to a congress on 'Atheism and Evangelization', 10 October 1980)

This was very much the view of Jacques Maritain (following Charles Maurras) in his *Three Reformers*. But if you believe that, you are more likely to devote energy to repressing the errors that have infiltrated the Church than engaging in courteous dialogue with those Promethean figures who have brought about this appalling state of godlessness. So the Secretariat for Non-Believers will fade into insignificance while the Congregation for the Doctrine of Faith will be exalted – which has happened.

That may explain why Pope John Paul found it necessary to set up a new curial office, the Pontifical Council for Culture. This took place on Ascension Day 1982 while no one was looking. The new body nestles under the wings of the Secretariat, and Poupard doubles up as its President. Its Secretary is the Canadian Jesuit and former Rector of the Gregorian, Fr Hervé Carrier. Its officially stated purpose is to 'encourage the dialogue and collaboration between the Church and cultures'. Among its first members were Sir William Rees-Mogg, former Editor of *The Times*, Leopold Senghor, poet and former President of Senegal, and Fr Theodore M. Hesburgh, President of Notre Dame. One woman, Sr Mary Braganza from India, has infiltrated the dozen. These distinguished names may give the impression that the Pope has only 'high culture' in view – string quartets and exhibitions of modern art. 'High culture' is certainly included in the project. The Pope says, quoting Pascal:

> Man infinitely surpasses man, witness the efforts of so many crea-
> tive geniuses to express in works of art and though the transcen-
> dental values of beauty and truth fugitively perceived as an
> expression of the absolute. (Quoted in Cardinal Casaroli's letter
> setting up the Council)

Again one needs to read Jacques Maritain's *Art and Scholasticism* to
understand that sentence (and a glance at the literary criticsm of
Charles du Bos would help too).

But John Paul is equally concerned with 'culture' in the
anthropological sense: it is the air we breathe, the assumptions we
automatically make, the set of values found in any particular society.
He calls it 'the living culture' and defines it as 'the ensemble of values
and principles which make up the ethos of a people'.

Undoubtedly this concern for culture (in both senses) is another
product of his Polish experience. Since all cultural activity in Poland
is officially state-controlled, to defend 'cultural values' is to defend
freedom. The experience of Solidarity showed that despite thirty-five
years of socialist indoctrination, Polish culture remained rooted in
Christian values. Film makers, actors, poets, artists, writers emerged
from their lairs, urged on by the actor-poet-dramatist from Kraków.

John Paul said this about the Pontifical Council for Culture:

> Where agnostic ideologies hostile to the Christian tradition
> inspire leading thinkers, it is all the more urgent for the Church to
> enter into dialogue with cultures in order to allow modern man to
> discover that God, far from being the rival of man, permits him to
> become himself most fully, and to grow in his image and likeness.

So the lesson applies just as much in the West as in the East. And the
aim of the Council for Culture is apologetic: its task is to dissipate
agnostic and atheistic misunderstandings. Against the claims of
'atheistic humanism' (summed up in Marx's aphorism, 'Man is the
supreme being for man'), it declares that there is indeed a Christian
humanism which alone can deliver the authentic goods. This is profoundly true. But how an annual jaunt of the great, the good and the
distinguished can help this process along is difficult to say.

Just across the courtyard of the Palazzo San Calisto is the Pontifical Council for the Laity (P.C.L.). It came into being in response to
Vatican II's decree on the laity (*Apostolicam Actuositatem*). Paul VI set

it up experimentally in 1967 as the *Consilium de Laicis*, and gave it its definitive shape in 1976 as the *Pontificium Consilium pro Laicis*. Laypeople, it goes without saying, form the immense majority of the world's 810,000 Catholics – 99.8 per cent according to one calculation. The Council's late arrival on the Vatican scene says something about how clericalized the Church had become. In the nineteenth century the laity had been seen as the grateful objects of clerical ministry. That was all going to change.

Paul VI defined the purpose of the P.C.L. as 'to work for the service and promotion of the lay apostolate by acting as a place of meeting and dialogue in the Church between the laity and the hierarchy, and between different forms of lay activity'. This did not mean, of course, that it was the only forum for such encounters, and parallel Laity Commissions were set up on the local level. But the P.C.L. was seen as both the international co-ordinating body and the voice of the laity in the Vatican.

It has two sections. Department I 'deals with questions concerning the laity as Christians living in the world and as members of the ecclesial community'. That sounds innocuous enough, but beware: the whole area is a theological minefield, littered with craters from earlier controversies as we shall see.

Department II is more practical. It deals with the Catholic international organizations (C.I.O.s) known by a variety of acronyms such as U.N.D.A. (radio and television), O.C.I.C. (films), and U.C.I.P. (journalists). In the early 1970s there was some argument about the use of the word 'Catholic' in the titles of such bodies; some wished to be more ecumenical than the Holy See was prepared to allow. There were disputes from time to time about the approval of new 'statutes' of organizations and the appointment of chaplains. Some C.I.O.s are also N.G.O.s (translated: some Catholic international organizations are recognized as non-governmental organizations by the United Nations). Two such are St Joan's Alliance, founded in 1911 (as the Catholic Women's Suffrage Association) to enhance the role of women in the Church and press for their ordination, and U.C.I.P., which was invited to comment on the ill-starred Unesco project for 'a New International Information Order'.

These Catholic international organizations are staffed by worthy people who have become, as it were, 'professional laypeople'. (The late Karl Rahner wanted to call all full-time Church professionals, whether ordained or not, 'clerics'. He had little support.) They have worked their way up through local, then national organizations to this topmost level of lay activity and representation. That is not to disparage them. They enjoy few or no material rewards, have their family life disrupted by having to attend endless international conferences, and are lucky if they get their expenses paid. The twenty-six full-time staff members of the P.C.L. mostly come from this milieu. They have acquired a taste for serving the Church.

The year 1984 saw a shake-up at the P.C.L., what the curial gossips called a *terremoto* – an earthquake. What happened was that the old guard was removed. Those who had served the P.C.L. from the beginning, either as members like Archbishop Derek Worlock of Liverpool, or as consultors like Australian Miss Rosemary Goldie, were ousted and replaced (though Worlock later made a comeback). This was largely the work of the relatively youthful German Bishop Paul J. Cordes (born 1934), vice-president of the P.C.L. Italian Cardinal Opilio Rossi shook his head and wondered where it would all end. He was promptly replaced by Cardinal Eduardo Pironio. Mgr Peter Coughlan, after experience in liturgy and non-Christian religions, has now settled down as under-secretary and is therefore the highest-placed English priest in the Curia.

Most laypeople in the Church know nothing about the P.C.L. It is difficult to think of any way in which it materially affects their lives. Nor do they usually think of themselves as posing a theological problem. But there has been a 'problem' about the laity since the 1950s when preachers, inspired by Pius XII, began to say to Catholics: 'You are the Church.' A radical equality in grace was asserted by Vatican II and laid down in the New Code of Canon Law: 'Flowing from their rebirth in Christ, there is a genuine equality of dignity and action among all of Christ's faithful. Because of this they all contribute, each according to his or her own condition or office, to the building up of the Body of Christ.'

The first problem about the laity is what practical consequences flow from these statements. How are they to be cashed? For it is obvious that clericalism does not go away simply because it has been denounced and that the laity do not 'come of age' and 'take up their rightful place in the Church' merely as a result of speeches to that effect. It is fair to say that the institutional consequences of speaking of the Church as the People of God were not realized. But at the same time a shimmering vision was dangled before Catholic eyes: 'The Church is not truly established and does not fully live, nor is it a perfect sign of Christ unless there is a genuine laity existing and working alongside the hierarchy.' (*Ad Gentes.*)

The second problem of the laity was one of definition. The easiest and most practical definition is that a layperson is not a cleric, that is not in holy orders. (Note that this definition places religious women and non-ordained brothers among the laity.) But no one felt satisfied with such a negative definition. Bishop Christopher Butler said that a layman was 'not just a monk in a bowler hat'. Said the Anglican writer Kathleen Bliss: 'Nobody wants to be an "is not".'

But the quest for a positive definition of the laity led to the idea that they have a special role 'in the world'. 'Certain things,' says the Council not very confidently, 'pertain in a particular way to the laity, both men and women, by reason of their situation and mission.' (*Lumen Gentium*, 30.) If we ask what things pertain in a special way to the laity, the answer is that 'a secular quality is proper to the layman' and that 'the laity, by their very vocation, seek the kingdom of God by engaging in temporal affairs. . . . They live in the world. . . . The layman is closely involved in temporal affairs of every sort.' (*Ibid*, 31.)

All this was well meant. It was defended as the 'liberal' view by progressive theologians. But it reintroduced into theology the dualism that had just been banished by making 'the People of God' the starting point. For it assigned to the priest, the ordained minister, the spiritual sphere while leaving the world to the laity. This recalled the theories of Catholic Action in the 1930s. Laypeople work in the order of creation (temporal tasks and so on) while priests work in the order of redemption (the sacraments and so on). The layperson then became the long arm of the priest, reaching the parts that the priest could not reach. This is bad theology because it makes an unworkable distinction: the priest cannot be excluded from the world (in which, as it happens, he lives); and the laity cannot be excluded from various forms of ministry within the Church.

What actually happened after the Council was that laypeople became increasingly involved in ministries or, it might be more accurate to say, began to conceive the work they were already doing in terms of ministry. A catechist, for example, might previously have thought of this teaching activity as her 'apostolate'. Now it took its place among the ministries. The Church has one mission but many ministries. In the United States and Canada there was a great proliferation of ministries. In one parish I found a minister of hospitality as well as voice ministers (who sang in the choir) and dance ministers. One had to discourage the boy who mowed the lawn from calling his activity 'the grass-cutting ministry'. In Chicago there was a whole conference devoted to the ministry of the clown ('fools for Christ'). There is a modishness or even a silliness about some of these developments; but they should not blind us to the fact that the explo-

sion of ministries has been a gift of the Spirit. The vast bulk of lay
ministers are either catechists or extraordinary ministers of the
Eucharist. All these ministries are, of course, 'non-ordained' ministries.

So Vatican II's theology of the laity is in some respects rather
dated. That is why 'The Vocation and Laity in the Church and the
World Twenty Years after the Second Vatican Council' (to give it its
snappy official title) will be the theme of the autumn 1987 Synod of
Bishops in Rome. It was intended to take place in autumn 1986 but
the unscheduled 'Extraordinary Synod' in 1985 caused it to be post-
poned: it is too expensive to hold an annual synod. This will give lay
Christians more time to study the preparatory document.

They may find it rather puzzling. For it warns of dangers that not
everyone will have experienced. Here is the principal one:

> In certain situations in some local Churches there exists a ten-
> dency to restrict apostolic activity to ecclesial 'ministries' only,
> while interpreting them according to a 'clerical image'. This can
> involve the danger of confusion in the correct relationship which
> should exist between clergy and laity in the Church. It can also
> lead to the impoverishment of the salvific mission of the Church
> herself, called as she is – in a special way by means of the laity – to
> carry out this mission 'in' and 'for' the world of temporal and
> earthly realities.

This is written in a kind of Vatican code. The members of the Pontifical Commission for the Laity will need to be able to crack it. If it
were really true that having a modest ministry in the Church led the
layperson to what the document elsewhere calls 'a negative flight
from the world', there might be something in this danger. But experience suggests that those most active in the Church are also most
active in the world.

The hidden agenda of the 1987 Synod is revealed in a quotation
from Pope John Paul's address to the Swiss Bishops in June 1984. He
urged them to avoid both 'the clericalization of the laity and the laicization of the clergy'. This point was first made by Cardinal Alfonso
Lopez Trujillo. He used it to attack those liberation-theology priests
who were deemed to have fallen into secularization, and those laity
who wanted to play a greater role within the Church. It may be that
Pope John Paul has something similar in mind. He always insists, for
example, that there is an essential distinction between the priestly
ministry and other ministeries. This enables him to revive the two-
realms theory, and so justify keeping the ordained priest out of poli-

tics ('his business is within the Church'). And, on the other hand, it permits him to prevent lay ministries from being considered as temporary halts along the road to the ordination of married men . . . and indeed women. The Synod document hints at this in the following question: 'In your local Church does the problem of ministries entrusted to the laity present itself? If so, in what way and for what reason?' So we are back to seeing the laity as a problem.

The Pontifical Commission for Justice and Peace (P.C.J.P.) is also housed in the Palazzo San Calisto. On 21 April 1973 Pope Paul VI compared it to a weathercock placed on the top of a church 'as a symbol of watchfulness' and said it would have the task of 'keeping the eye of the Church, her heart open, and her hand outstretched for the love she is called upon to give to the world'. Between 1967 and 1972 the International Commission helped to stimulate Catholic awareness on international issues: justice, injustice, torture, peace, hunger.

It spawned parallel national commissions which in some countries of Latin America were the only effective check on tyranny, and the only source of information. But the national commissions were not dependent on Rome, and went their own varied and radical ways. The international Commission became increasingly nervous about 'making statements' which might have some political content and eventually fell silent. When the Justice and Peace Commission of Rhodesia (as it then was) explained the nature of the Ian Smith regime to Bernadin Gantin, its President, he told them that he could do nothing. They would have to repeat their story to the Secretariat of State. P.C.J.P. lost its role and was reduced in one of its bulletins to counting up how many times 'the social doctrine of the Church' (or its equivalents) occurred in the speeches of Pope John Paul II.

However, in April 1984 the Cardinal Archbishop of Marseilles, Roger Etchegaray, became President of Justice and Peace and one began to hope for better things. Appointed to Marseilles in 1970 at the early age of forty-two, by 1975 he had been elected President of the French Episcopal Conference. He shocked traditionalist French Catholics by welcoming Algerian Muslims, who have a great devotion to Our Lady, at the local Marian shrine. Greeting Pope John Paul in Paris in 1980, he said that 'secularization' was not wholly bad and that the Church ought to learn its lessons. At the 1983 Synod he selected reconciliation with the Jewish people at the most important aspect of this theme. In all these ways he went against the grain of this pontificate. Yet he was summoned to Rome in April 1984. In his new post he has visited the Lebanon and other trouble spots, but otherwise has given no indication that he is anything other than the token Frenchman in the Curia.

He is, however, also *ex officio* President of the Pontifical Council *Cor Unum* (One Heart). Unlike Justice and Peace this is not at San Calisto but in the Apostolic Palace itself, a sign of how close it is to the Pope. 'It is,' says the *Annuario Pontificio*, 'the Pope's organ of charity.' It was set up in 1971 by Paul VI to 'harmonize' Catholic charitable work. It gives practical expression to solidarity. Its members therefore include the directors of fund-raising bodies such as C.A.F.O.D. (Catholic Fund for Overseas Development) in Britain, Catholic Relief Services in the U.S.A., and Secours Catholique in France. Absent for mysterious reasons is the German organization, Miserior; but present is Count Géraud Michel de Pierredon, Grand Hospitalier of the Knights of Malta. There have been murmurings that *Cor Unum* disburses money only for non-controversial projects that merely prop up the status quo. Since Cardinal Alfonso Lopez Trujillo is on the board, this is more than likely.

In an address to the plenary meeting of *Cor Unum* in November 1982, Pope John Paul discreetly alluded to this problem:

> One must not isolate charity from the other demands of the Beatitudes, and must bring out its relationship with justice – to which it cannot be reduced, and consider its specific contribution to the task of human promotion in relation to the socio-political projects on the civil authorities.

That seems to mean that if a government doesn't like your project you must think again, if not forget about it.

Pope John Paul also hinted at the existence of demarcation disputes:

> The task of your Council is certainly difficult and delicate. As a ministerial structure at the service of the Church's charity, *Cor Unum* relates to the local Churches, the episcopal conferences and bishops of various dioceses and their dependent organizations. Its task is not to replace them, nor to become a centralizing body, still less to take over their finances. It is at their disposal to help them make decisions in a more universal and better co-ordinated perspective. . . .

But co-ordination can so easily turn into control. So John Paul was trying to dissipate the anxieties of the national agencies. He assured them that *Cor Unum* works on their behalf and for the local churches. Then the dagger-blow: *Cor Unum* can perform this valuable service

because its 'more complete information and universal solicitude –
dependent on the Pope who gave it this authority and competence –
endow it with the charism of a disinterestedness and universal concern'. Perhaps they were more interested in the third world than the
second, in Africa more than Poland.

After this brief excursion into the Apostolic Palace, we return to
the Palazzo San Calisto for the Pontifical Council of the Family
(P.C.F.). Founded by Pope Paul VI in 1973 under the unpretentious
title of Committee for the Family, it acquired its present status only
on 9 May 1981, with the *motu proprio, Familia a Deo Instituta* (The family was set up by God). This was only four days before the bullets of
Mehmet Ali Agca nearly killed Pope John Paul II. Its membership,
not counting consultors, consists of twenty married couples. That
sounds promising. But they have all been checked for their reliability
on *Humanae Vitae*: that is, they are firmly opposed to artificial birth
control. It was largely because the P.C.L. was not altogether 'sound'
on *Humanae Vitae* – it admitted there was a problem of 'reception' –
that the Pontifical Council on the Family was split off and upgraded.
One saw its efforts at the 1980 Synod on Marriage and the Family.

In charge of this Council is French-Canadian Cardinal Edouard
Gagnon. His presence in the Curia in this post is mysterious. Born in
January 1918 in Port Daniel, he was Bishop of St Paul, Alberta, from
1969 to 1972. Since then he has been the specialist on family questions in the Vatican. An interview published in *The Wanderer* in 1983
gives a sample of his views. He thinks that disobedient bishops are a
problem and that 'whenever the bishops come to Rome, the Pope
tells them what he wants on morality and catechetics and so on. But
he doesn't have prisons to put them in, so many go back and don't
obey.' Gagnon evidently feels that a revival of pontifical prisons
would be welcome, since he believes that 'the Church is tolerating
material schism in the United States'. His chief remedy for our present lamentable state of affairs 'would be to change 90 per cent of the
teachers of moral theology and stop them from teaching. Because
they are teaching basically principles which lead to sexual abomina-
tions.' He exhorts the worried laity to delate errant bishops and
theologians to Rome. Curial postbags bulge with complaints.

So some parts of the new Curia are merely doing the work of the
old Curia. The high hopes of the post-conciliar period have been
frustrated. Enough of the rhetoric remains for one to glimpse the
dream of dialogue, but it is like a rare gleam of sunlight between
scudding clouds. How all this is presented to the world will be the
theme of the next chapter.

15

Communicating with the Global Village

The first comments of the Vatican on the mass media came in Gregory XVI's encyclical *Mirari Vos* in 1832. They were hostile. The Pope, like the other restored monarchs of Europe, was relieved that the era of revolutions was over but apprehensive that it might some day return. So he denounced the freedom of the press in his customary inflated style, writing of 'the appalling, never sufficiently execrated and destestable freedom of a press which diffuses among the people writings of every sort'. Reading newspapers was dangerous because it lodged ideas of liberalism and socialism in people's minds. So in this nineteenth-century perspective the press represented the hostile and dangerous world out there. The relationship of Church and world is mirrored in the relationship of Church and media.

But Gregory XVI was also worried by the way liberal and democratic ideas were infiltrating the Church. This was said to be happening in France in the Abbé de Lamennais' newspaper *L'Avenir*. Although Lamennais persuaded his editorial team 'respectfully to submit to the authority of the Vicar of Christ . . . and urge all their friends to do the same', this did not satisfy the Pope who in another irate encyclical, *Singulari Nos* (1834), denounced de Lamennais' apologia, *Paroles d'un Croyant* (Words of a Believer), declaring that 'the author, in captious phrases, attempts to attack and destroy Christian doctrine as We have defined it.' In particular de Lamennais had opposed 'the barrier that must be erected against the wild licence of free speech'. In all this the Pontiff and his Curia were acting as judge, jury and witnesses, and there was no right of appeal. The unfortunate de Lamennais died outside the Church, unshriven.

Gregory's successor, Piux IX, recovering from the year of revolutions in 1848, encouraged the then faithfully ultramontane Jesuits to found a fortnightly review called *Civiltà Cattolica* (Christian Civilization). They thought that the Devil ought not to have all the best stories. Its first editor, Fr Carlo Maria Curci, explained in 1850 that its aim was 'to counteract the ideological poison that intoxicates minds, and to propagate sound doctrine'. In its early years it published improving serial novels that could be safely read by pious provincial ladies. Curci himself, alas, was drummed out of the Society of Jesus in 1877 for saying that the loss of the temporal power of the Pope was a great blessing for the papacy. He paid the penalty for saying the right thing at the wrong time. However, he fared better than de Lamennais in that he was readmitted to the Jesuits on his deathbed. (See Pietro Pirri (ed.), *Pio IX e Vittorio Emanuele.*) *Civiltà Cattolica* is still in existence. It is much changed for the better though it is still irksomely censored in the Secretariat of State.

The Vatican daily newspaper, the *Osservatore Romano*, founded in July 1861, is another product of the period when the Catholic journalist was expected to be a propagandist and an apologist. It has changed rather less than *Civiltà Cattolica*. Perhaps it had less scope for change, for it is the house organ of the Vatican, and its principal function is to present pontifical and other Vatican texts. It had its moment of glory under Fascism when it was the only independent paper in Italy. It was often suppressed. But it is arguable that it is not a proper newspaper at all. It hardly ever attempts first-hand reporting, except when describing papal journeys. It has no news sense. It never investigates anything. Its first rule is caution and not letting the side down. That makes for dullness. 'Compared with *L'Osservatore Romano*,' *The Economist* once wrote, '*Pravda* positively bristles with gossip.' It is weak on facts but strong on opinions. Most of its articles implicitly editorialize. This was recognized by Pope Paul VI who, as the son of a Brescia newspaper editor, knew what he was talking about. He said that the *Osservatore Romano* 'reports on meetings before they have actually met' – to make quite sure nothing untoward leaks out.

Most administrations in the West pay at least lip service to 'open government' and the right of access to decision-makers. The Vatican does not. It remains a secretive organization, a closed shop. Most debates and options in the Church do not involve a clash of orthodoxy and unorthodoxy, they are about differences of opinion that are perfectly legitimate; yet there is no forum in which policies can be analysed and debated. The Synod of Bishops, which was meant to perform this role, has become a rubber stamp which in the end rallies, more or less grudgingly, to papal positions. Important decisions simply drop down from on high. No document actually exists until it is finally published, and the genesis (what is called the *iter* – journey) of any particular text remains impenetrable. No appointment is ever going to be made until it is made. No comment can be passed on the meaning of a papal text because that would mean that the spokesman was 'usurping the *magisterium*', that is, doing the teaching job of the Pope himself. The most the spokesman can do is to read it out again to make sure you have got it right.

Fr Romeo Panciroli, long-serving Press Officer at the Vatican until he was cruelly despatched to Africa as a Bishop late in 1984, became notorious among journalists for his *démentis*, or denials. Experience proved that they usually meant the opposite of what they said. Thus in November 1979 Panciroli was saying that the plan for a papal visit to Turkey was 'a wholly unfounded speculation' until the day the Pope announced it himself in St Peter's Square. But Panciroli did not blush. At the first special meeting of cardinals a few weeks earlier Panciroli said that the Pope's inaugural address would definitely not be made available at all, ever. The few zealous reporters still working at 8 p.m. discovered the text was waiting for them in the Press Office. Next day, Panciroli gravely explained: 'It was never intended to make the Pope's speech available, but when the cardinals heard it, they urged the Pope to publish it for the good of the Church.' I put this unlikely tale to a group of French cardinals three days later, and it was evidently the first they had heard of it. They just about managed to keep straight faces. Every Roman event produces a rich crop of such stories.

Sometimes they can be very damaging in their consequences. Thus the Vatican account of how the body of Pope John Paul I was discovered early on the morning of 29 September 1978 set David Yallop off on his murder investigation. There was a 'cover-up', he claims, from the outset. What really happened was not so much a cover-up as a muddle. The Vatican Press Office said that Pope John Paul had been discovered by his priest-secretary and that he was reading *The Imitation of Christ*. He was in fact discovered by Sr Vincenza and he was not reading *The Imitation of Christ*. Yallop, a very moral man, professes himself to be greatly shocked by these lies.

But to the Vatican mentality, it seemed inappropriate that the world should know Sr Vincenza regularly brought John Paul I his flask of coffee at 4.30 a.m., just as she had done in Venice, and he might well have been reading *The Imitation of Christ* in the middle of the night. The story was touched up, sanitized, made more edifying for public consumtion. This is not an attitude to truth one would wish to encourage, and in this case it was punished by a 'natural sanction': a nasty smell and the suspicion of foul play. But it illustrates Montini's remark on the *Osservatore Romano*: Vatican press statements describe not what happened, but what ought to have happened.

The key to this idiosyncratic concept of truth is that the defence of the institution prevails over all else. It is as though the possession of the Truth permits one to finesse with more humdrum truths. I became aware of this once when a letter from Cardinal Jean Villot, then Secretary of State, denounced me for 'offending against Truth and the Holy See'. He was responding to a denunciation from a missionary who had misunderstood a stroke of irony in *The Tablet*. But one can only simultaneously offend against 'Truth and the Holy See' if the two terms are seen as interchangeable.

Irony can prove a boomerang. Still, the risk must be taken. The greatest irony in this field is that the Church has to hand a perfectly good theology of social communications – this term is used to avoid the supposedly pejorative implications of 'mass media', for people should not be reduced to masses. It was formulated not by the Council document on the media, *Inter Mirifica*, which Cardinal John Carmel Heenan rightly pronounced 'not of conciliar calibre', but in the instruction intended to 'implement' that document. This was produced in 1971 by the Pontifical Council for the Means of Social Communication, and magnificently translated into English by the late Patrick O'Donovan of the *Observer*. It was an explosive little document. It rejects the mistaken notion that 'facts' exist somewhere out there and simply have to be picked up: 'Information does not simply occur, it has to be sought.' The obvious corollary was drawn: 'It is futile to talk about the right to information if a variety of sources for it are not made available.'

There is no reason to suppose that this principle should not be applied to the Church itself. On the contrary, the instruction says very clearly: 'The liberality which is an essential attribute of the Church demands that the news she gives out be distinguished by integrity, truth and openness, and that these should cover her intentions as well as her works.' That has not been taken to heart and meditated upon in the Vatican. Journalists there understand exactly what the instruction means when it notes, with commendable realism, that 'newsmen face formidable obstacles and these obstacles will sometimes include persons interested in concealing the truth.' Yes: we have met some of them. Of course there is a place for secrecy, but it should be restricted 'to matters that involve the good name of individuals or that touch upon the rights of people whether singly or collectively'. This document had a very tonic effect in the developed world, where relations between the press and the bishops improved as the bishops acquired professional press officers and were educated into some understanding of the media. There was always some friction, but its complete absence would have been a bad sign: it would show that the journalists were not doing their job properly. As my master, the late Robert Rouquette S.J., once advised, 'Do not get too close to top people in the Church – if you do you will have too much sympathy with their difficulties.' I have frequently ignored this advice.

But, by another irony, though there is some understanding of the media in parts of the new Curia, the lesson does not seem to have been learned in the departments professionally concerned with the media. Moreover, the pontificate of John Paul II has seen a step backwards. The Dutch Synod of January 1980, when the seven Dutch bishops were locked up in a fifteenth-century room until they signed forty-six propositions repudiating the positions they had adopted in the 1970s, was held in total secrecy. At an audience, the Pope explained to the fifty or so Dutch journalists who had come to Rome to cover this event the reason for the secrecy:

> I am sure you will understand that the Church, like all families, at least on certain occasions, needs to have moments of exchange, discussion and decision which take place in intimacy and discretion, to enable the participants to be free and to respect people and situations.

The Pope's confidence was misplaced. Frankly, the Dutch journalists did not understand. Did this mean that they were excluded from the 'family' of the Church? Had 'Church' come to mean once more 'the Pope and the bishops' and not the laity? It was difficult to avoid these implications. Moreover, the Dutch journalists suspected that the real reason for secrecy was to conceal the resistance of the Dutch bishops: all anyone would officially know about the Synod was its unanimous final communiqué. Order had been restored in the Netherlands.

The reader may be getting the impression that reporting the Vatican is a frustrating profession in which no honourable man or woman can for long engage without losing first their cool and eventually their sanity. This impression is well founded. But something can be frustrating and maddening without actually being impossible. Secrecy can never be absolutely watertight. An old saying has it that 'in Rome everything is a mystery and nothing is a secret.' Enough people are interested in leaking the truth to make news-gathering possible. The story of the Dutch Synod, for example, was given to me in melodramatic circumstances that I am not going to divulge. Even apart from such privileged insights, secrecy acts as a challenge to the resourceful journalist. He can also count on indiscretions, for the Vatican is like a village in which gossip is rife.

In the middle range of the Curia are plenty of men and a few women who are unhappy at being passed over, or whose draft document has been ignored, or whose Christian and pastoral feelings have been outraged. Given the right conditions and something to drink, they will speak, always on the understanding that the story must be unattributable. I have a private theory that celibacy has something to do with indiscretions: lacking a wife to whom they could unburden themselves, curialists will welcome a discreet, sympathetic outsider as someone with whom they can really relax and be reminded of the ordinary pastoral work of the Church to which the best of them, reluctant bureaucrats, still aspire.

Here one would have to speak of the 'informal Vatican', the places where contacts are made and information exchanged. The Lourdes grotto in the Vatican is a favourite resort of aged cardinals after the siesta. Marian piety can be happily combined with the latest news. Less frivolous is the Santa Marta Club, named after the palacè to the left of St Peter's where they meet for lunch, and familiarly known as the *Circolo* (meaning 'club'), which is sometimes credited with making all the vital decisions concerning appointments and documents. Restaurants in the Borgo Pio play an important role. The Secretariat for Christian Unity favours Roberto's. Others stick by Marcello's out of nostalgia for the Council, during which its garden was the scene of many famous encounters.

The most intriguing restaurant is L'Eau-Vive at 85 Via Monterone, which is run by a secular institute. It is dedicated to the ministry of gastronomy. The *cuisine* is mostly French, but various African and Creole dishes are also prepared by the team of multiracial cooks. It is a far cry from the soup kitchen at the convent back door. Every evening, towards 10.30, the *profiteroles* are set aside, the cigars put down and wine glasses ignored as the sister waitresses in elegant national costumes join the guests in evening prayer and the singing of the Lourdes hymn, *Ave, ave Maria.* The meal is then resumed with no sense of incongruity. Communists value the place and behave with proper respect.

The guest book enables one to work out just who was meeting whom and when. For example on the eve of the second conclave in

1978, Cardinal Franz König of Vienna entertained Cardinal František Tomášek of Prague at Eau-Vive: it would be astonishing if they did not talk of the possibility of a Polish pope emerging. The entire Yugoslav hierarchy, rejoicing in the capitalist fleshpots, dined here a year later. Archbishop Paul Marcinkus, financier ('You can't run the Church on Hail Marys'), was a regular until his movements were restricted by the Italian police. Pope John Paul himself dined here before he became Pope, to judge by his remark the sisters at an audience: 'You have prepared a Pope at Eau-Vive.' This consoled them because they were at the time being slanderously attacked. It is very difficult for a modern cardinal or curialist to be dissipated on a Renaissance scale. But a night out at Eau-Vive permits them innocently to rediscover the beauties of creation and culture (that is one of the meanings of *cuisine*) in a friendly setting while doing some useful if discreet business. One missionary prelate I dined there disappeared into the kitchen after the meal. 'I suppose you wanted to thank the cooks?' I said.

'No,' he replied, 'I wanted to invite them to my diocese.'

These informal meeting places play an important role. There is also a bookshop run by an enterprising *Monsignore*, formerly secretary to a cardinal, where coffee and the latest news is always available. He remains anonymous because he does not want to be deluged by ignorant reporters. However, one's credulity is strained by two fly-by-night Vaticanologists, Gordon Thomas and Max Morgan-Witts, who in order to conduct their researches into alleged C.I.A. influence on the Vatican claimed to 'have set up a network of secure restaurants in Rome'. Like other authors who write on Vatican conspiracies, they pretend that their lives are threatened by the C.I.A. or some other sinister agency. Their publishers find this helps to sell the books. But their life is not all hardship. In Rasella's this pair washed down their baby lamb and artichokes with a wine they call 'Capri Chianti' (which is like talking about 'Parisian Burgundy'). How long this lunch lasted can be estimated by the fact that at the end of it Fr Lambert Greenan O.P., the Ulsterman who edits the English edition of the *Osservatore Romano*, staggered off to say 'an early evening Mass'. 'Good luck, lads' was his cheerful parting shot. (See on your station bookstall: *The Year of Armageddon*.) Other authors claim their lives have supposedly been in jeopardy because they dared to 'tell the truth' about the Vatican.

The more immediate threat is that one will lose not one's life but one's credentials, the vital *tessera* or press card that gives access to the Vatican Press Office and its facilities. Changes in the organization of the Press office made this more likely than ever.

In December 1984 Fr Romeo Panciroli was banished and replaced by a forty-eight-year-old Spaniard, Dr Joaquin Navarro-Valls. This was presented as the first act of the 'dynamic' new President of the Pontifical Commission for the Means of Social Communications, Archbishop John J. Foley. Born in 1935 in a Philadelphia suburb, Foley can fairly claim to be the first President of this body who has actually worked in Catholic journalism. He was editor-in-chief of the Catholic *Standard and Times*, the Philadelphia archdiocesan paper, from 1970 until his present appointment. But there is journalism and journalism. To illustrate the point that Catholic journalists cannot be too careful, Archbishop Foley gave me an example from his own experience. He had once published an article in which he 'revealed' that letters asking for the Pope's prayers were daily pinned to the pontifical *prie-dieu*. This 'imprudence' resulted in an avalanche of letters under which the pontifical *prie-dieu* veritably disappeared. I must confess that I would not place this at the top of my list of 'problems that beset the Catholic journalist'. There are questions of truth that seen more important. Foley's prose style is more inspirational than informative. Writing in the journal of U.C.I.P. (the International Catholic Union of the Press) in December 1984, he said: 'In a way, Catholic journalists should be like candles, communicating the light of Christ's truth and the warmth of Christ's love and being consumed in the service of God.'

No doubt Joaquin Navarro-Valls will be able to live up to Archbishop Foley's stringent candle-burning requirements. He too is an experienced journalist, having been correspondent for the Spanish daily *ABC* in Rome. He was also President of the *Stampa Estera*, the Foreign Press Club, in Rome. He was presented to his colleagues as a modern Leonardo da Vinci, being a medical doctor and having done his apprenticeship as a bullfighter (too bad for animal lovers). But the great breakthrough, we were told, was that Navarro-Valls was the first layman to be director of the Vatican Press Office. What was not revealed was that Navarro-Valls is a member of Opus Dei. So the attempt to palm him off as an 'ordinary layman' simply did not wash. No ordinary layman has to report regularly to his 'director' (Opus Dei term for superior). No ordinary layman may go to confession only to an Opus Dei priest. And no ordinary layman can select which bishop he will come under (which is the practical effect of making Opus Dei a 'personal prelature'). That Navarro-Valls is personally charming, a vast improvement on Panciroli, and understands deadlines, may be splendid as far as it goes, but it cannot alter the fact that he is unlikely to promote the cause of truth-gathering in the Vatican.

For a start, any news about Opus Dei will be untrustworthy, concerned more with public relations than with conveying hard information. Navarro-Valls, for example, took up his post at the time Opus Dei was completing the takeover from the Oratorians of the complex of buildings surrounding the church of San Girolamo in the via Giulia. The Oratorians laid claim to it because it contained the room where their founder, St Philip Neri, had lived for thirty years. Paul VI had implicitly supported their claim by making the Oratorian Fr Giulio Bevilacqua, his old mentor, a cardinal and making San Girolamo his titular church. John Paul II showed his hand by assigning it to Cardinal Pietro Palazzini, whose friendship with Opus Dei we have seen. The Oratorians were now doomed. They could not afford to pay for the restoration work needed; aided by strategically placed friends on the Rome city council, Opus Dei stepped in with their unlimited resources to complete the work.

So, just across the Tiber from the Vatican, Opus Dei is already conducting a 'centre of higher ecclesiastical studies' linked with their University of Navarra in Spain. Their optimistic hope is that it will one day rival in importance universities such as the Gregorian (Jesuits) and the Angelicum (Dominicans). For anyone wanting to trace the rise of Opus Dei in this pontificate, this was an important story. But the Vatican Press Office had nothing to say about it.

Navarro-Valls' first act on taking office in January 1985 was to declare that Domenico Del Rio, the religious affairs writer for the Rome daily *La Repubblica*, would not be allowed aboard the plane taking the Pope to Latin America for a twelve-day visit starting on 26 January. What had Del Rio done to earn this punishment? Navarro-Valls did not explain. He may not have been responsible for the decision. One could only suppose that Del Rio had offended against the 'code of conduct' which says that accreditation may be withdrawn in case of 'incorrect behaviour on the part of the journalist towards the Church or the Holy See'. None of the 300 or so accredited journalists could remember this rule ever having been applied, though it had been frequently waved over the head of Bruno Bartoloni – a Vaticanologist by family tradition – whose mock-operatic outbursts of temper used to delight everyone even though they annoyed Fr Panciroli. But even when threatening Bartoloni with excommunication, Panciroli had a twinkle in his eye. Italians know how to fix things among themselves.

But there was nothing funny about the banning of Del Rio from papal plane. What had he done? It seemed that the trouble was caused by an article in *La Repubblica* which appeared on 29 December

1984. It was the first in a series of articles on the state of the Church twenty years after Vatican II. Headed by a photograph of Cardinal Joseph Ratzinger, smiling cherubically and holding his red biretta in his hands, it bore the somewhat cumbersome title: 'And the day of restoration came – a journey through the intelligentsia of dear old Catholic Europe'. 'Restoration' was the word used by Ratzinger in a famous interview in an Italian magazine, *Jesus*, in which he called for a return to pre-conciliar values. So Del Rio patiently went round Europe from Paris to Zagreb asking the theologians who made the Council what they thought of the policy of 'restoration'. Predictably enough, they had a low opinion of it. None of them shared Ratzinger's pessimism about the Council.

But to report this was surely not a crime. So again, one asked: why the ban? The *Osservatore Romano* finally vouchsafed an answer, thought it was not a very clear one: Del Rio had written an article that was 'rancid and full of sordid anti-clericalism'. The evidence? He had quoted the eminent French Church historian Emile Poulat as saying that 'the Pope is a religious leader who knows how to put on a show and understands perfectly the mass media.' That seems as true a remark as one has the right to expect in the circumstances. It could even be considered a compliment: at last we have a pope who understands the workings of television. Of course, if the judgement implied that the Pope was nothing more than a superficial showman then it would be offensive: but that interpretation lay in the eye of the beholder.

There was a brief Roman storm, a 'Del Rio affair'. The Italian Guild of Journalists protested to the Secretariat of State. Questions were asked in the Italian parliament about press freedom at the Vatican. Italians of a certain age remember that the last Italian leader who suppressed press criticism was Benito Mussolini. None of these protests made any difference. Del Rio was stood in the corner like a naughty boy, while his place on the papal plane was taken by Alberto Michelini, the well-known television commentator who, by a remarkable coincidence, was a member of Opus Dei and of the European Parliament.

It seems that a new crime has been invented, that of *lèse-papauté*.. It is enough to have a legitimate difference of opinion to be removed or silenced. Fr Virgilio Levi, deputy editor of the *Osservatore Romano*, was promptly sacked for saying that the Church in Poland was quietly dropping Lech Walesa. The editor of *Civiltà Cattolica*, Fr Bartolomeo Sorge S.J., a man of impeccable orthodoxy and at the same time an influential figure on the Christian Democratic scene, was despatched in July 1985 to distant Palermo. His crime was that he did not share the Pope's enthusiasm for *Communione e Liberazione*, a mass youth movement with an ideology close to that of Opus Dei, which is regarded by some as the hope of the future. In exile Sorge can meditate on the fate of his predecessor, the founder of *Civiltà Cattolica*, mentioned at the start of this chapter. He too had the misfortune to say the right things at the wrong time.

We might conclude that in 150 years the wheel has come full circle and that we are back to journalism as propaganda. But there are two important differences. No one can possess a total monopoly of Vatican news any more, so there is room to move within the interstices of incomplete control. And enough people have learned from Vatican II a vision of the church which makes the current Vatican approach look harmful, misguided and doomed. Keep faith with the vision: there will be another pontificate and it will be different. The final chapter will suggest how.

16

The Next Council: Lateran VI

The year is 199–. Pope Benedict XVI, a French Benedictine monk, has astonished the world by moving his headquarters out of the Vatican. His next surprise was to go to Moscow to exchange the kiss of peace with the Russian Orthodox Patriarch. Finally he summoned an Ecumenical Council which he insisted on calling Lateran VI instead of Vatican III as most commentators expected.

Pope Benedict explained all these moves in his inaugural address to the council. The author was able to get hold of the authentic transcript of the text. It differed notably from the version published in the Osservatore Laterano.

My dear sisters and brothers,
Gaudet Mater Ecclesia hac in celebratione.

I wanted to use the ancient Latin words to open this Sixth Lateran Council: Mother Church rejoices in this celebration. These words were used by Pope John XXIII as he inaugurated the last Council in October 1962. They remind us that above all else a Council is a celebration of the faith of the Church.

Soon enough, there will be the cut and thrust of debate – real debate, out in the open, not mere shadow-boxing. But the context of the debate will be the continuing Christian story, told and ever retold in our midst, making sense of our own stories, his-stories and her-stories, making us a community, constantly applied to new situations by new generations, *per omnia saecula saeculorum*, for all the ages of ages. Yes, *Amen.* May our celebration of faith not be self-indulgent navel-gazing. May it bring joy and a little more peace to a troubled world that looks to us for – quite literally – 'God knows what'.

You know the reasons that led me to leave the Vatican and install myself here at the Lateran. Popes lived here for over a millennium. They moved into the Vatican only in 1377 when my venerable predecessor of distinctly unhappy memory returned from exile in Avignon, France. So from the outset the Vatican was associated with the pomp of the Renaissance and the polemics of the Counter-Reformation.

It seemed to me that the only way to break with such associations was to move out. But where to? The Lateran is where the Bishop of Rome properly belongs. All my grander titles take their origin in this one. It is therefore fitting that the Bishop of Rome should live among the people of Rome and amid the swirl of its traffic rather than in a palace on a hill surrounded by a high and impenetrable wall.

The Vatican Palaces make excellent museums, and the once squabbling Unesco suddenly became peaceful and purposeful when it was invited to administer them. And St Peter's with its precious bones is still ours, inalienably. But now I live here, 'over the shop'.

Though the cathedral of the Rome diocese is known as St John Lateran, its original dedication was to Our Saviour. Since the whole of Christian life needs to be focused on Jesus, Our Lord and Saviour, this ancient dedication directs us along the right road. It is John the Baptist himself who is reported to have said, 'He must increase, but I must decrease.' (John 3:30.) So it is as Bishop of Rome that I have invited you here to this Basilica of St Saviour for this Sixth Lateran Council.

Simply by coming here – and before we have opened our mouths or had our first serious row – we make a statement of intent. It is not nostalgia that makes us pay attention to the past. We value tradition, but we are not its prisoners. Those who profess to ignore history are condemned to repeat its mistakes. With Pope John XXIII and Cicero I believe that history is the teacher of life (*magistra vitae*).

Not all the associations – the 'vibes' they used to be called in my youth – of the Lateran Basilica are good ones. You came in here this morning, in solemn procession, through perhaps the oldest doors in the world still in use: the great bronze doors that once guarded the entrance to the Roman Senate. Through those doors strode grave men in togas to debate the fate of the known world while in distant Palestine another obscure Jew was crucified. What a link with the past!

Three centuries later the Emperor Constantine had this church and the first St Peter's built. How abused Constantine has been. He has been blamed for subordinating the Church to the State, and thereby turning Christians into conformists and conservatives. He has much to answer for. But that is not the last word on the subject. Perhaps one day I'll try to rescue Constantine.

The Lateran has other memories. Five Councils were held here.

The last was in 1512. It was possibly the most ineffectual Council in
the life of the Church. Held on the eve of the Reformation, just three
years before the Augustinian Friar Martin Luther nailed up his
theses, it failed dismally to reform the Church 'in head and members'
(as the current phrase was).

Today we are better placed to understand the Christian and
prophetic content of Friar Martin's protest; and so we will have to
complete here the work left unfinished in 1512. At the opening session of Lateran V, the equivalent of this, the preacher was Giles of
Viterbo who, as it happened, was General of the Augustinians. 'Man
must be transformed by the holy,' he declared, 'and the holy must
not be transformed by man.' Not a bad motto for us, provided we
know what the terms mean.

But as we pick up all these threads of so long ago, history has for us
a much broader lesson. Above all it teaches that this Church of ours
is a pilgrim Church. And on its journey through the centuries it picks
up burdens that make it more difficult to reach its goal. Institutions,
devised in one era no doubt for good reasons, become handicaps,
impedimenta, in another.

Yet we so rarely discard anything. We are squirrels, spiritual
hoarders. We find it so hard to let go of anything, to let go in God as
the mediaeval German mystics called it: *Gelassenheit*. We need *Gelassenheit* to let go of the lumber of our institutions. It will be part of our
task here to ensure that the Pilgrim Church emerges leaner, fitter
and more uncluttered so that she can go forward with greater spring
in her step.

I will not hide from you that there was great opposition to the project of another Council. It did not come merely from the Roman
Curia, always suspicious of foreigners in Rome – *questa gente da fuori*,
as we are called. Many of you, when consulted, had objections.

Some of you said rather wearily: 'This comes much too soon after
Vatican II which has not yet been assimilated. The idea of another
Council is premature. One a century is quite enough.' I see the point:
in the previous pontificate there were some pessimists who held that
Vatican II had failed. But I believed that it was rather we who had
failed the Council. One council a century was not a bad principle in
a more leisured age. But in this century 'history is accelerating' (as
Vatican II itself noted) and the pace of change has been frantic. So
aggiornamento, bringing up to date, is itself quickly dated. 'Modern' is
an epitaph.

The other main objection was simply that councils cause trouble.
Intended to forge unity, they create divisions. After any council there

are always two interpretations possible: the forward-looking which stresses what is new, and the conservative which stresses what has been repeated. Certainly this happened after Vatican II; and it will no doubt happen again. But we cannot refuse the risk. As John XXIII remarked, there would be no point in assembling a council merely to repeat what was already known. There is a link between renewal and innovation that is more than merely semantic.

So, despite such objections from grave and weighty persons, I decided to go ahead with this project. Why? In simplest terms this Council is summoned in order that the Catholic Church may become still more Catholic. *Lumen Gentium* says that the function of the Chair of Peter – that's where I'm sitting – is to 'preside over the assembly of charity and protect legitimate differences'.

As I meditated on this text, this job description of the vicar of Peter, it came home to me that legitimate differences were not sufficiently protected in the Church and that we should go much further along this road. 'Legitimate' is a weak and weasel word: it tends to mean 'what I agree with'. There is, for instance, 'legitimate pluralism' for theologians in the Church; but just how much pluralism is that? How much is legitimate? It seemed to me that I must not only defend and protect legitimate differences, however defined, but encourage them, cherish them and extend their range.

The basic question is about the nature of authority – yours and mine – in the Church. It exists for one purpose only, according to *Lumen Gentium*: 'in order that all may unite freely and yet in order'. In the past, and for understandable reasons, we have stressed order rather than freedom, uniformity rather than diversity. We have been stationmasters checking the clock, rather than prophets discerning the signs.

At this point many get alarmed – and write me distressed memos. They think that the unity of the Church is being put in jeopardy. They fear that these disparate local churches, impelled by some centrifugal force, will fly off into chaos unless kept firmly under control. Control by whom?

I am not the sergeant-major of the Church. I am not the headmaster of an unruly school. The relationship between the Bishop of Rome and his fellow bishops cannot be that between a dictator and his minions. We cannot stress it too much: our unity is a unity of communion or *koinonia*. Diversity only threatens the Church if our model of unity is one of uniformity.

Even throughout the period of the greatest centralization in the Church, after Vatican I, when the Roman colleges seemed to be mass-producing bishops and bureaucrats, there were still the Eastern churches, usually small and often persecuted, who kept alive the principle that true Catholicism meant not uniformity but 'reconciled diversity'. I see them nod in agreement.

Their witness has been precious to us. Their martyrdoms have been eloquent. In a time of increasing centralization, when it almost seemed as though the aim was to make every local church a carbon copy of the Roman Church, they taught us what Catholicism was. They represented an alternative model of unity. They taught the Bishop of Rome that he was an enabler rather than a dictator.

Let me apply this to one practical question. Does the unity of the Church entail that the appointment of bishops should be centralized? You yourselves may think so. You have nearly all been appointed by me or my predecessors.

Yet it is evident that I cannot have the detailed knowledge of every situation that would be required to make wise choices. Superhuman powers would be needed for that. I believe that I have divine assistance, just as you have, but it does not endow me with magical qualities.

Is it essential for the unity of the Church that I should be obliged to scrutinize week by week, sometimes day by day, lists of names of people whom I do not know personally and who have to be judged on the basis of second- or third-hand reports from witnesses who are not altogether impartial?

There is nothing in divine law which says that all bishops have to be appointed by me. In fact, centralized appointment is a modern thing. Until 1820, the majority of your predecessors were appointed by some other method, usually involving election by the cathedral chapter.

Some may say – they already have – 'Renounce this power, and you will strike a blow at the heart of the Church's unity.' But why should this be? Is not this fear based on a false concept of unity? Of course my role is to express and embody the unity of the Church. But it would be blasphemous to forget that the deeper cause of our unity is 'the Spirit poured out in our hearts' whereby we are impelled to come together. We constantly invoke the Holy Spirit when we sing, as we shall every day at this Council, *Veni, Creator Spiritus*. Can we not accept that our prayer has been heard and trust the Spirit?

There are many ways of expressing the Church's unity other than by the appointment of bishops. Though I have deliberately travelled much less than my predecessor, John Paul II, you have seen me on your television screens. You have been here regularly for synods,

general and particular, which – I have to confess – convinced me that
a council was needed. I conclude that the attempt to impose uniformity on the Church by keeping a tight rein on the appointment of
bishops has by now fulfilled its historic purpose. It should therefore
be abandoned. As of now, it is abandoned.

It is not that the old system was utterly wrong: it is simply that
such a method of expressing the Church's unity has had its day.

I see journalists – no doubt agency journalists – rushing out to file
their stories. They should be patient. I haven't finished yet.

As for what system you will follow, whom you will consult, how the
laity will be brought into the process of bishop-making: these will be
matters for you to discuss and decide in this Council. There need be
no common system all over the world. Some of you in totalitarian
countries – of the left or the right – welcome the help of an outsider
like the Bishop of Rome which frees you from total subordination to
the local satraps. If any of you want such an element of 'recognition
by Rome' to be built into your arrangements, then say so clearly.

Certain other consequences will immediately follow from this
decision. The Congregation of Bishops here in Rome will be wound
up. It is superfluous. Those who have so often complained about 'the
shortage of priests' in this diocese of Rome will now have a chance to
work pastorally in it. This will be the first step towards turning the
Roman Curia into the Secretariat of the Church.

It is equally clear that the whole network of papal nuncios, inter-
nuncios and apostolic delegates will need scrutiny. One of their main
functions has traditionally been gathering intelligence about episcopal candidates and selecting, after rather elusive 'consultations',
the *terna* for the Congregation of Bishops.

With this function gone, I am tempted to abolish the Vatican diplomatic service altogether. I will tell you what I think, and leave you
to decide.

The Vatican diplomatic service has proved its usefulness here and
there. But I cannot get round the theological difficulty: why should
there be an intermediary between the local church and the Chair of
Peter? Inevitably the intermediary, whatever his merits or intentions, tends to act as a spy on behalf of his superiors – in this case,
myself. But I do not want such secret information. When anyone
offers secret information, I say: burn it.

Information in the Church should be communicated face to face.
When we say that the Church is a communion, we claim to privilege
a form of communication that is direct, unshifty, as honest and truth-
ful as we can make it.

There is a second theological difficulty. Most nuncios, inter-nuncios and apostolic delegates have the title of archbishop. They are given titles of defunct sees in Asia Minor or elsewhere. A bishop without a people, a community, a constituency and a territory is an anomaly, a monstrosity. Yet for years we have forced good men into this position. Has the time come to release those trained in diplomacy – only about two hundred – for the pastoral work they say they aspire to?

But once again, I do not want to *impose* changes. I would understand if a particular episcopal conference wishes to retain its Vatican diplomat as a buffer or *cordon sanitaire* against the encroachments of the state. You are free to request that. But I do not think it should be the normal practice.

I see some more reporters hastily departing. I warn them that they risk missing the juiciest bits. I've talked about accretions, the deposit of centuries, the barnacles on St Peter's Barque. I've just scraped off two of them. There are plenty more. But it is not a matter of being destructive or iconoclastic for its own sake.

The criterion will be: does this change make for a more effective and more evangelical ministry? Bishops exercise and oversee ministry in the Church. Anything which opens up that ministry to a fuller, wider, deeper service of humanity is progress in the Lord.

You will have to discuss what that implies for other 'ministries' in the Church. You will remember how the Synod of autumn 1987 opened our eyes in this matter. It became evident, and was a sign of the Spirit in our time, that there are many ministries within the one mission of the Church. Who is called to them, women and men, and how liberty, discipline, and tradition are to be combined will be high on your agenda. I do not wish to pre-empt that debate. I will merely ask you to note that interventions declaring that 'nothing shall ever happen for the first time' will cut little ice with me.

A Canadian theologian, Joanne Dewart, once explain that 'tradition' in the Church did not mean a house-museum which carefully preserved, say, the nineteenth-century past, but was more like a rather untidy lived-in home. The house-museum never changes; it is fixed for all time. But there is always something happening in the home: a new kitchen, a glazed porch, pointing the brickwork. You get the idea.

This brings me to my own Petrine ministry which by a curious oversight totally eluded examination at the last Council. My greatly esteemed predecessor, Pope Paul VI, confessed, in an anguished moment, that he knew his own office was an ecumenical obstacle.

But he did not see what he could do about it. He was bound, by oath, not to put in jeopardy the patrimony he had received.

I do not claim to be wiser than my predecessors. But sometimes experience helps us see things in a new light. When that happens, the words of Pope John XXIII, written just before his death, apply: 'It is not that the Gospel has changed; it is that we have begun to understand it better.'

So I wondered if there was anything I could legitimately do to make my office less unacceptable to those Christians with whom we share faith, hope and charity, these three. After all, this common inheritance is mind-boggling enough to make certain differences, mere products of the last 800 years, take second place if not fade into insignificance.

It was only when I came here to the Lateran that I began to understand. I had gone back, in some sense, to a period when such differences did not exist or were only beginning to. So my imagination was released. If one law of history states that functions accumulate as centralization grows, another states simply that what is done in human freedom can be undone in human freedom.

In short, there can be decentralization and the voluntary, unforced surrender of accumulated functions. We can actually change things. Sociologists tend to say that it cannot be done, because nobody – or no body – commits institutional suicide. In this case they are mistaken.

The 'tradition' on which we base ourselves does not in any case provide a blueprint for the papal office in precisely the way it has worked out. There is an aspect of indeterminacy in what we have inherited. Tradition, if you forgive the coinage, provides not a blueprint but a 'greenprint' – the living guidance of the Spirit rather than the dead hand of the past. In such matters a small departure from precedent can be as important as a major one. That is why I began with the appointment of bishops. It is a real and symbolic change. It restores to your local churches what properly belongs to them. I can claim to be a better 'traditionalist' that those who will inevitably say that, like King Lear, I am a foolish old man who will soon regret throwing away my authority.

But look at what is gained by this simple decision about the appointment of bishops. It will make your local churches more aware of their dignity and worth. It will involve treating them as grown-up and mature. It will make my relationship with you one of genuine brotherhood rather than that of lord and feudal servant. Nor do I think you will esteem me any the less.

So the renunciation of power does not have to lead to the diminution of authority. But how much further can the renunciation of power go? Where does one stop on this slippery slope? The answer is: where common sense tells you to stop. Unlike my monkish predecessor, Pope Celestine V, I am not proposing to resign.

But I can impose on myself a self-denying ordinance. We do not, for example, need solemnly to repeat Vatican I – even supposing there were a canonical way of doing so, which there is not. However I could say that I do not propose to exercise the charism of infallibility which Vatican I attributed to the Church, and then to the Pope via the Church. I could say that; nor is it really very shocking.

All popes in the last half-century have said it in effect, notably Pope John XXIII who made it explicit in private. It ought to be possible for me to say in public: I am not denying that I have this power, but I assure you that I do not intend to use it. Is it not true that this aspect of Vatican I's teaching has in practice fallen into abeyance? Can one not ratify this state of affairs and give it a more formal basis?

There is no evidence that Pope John XXIII had any less authority in the Church because people knew that he would not rely on infallibility. Rather the contrary. His authority grew because his teaching, his *magisterium*, was relevant to the world's problems. He did not need to depend on the big stick in the background.

If you think such language is offensive, consider this: in 1830 Pope Gregory XVI said that in the crisis after the French Revolution he had to wield the stick (only he called it a rod). In 1962 Pope John said that he had laid aside that stick (only he called it a rod). If in the Church we can call a spade a spade, we ought to be able to call a stick a stick.

Some will interpret this discourse as meaning that I am staking a claim to the world leadership of the ecumenical movement. Let me assure you that I am. If tomorrow's headlines say 'POPE BIDS FOR TOP POST', I would have no complaint, provided we are all prepared to think beyond headlines and understand that this ambition is one of service rather than power. I am not stooping to conquer.

Throughout the 1970s and 1980s our Christian brothers and sisters were saying, not always in chorus but with enough insistence for us to pay attention, that the unity of the Church should be visibly expressed and embodied, and that a reformed and evangelical papacy could provide this service for a united Church. The Lutherans were the first to say that.

The Anglican position was well known. The Bishop of Rome has been the historical focus of Christian unity – and there are no other candidates for the job. But for the Bishop of Rome to fulfil this function today, Anglicans wanted to be convinced that he would excercise his authority with respect for collegiality – and not just act as an isolated monarch at the apex of the hierarchical structure. By this Council we are going some way towards meeting these reasonable demands.

With our Orthodox brothers and sisters there were fewer theological obstacles to be overcome. Intercommunion was already established. The Orthodox, moreover, have a keen sense of the meaning of 'gestures'. They fully understood the meaning of my visit to Moscow and the kiss of peace exchanged with the Moscow Patriarch at Zagorsk.

It was not a piece of theatre. It was the recognition of a brother patriarch by another brother patriarch. By the same token it was a recognition that our Churches are 'sister Churches'. It sealed our reconciliation and asserted our equality. What was sketched out by the visit to Constantinople of Pope John Paul II in 1979 was confirmed and completed by my visit to Moscow in 199–. Peter remains the elder brother of Andrew, patron of the Church of Constantinople, from which all the Orthodox Churches derive their faith.

Permit me a disgression. I wish to say something about the pontificate of my predecessor, Pope John Paul II. It is customary for popes to call their predecessors 'venerable'. If I withhold this title in a formal and routine fashion, it is only in order to use it more precisely. I have often asked myself what God meant by the election of Karol Wojtyla, Pope John Paul II. These are mysterious questions, hidden in the designs of Providence. But we ought, I feel, to be able to say something about them – to indicate at least a direction, a trend, a current.

Most of you here were appointed bishops by John Paul II and some cardinals. In that sense you owe a personal debt to him. It may not be entirely a matter of gratitude. Personally, I would have been happy to have been neither bishop nor cardinal. I would have preferred to retire to fish, pray and prepare for death. Many of you would say something similar. Those of you who do not could be taxed with unscriptural ambition.

But it fell out otherwise for all of us. I do not know how you now think of my predecessor, John Paul II. He said many things. He was prolix. He was, to be frank, long-winded. He seemed to know by looking into his heart exactly what the Church needed. He was not naturally sympathetic towards the Western world which many of us either come from or aspire to join. He was a man from the East.

I puzzle over the providential meaning of his pontificate. John Paul II thought he inherited a Church in disorder and aimed to give it shape, character, and discipline. It was the policy of 'restoration' advocated by the late lamented Cardinal Joseph Ratzinger whose unaccountable breakdown was such a tragedy.

But the real achievement of my predecessor, I believe, was contained in his fourth encyclical, *Slavorum Apostoli*, which did not get the attention it deserved. John Paul II, the first Slav Pope in history, wanted to redress the balance of the Church. It was too 'Western' in the sense of too rational, too juridically minded, too 'Roman' in short. We needed the Oriental tradition, which is equally Catholic but more mystical, intuitive and trusting in the Holy Spirit.

What had been driven apart in 1054 – I know the date is conventional but it is also convenient – he tried to bring together in 1985. There are some problems that only a Slav could perceive. And there are some problems that only a Slav could resolve.

I suppose I became aware of this during my visit to Moscow which caused such uproar in the media. It would not have been possible unless John Paul II had prepared the ground. My visit there built on and exploited a process that had been burrowing away for a long time. I think I can tell you this without illusion.

There are new attitudes abroad in the Soviet Union. The decision of the Communist party to harness rather than to harass the Orthodox Church came as a complete surprise; but it had its parallel between 1942 and 1945 when the devastations of 'the Great Patriotic War' (as the Russians always called it) led even Stalin to seek the help of the Church.

There was a complete crisis, but of an internal nature, in the late 1980s, and a similar solution was sought in the name of national cohesion. The leaders of the Soviet Union, however, will forgive me for saying that the embrace of the State is always ambivalent for the Church. The hug of the bear tends to crush. That is the gist of the Constantinian problem.

Even so, the change of policy in the Soviet Union was welcome as a way out of the impasse. That was why I felt able to go to Moscow and embrace the Patriarch. It is important to begin the journey together – even if the motives at the start are mixed. That is how most journeys begin. Motives get purified along the way.

Of course our Ukrainian brothers in exile find all this hard to understand. They see no prospect of returning to their homeland. They think that I have betrayed them by shaking hands with, and even embracing murderers. They say it is an insult to their martyrs that the Bishop of Rome should be friendly with those who destroyed the Catholic Church in the Ukraine.

I doubt whether anyone can put their minds at rest. I beg of them to recognize this truth. The generation which perpetrated this crime – it was a bloody crime – has largely passed away. Their successors inherited a situation they did not create, and perhaps did not want. They should be given the benefit of the doubt, for if the common Christian faith cannot reconcile those who hold it, how can we hope to reach out towards those who do not?

Am I simply saying that the Ukrainians have to accept defeat graciously? Yes and no. I do not have to tell the Ukrainian Catholic Church that the Passion of Christ not only looked like but was a defeat, and yet without it there would have been no resurrection.

So I am brought, finally, to international themes and to 'the world'. In the New Testament 'the world' is an ambivalent place: sometimes to be avoided, sometimes to be embraced because 'God so loved it as to send his only-begotten Son.' For the Christian the world is home, and yet not quite home; ours and yet not entirely ours; both friendly and hostile.

Now in a paradoxical way this Christian sense of being 'strangers' in this world has been strengthened by the overhanging nuclear threat. It has obliged us to live in the provisional. We can better understand St Paul feeling that the end of the world was close and that we have here 'no abiding city'. Eschatology has been given back to us.

When I became Bishop of Rome I took the name Benedict. This was because I am a monk of his order, because his motto was *Pax*, and because the last Pope Benedict was a man utterly committed to peace. In World War I he annoyed all the belligerents by describing their conflict as 'a useless slaughter'. He was accused of demoralizing the troops.

In choosing this name I wanted to take up at the end of the century the torch Benedict lit at its start. But peacemaking has now passed beyond the stage at which exhortation is much use. It has entered the highly technical realm of conflict resolution and became an interdisciplinary study. There is nothing specially Christian in that.

But Christians can, I believe, contribute some crucial elements to the peace process: a motive to work for it, a sense that 'the enemy' still has his rights and dignity, and above all hope. Hope you know, is not just an attitude which waits for something to turn up or – in this case – to go away.

Hope is a positive response to the promises of the Lord. He has said he will be with us as strength and light. We ratify that every time we pray and say 'Yes, Amen'. Christ, says St Paul, is the 'Amen' to God's promises. It may be that in our time God appears to us more as the God of hope rather than the God of Providence. He too was a greenprint rather than a blueprint.

I don't have to tell you the history of the last decade. The fact that a nuclear war has not happened is attributable not to any sudden access of virtue, but to the certain knowledge that there could be no winners. What exhortation could not bring about, enlightened self-interest did.

It was not merely that mutual assured destruction was a prospect from which not only peoples but even leaders on both sides recoiled. It was the certainty that even a successful and pre-emptive first strike would not secure those who made it from devastation. A thick smoky layer would spread over the whole northern hemisphere extinguishing flora and fauna, and so the means of life, in a new ice age. That proved to be the ultimate deterrent.

So we survived, perilously and anxiously, until today and can now glimpse the end of the century. We still live on the edge of the abyss; but even if we fall into it, we fall into the hands of the Lord.

'The world and everything in it is the Lord's,' says the psalmist. So it is, including the abyss and including human freedom. Without freedom we would have no dignity, no responsibility. Sometimes it seems that the burden of freedom is almost too great to bear. We might be tempted to envy the robot or the computer. But not for long.

Of course the fact that we have escaped annihilation does not mean that the world has been at peace. On the contrary, fierce and bitterly cruel ideological wars have been fought in so many frontier regions where the superpowers imagined their interests were threatened, but kept their distance.

Many of you have experienced such wars personally. You know that those who suffer usually feel: 'This is someone else's war, why don't they fight it elsewhere?' And you know about the terrifying new weapons that can maim and blind without the merciful release of death. Well below the nuclear threshold, there is still work for peacemakers. They are more than ever blessed.

But all is not despair. The North-South conflict never turned into the outright war that many feared. The threat of oil running out moderated the aggressiveness of the Islamic revival: Islam has embarked on its *aggiornamento*. Political ideologies have declined as they commanded less and less conviction.

This Council will have to look at these and other 'signs of the

times' as this twentieth century draws to a close. What is the Spirit
trying to say to us through these divinely coded events? Can we tell
and retell the Christian story in such a way that it begins to draw
together and make sense of late twentieth-century experience? That
is the measure of our task.

I began, aptly enough for a Benedictine, in St John Lateran, the
Church of Our Saviour, in the past and with intra-Church questions.
No doubt others would want to start in the present which writes the
agenda for the Church. The important thing is to establish the connection.

For I think we are called to be utterly radical and utterly contemporary. To be radical is to be related, originically, to one's roots. A
Christian cannot cut himself off from his roots without becoming
superficial. But then, from within that living tradition, the Christian
eye must be cleansed to see the contemporary world in all its rich
potential for grace.

So we are going to need a combination – not everyone finds this
easy – of conviction and open-mindedness. I think this Council can
realize its goals.

There is only one more thing to say. An old patristic maxim said:
'*In necessariis unitas, in dubiis libertas, in omnibus caritas*' (In necessary
things unity, in doubtful matters freedom, in everything charity).
The conciliar art is to discern the difference between the essential
and the non-essential, while dwelling all the time in charity, the gift
of the Holy Spirit.

This is the blessing I call down upon us all.

Forgive me for going on so long. You will be late for lunch. But it is
only once or twice a century that one has such an opportunity to say
what is in one's heart. *Dixi*. From now on the Council and the future
are in your hands.

Bibliography

Abbott, Walter M., S.J. (ed.), *The Documents of Vatican II*, G. Chapman, London, 1966.

Acton, Lord, *Essays on Church and State*, (ed.) Douglas Woodruff, Hollis & Carter, London, 1952.

Adam, Karl, *The Spirit of Catholicism*, Sheed & Ward, London, 1929.

Adista, Rome news agency specializing in the Vatican.

Andreotti, Guilio, *A Ogni Morte di Papa*, Rizzoli, Milan, 1980.

Andrieux, Maurice, *Daily Life in Papal Rome in the Eighteenth Century*, George Allen & Unwin, London, 1968.

Annuario Pontificio, the Vatican handbook published by the Libreria Editrice Vaticana.

Atheism and Dialogue, quarterly of the Secretariat for Non-believers, Rome.

Boff, Leonardo, O.F.M., *Church: Charism and Power*, S.C.M. Press, London; Orbis, New York, 1985.

Bollettino, the daily bulletin of the Vatican Press Office.

Briefing, documents and news releases from the Catholic Media Office, London (U.S. equivalent: *Origins*, Washington).

Brown, Raymond E., *Crises Facing the Church*, Paulists and Darton, Longman and Todd, 1975.

Caprile, Giovanni, S.J., *Karol Wojtyla e il Sinodo dei Vescovi*, Vatican Press, 1980.

Cardinale, Hyginus Eugene, *The Holy See and the International Order*, Colin Smythe, Gerrards Cross, 1976.

Chadwick, Owen, *The Popes and European Revolution*, Clarendon Press, Oxford, 1981.

Clark, Kenneth (Lord), *Civilisation, A Personal View*, B.B.C. Publications and John Murray, London, 1969.

Congar, Yves, O.P., *Diversity and Communion*, trans. John Bowden, S.C.M. Press, London, 1984.

Cornwell, Rupert, *God's Banker, An Account of the Life and Death of Roberto Calvi*, Gollancz, London, 1984.

Creighton, Mandell, *A History of the Papacy from the Great Schism to the Sack of Rome*, 5 Vols., Longmans, Green, London, 1897.

Davies, J.G., *Liturgical Dance: An Historical and Practical Handbook*, S.C.M. Press, London, 1984.

Delooz, Pierre, S.J., 'Towards a sociological study of canonised sainthood in the Catholic Church' in *Saints and their Cults, Studies in Religious Sociology,*

Folklore and History, (ed.) Stephen Wilson, Cambridge University Press, Cambridge, 1983.

Eagan, Joseph P., *Pilgrim from Canterbury*, Atonement Friars, Garrison, New York, 1972.

Empie, Paul C. and Murphy T. Austin (eds.), *Papal Primacy and the Universal Church*, Augsburg Publishing House, Minneapolis, 1974.

Fitzgerald, Penelope, *The Knox Brothers*, Macmillan, London, 1977.

Fremantle, Anne, *The Papal Encyclicals in their Historical Context*, Introduction by Gustave Weigel, S.J., Mentor-Omega, New American Library of World Literature, New York, 1956; revised and enlarged 1963.

Frossard André, *Be Not Afraid! André Frossard in Conversation with John Paul II*, Bodley Head, London, 1984.

Graham, Robert, S.J., *Il Vaticano e il Nazismo*, Cinque Lune, Rome, 1975.

Granfield, Patrick, O.S.B., *The Papacy in Transition*, Doubleday, New York, 1980; Gill and Macmillan, Dublin, 1981.

Grootaers, Jan, 'Quelques données conernant la rédaction de l'encyclique Humanae Vitae' in *Paul VI et la Modernité*, Ecole Française de Rome, 1984.

Gross, Jan Tomasz, *Polish Society Under German Occupation. The Generalgouvernement 1939-1944*, Princeton University Press, Princeton, New Jersey, 1979.

Guarducci, Margherita, *Saint-Pierre retrouvé, le martyre, la tombe, les reliques*, Saint-Paul, Paris–Fribourg, 1974.

Guitton, Jean, *Dialogues avec Paul VI*, Fayard, Paris, 1967.

Hasler, August, *How the Pope became Infallible*, Doubleday, New York, 1981.

Hastings, Adrian (ed.), *Bishops and Writers, Aspects of the Evolution of Modern English Catholicism*, Anthony Clarke, Wheathampstead, 1977.

Haynes, Renée, *Philosopher King*, Weidenfeld & Nicolson, London, 1970.

Hebblethwaite, Peter, *The Runaway Church*, Collins, London, 1975; revised and enlarged, 1978.

Hebblethwaite, Peter, *Christian-Marxist Dialogue and Beyond*, Darton, Longman & Todd, London, 1977 (U.S.: *The Christian-Marxist Dialogue, Beginnings, Present Status and Beyond*, Paulist Press, New York, 1977).

Hebblethwaite, Peter, *John XXIII, Pope of the Council*, G. Chapman, London, 1984; pb., 1985 (US.: *Pope John XXIII, Shepherd of the Modern World*, Doubleday, New York, 1985).

Heenan, John Carmel, *Not the Whole Truth*, Hodder & Stoughton, London, 1971.

Insegnamenti, see Paul VI.

John XXIII, Pope, *Journal of a Soul*, revised edn., G. Chapman, London, 1980.

John Paul II, Pope, *Love and Responsibility*, Collins, London, 1981.

John Paul II, Pope, *The Acting Person, Analecta Husserliana, The Yearbook of Phenomenological Research*, Vol. X, D. Reidel, Dordrecht, Holland, 1979.

Keohane, R.O. and J.S. Nye (eds.), *Transactional Relations in World Politics*, Cambridge, Massachusetts, 1972.

Kenny, Anthony, *A Path from Rome*, Sidgwick & Jackson, London, 1985.

Küng, Hans, *Infallible?* Collins, London, 1971.

Küng, Hans, *Why Priests?* Collins, London, 1972.

Longford, Elizabeth, *Pilgrimage of Passion*, Weidenfeld & Nicolson, London, 1979.

Machiavelli, Niccolò, *The Prince*, trans. and with intro. by George Bull, Penguin Books, Harmondsworth, 1961.

Maritain, Jacques, *Three Reformers*, Sheed & Ward, London, 1928.

Maritain, Jacques, *Art and Scholasticism*, Sheed & Ward, London, 1930.

Martin, Malachi, *Three Popes and a Cardinal*, Hart-Davis, London, 1973.

Mercier, Désiré, *Per Crucem ad Lucem*, Bloud & Gay, Paris, 1917.

Murphy, Francis X., C.S.S.R., *The Papacy Today*, Weidenfeld & Nicolson, London, 1981.

N.C. News Service, international news agency run for the U.S. Bishops.

Oliveri, Mario, *The Representatives. The Real Nature and Function of Papal Legates*, Van Durran, Gerrards Cross, 1981.

Origins, see *Briefings*.

Parpagliolo, Luigi, *Italia negli scrittori italiani e stranieri*, Vol. 5, *Roma*, Morpurgo, Rome, 1937.

Pascal, Blaise, *Pensées*, trans. A.J. Krailsheimer, Penguin, Harmondsworth, 1966.

Paul VI et la Modernité dans l'Eglise, Ecole Française de Rome, 1984.

Paul VI, Pope, *Insegnamenti di Paolo VI*, 16 Vols. plus index, Libreria Editrice Vaticana,

Pawley, Bernard and Margaret, *Rome and Canterbury through the Centuries*, Mowbrays, London, 1974.

Pin, Emile, *La religiosità dei Romani*, Dehoniane, Bologna, 1975.

Pirri, Pietro, S.J. (ed.), *Pio IX e Vittorio Emanuele dal loro Carteggio Privato*, Gregorian University Press, Rome, 1961.

Pomian-Srzednicki, Maciej, *Religious Change in Contemporary Poland*, Routledge & Kegan Paul, London, 1982.

Poupard, Paul, *Il Vaticano Oggi*, Borla, Rome, 1968.

Riccardi, Andrea (ed.), *Pio XII*, Editori Laterza, Rome-Bari, 1984.

Ratzinger, Joseph, *Rapporto sulla Fede*, Edizioni Paoline, Milan, 1985 (English trans.) *The Ratzinger Report, An Exclusive Interview on the State of the Church with Vittorio Messori*, Ignatius Press, San Francisco, and Fowler Wright, 1985.

Rouquette, Robert, S.J., *La Fin d'une Chrétienté*, 2 Vols., Cerf, Paris, 1968.

Scott, Christina, *A Historian and his World, a Life of Christopher Dawson*, Sheed & Ward, London, 1984.

Seton-Watson, Christopher, *Italy from Liberalism to Fascism*, Methuen, London, 1967.

Tardini, Domenico, *Pio XII*, Vatican Press, 1960.

Wall, Bernard, *Italy, a Personal Anthology*, Newnes, London, 1964.

Walsh, Michael J. (compiler), *Vatican City State*, Vol. 41 of the World Bibliographical Series, Clio Press, Oxford; Santa Barbara, California, 1983.

Zizola, Giancarlo, *Quale Papa?*, Borla, Rome, 1977.

Index